D1756201

THE HONOURABLE WOMEN OF THE WAR
AND WOMEN'S WHO'S WHO.

SWANSEA LIBRARIES
WITHDRAWN
6000224268

THE HONOURABLE WOMEN

OF THE

GREAT WAR

AND

THE WOMEN'S (WAR) WHO'S WHO.

Published for Subscribers only, £6 6s. per copy.

P. CAMPION.

The Naval & Military Press Ltd

Published by

The Naval & Military Press Ltd
Unit 10 Ridgewood Industrial Park,
Uckfield, East Sussex,
TN22 5QE England

Tel: +44 (0) 1825 749494
Fax: +44 (0) 1825 765701

www.naval-military-press.com
www.military-genealogy.com

*In reprinting in facsimile from the original, any imperfections are inevitably reproduced
and the quality may fall short of modern type and cartographic standards.*

ERRATA.

THE work of preparation involved in the compilation of a volume such as this, covering over two years, renders it impossible in every case to embody the latest information, many of the personal references necessarily having been in type for some little time.

In the notes on LADY AYKROYD (the wife of Sir William Henry Aykroyd, Bart.), the fourth paragraph should read :—At the outset of the conflict, she enlisted the ready sympathy of her husband in the cause of the Belgians, and together they partly furnished and equipped one of their houses—Oakwood, Bradford—as a refuge for thirty-two Belgians.

The COUNTESS FITZWILLIAM resigned, during the war, the Presidency of the Women's Unionist Association for Yorkshire.

MRS. LOUIS H. GRUBB, the daughter of Col. Alexander Grubb, late R.A., of Elsfield House, Hollingbourne, Kent, formerly of Cahir Abbey, Cahir, co. Tipperary, married Louis H. Grubb, Esq., D.L., of Ardmayle, Cashel, co. Tipperary, in December, 1899.

MRS. WINGFIELD DIGBY has been President of the Red Cross, Sherborne Division, since its inception, and for more than two years there was an hospital at Sherborne Castle under her supervision.

FOREWORD.

THE Great War, which swept over Europe, has run its course and spent its fury.

> " The tumult and the shouting dies,
> The captains and the kings depart."

The smoke has rolled away, and we are able with a clear vision to appraise the mighty work done by British men and women for the honour of their country. And all the horrors of war—anguish and terror and revolting cruelty—cannot quench the splendour of fine deeds which is the sum of that work—deeds of high courage—exquisite chivalry, nor we nor our children's children shall ever forget.

The record of our men in France and Flanders and the East is famous for ever, and though in its glorious, pitiful entirety the tale may never be told, doubtless each of us has in his heart some sacred fragment of history which shall not be lost in the years to come.

As for the women, surely no more adequate tribute can be given them than that they were worthy kinswomen of our soldiers and sailors. High and low, gentle and simple, with one accord they flung aside all selfish considerations and gave themselves whole heartedly to patriotic service. Thus we find many women of distinction, of gentle birth and cultured tastes, abandoning gladly the ease and amenities of their sheltered lives to devote days and nights to strenuous, rough and unaccustomed work, in order that our scarred and maimed fighting men home from the battle fronts might be given the care and attention which was their due.

In the following pages will be found the war-record of many such noble women, deserving of the praise and gratitude of all who love their country.

ROYALTY AND WAR WORK.

QUITE fittingly, Queen Mary took her place at the head of the Women War Workers of the Nation. And as we sail into smoother waters after the storm and stress of those terrible times we have to admit (with pride and pleasure) that none of the women of the Empire showed to better advantage, or took a more exalted view of the demands of patriotism, than the First Lady in the Land.

The War has brought home to us as few things could that the rough path of service is the only road to real greatness, and surely royal dignity could not be better maintained or expressed than by the attitude of unwearied kindness and unflagging devotion which characterised the Queen and the Royal Family generally during the War.

Patriotism, like most of the other virtues, begins at home, and Queen Mary in her own household was quick to give the lead in voluntary submission to the restraints imposed by the various " Controllers "—restraints irksome but very necessary for the conservation of our food and other supplies ; while to the end that all available service should be utilized in the national interest, the young Princess and her brothers were taught to perform many useful tasks which would ordinarily fall to servants.

To detail the War-time activities of the Royal ladies would require a volume in itself. Queen Mary's patronage of, and close association with, the various women's auxiliary forces ; her constant thought and care for the fighting men, and her strong womanly sympathy for those wounded and maimed ; Queen Alexandra's connection with the nursing service to which she gave her name— Queen Alexandra's Imperial Military Nursing Service—and the ready exercise of her gracious influence in many other directions ; the charming, girlish personality of the Princess Mary, devoted so earnestly to national service—these are too well known to require dwelling upon.

And there are other royal personages whose record is scarcely less admirable—among them Princess Beatrice, the ever-popular Princess " Pat," Princess Arthur of Connaught and Princess Louise, Duchess of Argyle.

LIST OF CONTENTS.

LIST OF CONTENTS.

C

LIST OF CONTENTS

LIST OF CONTENTS

LIST OF CONTENTS

LIST OF CONTENTS

LIST OF CONTENTS

LIST OF CONTENTS

LIST OF CONTENTS

W

LIST OF ILLUSTRATIONS.

QUEEN MARY
QUEEN ALEXANDRA

PRINCESS ARTHUR OF CONNAUGHT

A

ABEL-SMITH, MISS GLADYS
ABINGER, LILA LADY
ALEXANDER, MRS. HARVEY
ANDERSON, MISS M. J.
ANSTRUTHER-GOUGH-CALTHORPE, THE HON. MRS.
ASHBY, MRS. W. W.
ATHERSTONE, MISS P. G.
AYKROYD, LADY

B

BAIRD, MRS. OF DURRIS
BARTHOLOMEW, THE LATE C. W., ESQ.
BARTHOLOMEW, MRS.
BEDFORD, THE DUCHESS OF
BIRRELL, MISS A.
BOLITHO, MRS.
BOWEN, MRS. G. W. H.
BOYNE, THE VISCOUNTESS
BRANDT, MRS. A. P.
BRINKLEY, MISS M. A.
BRINKLEY, MISS V. K.

LIST OF ILLUSTRATIONS

LIST OF ILLUSTRATIONS

LIST OF ILLUSTRATIONS

LIST OF ILLUSTRATIONS

LIST OF ILLUSTRATIONS

LIST OF ILLUSTRATIONS

H. M. Queen Mary

H. M. Queen Alexandra

Princess Arthur of Connaught

Lady Abinger

Mrs. Ashley

MISS GLADYS ABEL-SMITH.

MISS GLADYS ABEL-SMITH is the daughter of Colonel and the Hon. Mrs. Abel-Smith, of Woodhall Park, Hertford, a family who for generations have always been keenly active in the public service, and have from time to time contributed distinguished members to the House of Commons.

Miss Gladys Abel-Smith's mother, before her marriage, was the Hon. Isabelle Anna Brownlow, the fourth daughter of the second Lord Lurgan.

Miss Gladys Abel-Smith was a member of a V.A. Detachment since 1913, and nursed in her parents' Auxiliary Hospital at Woodhall Park, staffed by No. 4 V.A.D., Herts, since 1914, and at other V.A.D. hospitals in the neighbourhood. She has also done canteen work in London. Poultry, gardening, tennis, and golf are her favourite recreations.

MRS. HARVEY ALEXANDER.

MRS. HARVEY ALEXANDER was Commandant of V.A.D. Detachment, Dorset/64. She also worked a Hospital from October, 1914, to March, 1915, at Hill House, Yetminster, with twelve beds, and from March, 1915, to December, 1918, at The Grange, Chetnole, which contained thirty-two beds.

This institution formed one of the Sherborne Group Red Cross Hospitals, and all cases received belonged to the " direct overseas " class.

Mrs. H. Alexander is the daughter of Charles Glynn Prideaux-Brune, Esq. (of Prideaux Place, Padstow, Cornwall), and Ellen Jane Prideaux-Brune, daughter of the 1st Baron Carew. In April, 1890, she married Col. Harvey Alexander, D.S.O.

MRS. H. W. ALLAN.

THE daughter of the late T. Rodwell, Esq., and Mrs. Rodwell, of Monkseaton, Northumberland, and married to H. W. Allan, Esq., M.R.C.S., L.R.C.P., in April, 1900, this lady has given practical proof of her sympathy with the sacred cause of the alleviation of the sufferings of our brave wounded heroes, by devoting her services as a V.A.D. nurse from the time of the opening of the " Cedars " Red Cross Hospital, Wells, Somerset, in February, 1915, until June, 1916, when she was appointed Lady Superintendent and later Quarter Master.

THE HONOURABLE
MRS. ANSTRUTHER-GOUGH-CALTHORPE.

DURING the years of the Great War when England passed through an epoch of distress and unparalleled trial, her loyal sons gallantly went forth, sacrificing everything to uphold her honour. Unflinchingly, upon the bloodstained battle-fields, they withstood the onslaughts of the enemy. Their heroism and noble endurance will ever be gratefully remembered.

At home, many of the fairest women of Great Britain also willingly sacrificed ease, comfort and lives of luxury in order to tend the wounded fighting men who had crowned themselves with glory over-seas.

The Hon. Mrs. Anstruther-Gough-Calthorpe performed much valuable and honorary war work as Vice-President of the B.R.C.S., Hartley-Wintney Division of Hampshire, in which there were five Hospitals ; President of the Ladies' Committee of the Cottage Hospital, Fleet ; District Registrar for the Hartley-Wintney District regarding the work of women in agriculture ; Member of the local sub-committee, War Pensions, Odiham Division of Hampshire and Almoner for the Parish of Elvetham for both men and women ; a member of the Hartley-Wintney War Hospitals Supply Depot (Queen Mary's Needlework Guild) ; Treasurer for the Elvetham War Savings Association ; and during the war entertained over 100 overseas officers at her own home, Elvetham Hall.

The Honourable Mrs. Anstruther-Gough-Calthorpe is the eldest daughter of Augustus Cholmondeley, 6th Baron Calthorpe, and of Maud Augusta Louisa, younger daughter of the Honourable Octavius Duncombe ; and on October 11th, 1898, married Fitz-Roy Hamilton Anstruther Gough-Calthorpe, Esq., only son of Colonel Robert Lloyd-Anstruther, and of Gertrude Louisa Georgina, eldest daughter of Francis Horatio FitzRoy, Esq.

Recreations : Riding, driving, motoring, lawn-tennis, bridge, etc.

LILA LADY ABINGER.

BEFORE the war Lila Lady Abinger had devoted much of her time and influence to patriotic work. Her Ladyship is a member of Queen Alexandra's Committee of Queen Victoria's Jubilee Nurses Association, President for Hampshire of the Imperial Service College and of the British Women's Patriotic League, Vice-President of the Girl Guides' Association, etc.

During the early part of the war Lord and Lady Abinger converted their residence, Rownhams House, into a Convalescent Hospital for wounded evacuated from Cosham Military Hospital.

Her Ladyship performed V.A.D. work, St. John's, Hants, No. 200, 1914-17, and in March of the following year toiled with the French Red Cross at the Hopital Militaire, 23, and later in the Marne with Ambulance 5/66.

Lila Lady Abinger, who is the daughter of the Rt. Hon. Sir William Arthur White, P.C., G.C.B., G.C.M.G., of H.M. Diplomatic Service, married in 1899 the 5th Baron Abinger, who died on active service in May, 1917. His Lordship was Commander, R.N.V.R., from 1915-17. Her Ladyship's club is the Halcyon, Cork Street.

MRS. W. W. ASHLEY.

THIS gifted and versatile lady, the wife of Colonel W. W. Ashley, M.P., of Broadlands, Romsey, has devoted herself largely to war and post-war work. She is especially interested in the Women's Section of the Comrades of the Great War (of which organisation Col. Ashley is practically the founder), and is herself a member. She is one of the two lady Vice-Presidents (the other being Lady St. Cyres) of the Christchurch and Hampshire Conservative Association, Chairman of the Women's Constitutional Association for Christchurch and Hampshire, and is a member of the Executive Committee of the Society for the Prevention of Cruelty to Children.

During the war she was a member of the London Committee appointed by the Ministry of Information to supervise the entertainment of American troops stationed in this country. Each day a hundred officers had tea at Broadlands, and probably about seven hundred were entertained to dinner during the summer by Col. and Mrs. Ashley.

Mrs. Ashley (who before her marriage with Col. Ashley was the Hon. Mrs. Forbes-Sempill) is a daughter of Walter Spencer, Esq., of Fownhope Court, Hereford.

A

MISS MARGARET JANET ANDERSON.

THE daughter of a soldier—Colonel J. W. M. Anderson (retired), Indian Army—Miss Margaret Janet Anderson naturally has very keen sympathies with all that appertains to the welfare and the care of our brave wounded heroes. Before the war she passed her days as a typical young English gentlewoman, skilled in and very fond of all out-of-door games and pursuits, especially tennis and fishing. She also developed considerable ability in etching, and twice had a small exhibit in the Edinburgh Royal Academy (1913 and 1917). She was a " war worker " in Etal Manor Hospital (13 North End), Cornhill-on-Tweed, Northumberland, from its opening in July, 1915, first as an ordinary member, taking her turn periodically with the other nurses, subsequently, being very fond of cooking, and the post being vacant, she offered herself and was accepted as (voluntary) cook ; and she remained in that position since (except for the four summer months, during which time she continued at the Hospital but not in the kitchen). Her position in the Detachment was Section Leader.

MISS PHILLIS GRANT ATHERSTONE.

THIS lady, the daughter of Mr. and Mrs. Atherstone, of " Ellande," Albany, South Africa, became proficient before the war as a hospital nurse ; and from August, 1915, for two years, was night sister at the Sussex Lodge Hospital, Newmarket ; whilst at the time of the earlier preparation of this volume (1918) Miss Atherstone was performing day duty.

THE COUNTESS OF ALBEMARLE.

THE Countess of Albemarle held and still retains the position of Vice-President of the Red Cross, Guildcross Division, Norfolk. She was also a member of the V.A. Detachment, No. 14, Norfolk, and was on the Coldstream Guards and other Prisoners of War Committees.

For her services, her Ladyship has had the distinction of being " mentioned " in the " Roll of Honourable Service " during 1919.

Lady Aykroyd

Miss Broadhead

Mrs. A. E. Browne, O.B.E.

Miss Anderson

Miss Gladys Abel-Smith

Mrs. Harvey Alexander

The Hon. Mrs. Anstruther-Gough-Calthorpe

LADY AYKROYD.

LADY AYKROYD, of Cliffe Hill, Lightcliffe, nr. Halifax, has long been prominently associated with many well-known institutions of a charitable nature. Her influence, strong personality and sound, practical common-sense have been largely instrumental in achieving the success which has attended those institutions with which she has been connected.

For many years she has been President of the Hipperholme and Lightcliffe Habitation of the Primrose League, the President of the Hipperholme and Lightcliffe Habitation of Young Helpers' League, and in particular has been untiring in her energies as President of the Hipperholme and Lightcliffe District Nursing Association, which has been a boon and a blessing to this agricultural neighbourhood.

Her war-work was but a continuation of those peace-time activities in which she had hitherto spent herself, directed into new channels.

At the outset of the Conflict she enlisted the ready sympathy of her husband in the cause of the Belgians, and together they furnished and equipped one of their houses—Oakwood, Bradford— as a refuge for twenty-two Belgians.

When the calls of the Red Cross for war dressings were so imperative and insistent, Lady Aykroyd, with characteristic energy, got together a number of local ladies, who formed themselves into a War Hospital Supply Depôt at her house, under the direction of the Queen Mary's Needlework Guild. This organisation from the beginning met with marked success, due in a large measure to Lady Aykroyd's capability and tact. The work of the Depôt in supplying some 80,000 dressings evoked high commendation from the Guild Headquarters.

Lady Aykroyd is a daughter of the late E. W. Hammond, Esq., J.P., of Horton Hall, Bradford, and wife of Sir William Henry Aykroyd, J.P.   Club : Bradford Ladies' Club.

MRS. E. ARMSTRONG.

MRS. ARMSTRONG has for many years been Matron of the Victoria Hospital, Cork, which in September, 1914, opened a new ward with thirty-three beds for wounded and sick soldiers, and six private rooms for officers. Throughout the war she has done a great deal of work for military patients.

Mrs. Armstrong is the widow of the late G. W. F. Armstrong, Esq., M.D., R.N.

MRS. J. ARKWRIGHT.

ON the outbreak of war Mrs. Arkwright immediately offered her daily services at the Epping and Bishops Stortford Infirmary. From there she went to the West Ham Infirmary and to the Colchester County Hospital, where she carried on equally valuable and indispensable work. Mrs. Arkwright then went to her own hospital at Harlow, and subsequently to the Middlesex Hospital. After a time she took up residence at Worthy Manor, Porlock Weir, Somerset, and whilst there willingly applied her services at the Minehead V.A.D. Hospital.

Mrs. Arkwright was a member of the Harlow V.A.D. Hospital in 1914. Only during the period when her three sons were on leave did Mrs. Arkwright's labours cease. Two of her sons are midshipmen and one is in the R.F.A.

MRS. O. W. ANDREWS.

AT the outbreak of the Great War none responded more splendidly to the country's call than the women of the British Empire. All classes of Society placed themselves at the nation's service, and alike from the mansion and the cottage homes of England, women gladly volunteered to perform work which hitherto had been regarded as altogether outside their sphere.

During 1914-15 Mrs. Andrews was engaged in various duties for the Red Cross Supply Depôt, including the holding of sewing meetings, making garments for and acting as Local Representative of the S. and S.F.A. for St. Briavels, Gloucestershire.

For the same district this lady also acted as Hon. Treasurer of the War Savings' Association and Nursing Association, in addition to being Superintendent of the local branch of the Child Welfare Committee.

Mrs. Andrews also served as Hon. Secretary to Lord Denton's Charities Committee at St. Briavels, and local representative for Naval and Military War Pensions (Sydney Sub-Committee), besides being a member of the Civil Liabilities Committee.

Further, this indefatigable lady undertook for four years the charge of " Our Day " throughout the St. Briavel's district, and also acted as Secretary to her husband, Surgeon Capt. Andrews, C.B.E., R.N., in connection with Public Health work under the L.G.B. (now the Ministry of Health) and " carried on " during his absence on Service.

Mrs. Andrews is the daughter of A. M. Ferrar, Esq., J.P., and D.L., of Torwood, Belfast, and in 1894 was married to Surgeon Capt. O. W. Andrews, of St. Briavels, Glos.

MRS. A. E. BROWN, O.B.E.

MRS. A. E. BROWN'S war work has been associated with the Aux. Hospital at Reigate, which she opened in connection with the 3rd London General Hospital, Wandsworth, and during its career of three-and-a-half years patients were sent from the Military Hospital, Lewisham, and the 4th London General Hospital, Denmark Hill. This institution opened with twenty beds and at the time of closing in May, 1919, the number had grown to fifty.

Over 1,500 wounded passed through Mrs. Brown's hands without one death. She was the donor of a house with a beautiful garden, also an ambulance, converted from her own car, truly a practical form of self-denial.

During the whole period this Hospital was maintained with the same matron, Miss Mary Johnston, who devotedly gave her services at a very small salary and was rewarded with the R.R.C., and staff, who faithfully and cheerfully co-operated with Mrs. Brown in "doing their bit" for their country.

MISS GRACE ISABEL BROADHEAD.

FOR nine months in 1914, Miss Broadhead worked assiduously among soldiers' and sailors' wives and children in London. Then in May, 1915, she was called to the Royal Herbert Hospital at Woolwich, and worked there until December, 1915, when she was sent on H.M.H.S. "Aquitania," which sailed to Mudros. Later on she was ordered to the Prees Heath Camp, Whitchurch, afterwards returning to her original Hospital at Woolwich. In 1917 Miss Broadhead was "mentioned" for her valuable services; Asst. Nurse in 1918; A.R.R.C., 1919.

She is the daughter of the late Walter Broadhead, Esq., of Halifax.

MISS M. A. BRINKLEY.

MISS MAUD AGNETA BRINKLEY is the eldest daughter of the late Major Charles M. E. Brinkley, of the 4th Dragoon Guards, and of Mrs. Brinkley, of Boderw, St. Asaph, N. Wales, and at the time of the earlier preparation of this volume (1918) had been a V.A.D. nurse for over two years at the Rhyl and District Red Cross Hospital ; also for brief periods at two other hospitals. She has been a member for over six years of the St. Asaph Detachment, Flint 2, and takes the keenest interest in her work. Miss Brinkley and her sister belong to a distinguished military family. Their grandfather, Major Thomas Everard Hutton, 4th Light Dragoons, was one of the " 600 " and was wounded very severely in that famous charge. Their great-grandfather, Major Turner, of the King's Dragoon Guards, was severely wounded at Waterloo. Miss Brinkley is also a great-niece of the late Captain Alfred Hutton, King's Dragoon Guards, the well-known authority on fencing.

She and her sister were both " mentioned " in the list of October 20th, 1917, for valuable services rendered by V.A.D. members.

MISS VIOLET KATHLEEN BRINKLEY.

THE second daughter of the late Major Charles M. E. Brinkley, of the 4th Dragoon Guards, and of Mrs. Brinkley, of Boderw, St. Asaph, Miss Violet Kathleen Brinkley rendered efficient and valuable services as V.A.D. nurse for a year at the Rhyl and District Red Cross Hospital, and for one year at the War Hospital, Combe Park, Bath, where (in 1918) she still is. Miss Violet Brinkley has for over six years been a member of the St. Asaph Detachment, Flint 2, of which Miss E. C. Pilkington, A.R.R.C., was Commandant since its formation. Miss Violet Brinkley, like her sister, is a keen war worker, and has applied to be sent abroad. She was " mentioned " in the same list, October 20th, 1917, as her sister.

MRS. G. W. H. BOWEN.

THE daughter of the late Richard Chamberlain, Esq., and married January 16th, 1896, to George William Howard Bowen, Esq., J.P., D.L., this lady who in pre-war time found much recreation in fishing, gardening and motoring, was since its opening on November 5th, 1914, the earnest and very efficient Commandant of the Red Cross Hospital, Ickleton, Gt. Chesterford, Essex ; and also acted as Quarter Master since January, 1916.

Mrs. Bowen was offered but declined the Order of the B.R.C.S. She was " mentioned " in the Secretary of State's war list, October 22nd, 1917.

The Lady Byron, D.C.B.E.

Mrs. G. W. H. Bowen

Miss M. A. Brinkley

Miss V. K. Brinkley

THE LADY BYRON, D.C.B.E.

THE LADY BYRON, the daughter of the late Thomas Radmall, Esq., of St. Margaret's, Twickenham, married the 11th Baron, who died in 1917, and has a record of war activities which has rightly evoked the gratitude of the nation, and which has been well summed up in the words of one chronicler, " This woman of understanding is beloved by thousands who have never seen her, but who have come to regard her name as the synonym for all that is generous and compassionate in life, kindness in the truest sense of the word, inasmuch as it is essentially practical."

Indeed, practical good war work has throughout the colossal conflict been her constant aim. Her first war service was in behalf of tired nurses ; and realising that the invariable formula, " change of air, rest, freedom from worry," is not within the reach of all, she founded " The Blue Bird's Nest," a delightful house on Parliament Hill, as a Home of Rest for War Nurses ; blue, in all shades, being predominant in the decoration and furniture of that charming home.

Lady Byron, also recognising that socks for our sailors and soldiers was one of the greatest needs engendered by the war, instituted a Sock Fund which provided the sister forces with 30,000 pairs ; and instead of placing her orders with the shops, she entrusted them to two of our Blind Schools, and this human touch is another index to Lady Byron's character, so essentially womanly, and no wonder, therefore, that the sightless ones often think of and bless their Lady of Compassion.

Whilst cigarettes and tobacco were being profusely supplied to our troops, Lady Byron discovered that our men were suffering from the shortage of matches. She promptly despatched to them 100,000 boxes, each inscribed with the words, " A Match for a Matchless Soldier," and of course these match boxes became much-prized possessions. Footballs and quantities of sweets were also sent in generous supplies to the front.

Lady Byron has made large patriotic personal sacrifices in aid of the war—in 1917 she gave a panel of old French tapestry, which fetched £220 at a Red Cross sale ; in 1918 a " Cat's-eye " diamond pendant, with earrings to match, a set which cost £1,500 thirty years ago.

At Byron Cottage, her old-fashioned residence on Hampstead Heath, where the grounds are especially charming, its chatelaine welcomed in the summer-time to her breeze-swept and sun-kissed garden, many mothers of our fighting men and women toilers in our midst.

B

Lady Byron's energies have also been devoted to the interests of the National Land Council and those of the Italian League; she is also on the Committee of the British Empire Union and the National Political League. In 1917 she was created one of the first Dame Commanders of the British Empire.

To quote again from another writer, concerning this delightfully feminine and yet intensely practical War Helper, " Lady Byron is beautiful with that fascination produced by a combination of appealing features, extraordinary aliveness and the gift of eternal youth; the face which makes one say, Who *is* she ? And as befits the woman of Society, Lady Byron wears her beautiful gowns with infinite distinction."

MRS. BAIRD OF DURRIS.

MRS. BAIRD, of Durris, Kincardineshire (daughter of Mr. and Mrs. Frederick Villiers, of The Shieling, Ayr), started her Hospital in October, 1914. She acted as Matron, personally doing the nursing and taking charge of the management. Mr. Baird was the treasurer and secretary.

The Hospital was an Auxiliary Red Cross Hospital, conducted entirely by the local V.A.D., consisting of girls and women on the Durris estate, under their Commandant, Mrs. Norman of Ardoe. During the last two years of the war they had nearly all stretcher cases, sent from the 1st Scottish General Hospital, Aberdeen. Mrs. Baird's Hospital was not closed until March, 1919. There were sixteen beds, and altogether, 778 patients passed through the institution, which was carried on in a private hall provided by Mr. Baird for Territorial and local purposes on the estate.

MRS. A. P. BRANDT.

WITH one accord and with great womanly compassion for the sufferings of our wounded heroes, all classes and grades of the gentler sex worked ungrudgingly and unsparingly throughout the four years and a half of the Great War, and no section of women have rendered more willing or efficient patriotic service than those who represent the independent families of England.

Mrs. Brandt, the wife of A. P. Brandt, Esq., of 15, Queen's Gate Gardens, was greatly interested, long before the war, in the welfare

Mrs. A. P. Brandt

Mrs. Baird of Durris

Mrs. Brandt's Hospital at Castle Hill, Bletchingley, Surrey

The Viscountess Boyne

of children's hospitals; and at the beginning of the great conflict with Germany, she opened at Bletchingley Castle, which possesses all the advantages of a beautiful country estate, and maintained there, a private hospital for wounded soldiers. It was a Relief Hospital first for the London Hospital and then for Bethnal Green, under the War Office and Red Cross Society. It was conducted at her own expense until the end of the war, the institution being among the very last to close, and Mrs. Brandt found time and energy also to devote towards the interests of the Baby Welfare Centre in addition to invalid kitchens.

MISS AGNES BIRRELL.

MISS AGNES BIRRELL, who was " mentioned " in Despatches in 1917, is the daughter of the late Alexander Birrell, Esq., of Glasgow; and before the war took the I.S.T.M. certificate in 1903. From 1914, Miss Birrell was attached to the A.P.M.N.C. in the 3rd Scottish General Hospital at Glasgow, where she was appointed head masseuse in 1916.

THE VISCOUNTESS BOYNE.

THE VISCOUNTESS BOYNE, who is a Lady of Grace of St. John of Jerusalem, acted as Director of an Auxiliary Hospital, with 126 beds, at her own house, Brancepeth Castle, Durham, for a period of four years, during which time 4,090 patients passed through the institution. In addition to performing these arduous duties, her Ladyship held the following important positions :—President of the County Branch of the British Red Cross Society; Assistant County Director of the V.A.D.; Chairman of the Durham Women's War Agricultural Committee; District Commissioner of the Girl Guides; President of two Women's Institutes; and she has also served on two local Pensions Committees.

The Viscountess Boyne, whose recreation is hunting, is the daughter of the Earl of Harewood, and on October 4th, 1906, married Viscount Boyne, and has four sons.

Her Ladyship is a member of the Forum Club, Grosvenor Place, London.

THE HON. MRS. BURN, O.B.E.

THE HON. MRS. BURN, the daughter of Lord and Lady Leith of Fyvie, of Fyvie Castle, Aberdeenshire, and wife of Col. Charles Rosdew Burn, M.P., (U) Torquay Division, Devon, devoted her residence, Stoodley Knowle, Torquay, to the use of wounded officers, equipping it as a First Line Hospital shortly after the outbreak of war.

Col. and Mrs. Burn have naturally always taken a keen interest in the soldier's welfare, the Colonel having a lifelong connection with the Army. He is an A.D.C. to His Majesty the King, and acted throughout the War as King's Messenger to the various fronts. In October, 1914, their eldest son, Arthur Herbert Rosdew Burn, The Royal Dragoons, was killed in action whilst serving in his father's old regiment in Flanders at the first battle of Ypres.

The Hon. Mrs. Burn, who has been a member of the V.A.D. Devon 22, for many years, went to France in September, 1914, with a Red Cross unit for special work. Upon her return she at once opened her hospital. Excellent first line work was carried on until June, 1918, when she was reluctantly compelled to close.

Their Majesties the King and Queen visited Stoodley Knowle in September, 1915, showing great interest in the work, and expressing their appreciation of it and the hospital. In November, 1916, Prince Albert also visited the hospital, and was delighted with his visit. Between October, 1914, and June, 1918, 841 officer patients were admitted.

The Hon. Mrs. Burn acted as Matron and Commandant; is also a Lady of Grace of the Order of St. John of Jerusalem, and an Officer of the British Empire, and has twice been mentioned in dispatches. Prior to the War Mrs. Burn took an active interest in political work, both in East Aberdeenshire and at Torquay, where Col. Burn was returned a member in 1910.

The Hon. Mrs. Burn

Miss Burn
(now Mrs. Conyers Lang)

MISS BURN.

(now MRS. CONYERS LANG.)

ON the outbreak of war Mrs. Conyers Lang, who had already showed an interest in Red Cross Work, became a V.A.D. in Devon/22 Red Cross Detachment, and served for eight months as a nursing V.A.D. in the Town Hall Red Cross Hospital, Torquay.

Later she did excellent service in her mother's hospital for officers at Stoodley Knowle, Torquay (a " First Line " Hospital from October, 1914, to 1918).

Still later she performed duty as a nurse for several months with the French Red Cross in France.

Mrs. Conyers Lang is a daughter of Colonel Burn, O.B.E., A.D.C. to the King, M.P. for Torquay, and the Hon. Mrs. Burn, O.B.E., Lady of Grace of St. John of Jerusalem. On November 4th, 1916, she married Captain Conyers Lang, 1st Devonshire Regiment, son of Colonel Lang, late of the Devonshire Regiment.

Her recreations are yachting, shooting and fishing, travelling, and country life pursuits generally.

MRS. W. E. T. BOLITHO.

MRS. W. E. T. BOLITHO, at the outbreak of the war, was at Invergordon Castle, Ross-shire, N.B., and there promptly inaugurated a Hospital Supply Depôt in addition to working at various canteens, stations and munition works, and at the local Y.M.C.A., of which she was Convener. Mrs. Bolitho generously helped to entertain naval officers and their wives, starting football, hockey and tennis for junior naval officers. Tea, billiards, music, etc., were provided, with Mrs. Bolitho's assistance, for the entertainment of the 3rd Batt. Cameron Highlander Officers, quartered at Invergordon.

Mrs. Bolitho, who is the daughter of Robert Bruce Æneas Macleod, of Cadboll, married W. E. T. Bolitho, Esq., of Polwithen, Penzance, on 21st June, 1888, and takes a keen interest in local charitable works and various sports, including hunting.

Her house at Penzance was let to the Royal Naval Air Force during the latter part of the war. Lt.-Col. W. E. T. Bolitho was serving with the Royal S. Devon Yeomanry at home and in Ireland, from August, 1914, to November, 1918.

MISS DOROTHY ANSTRUTHER BOWDEN.

THE daughter of the late Rev. and Mrs. Bowden, of Christchurch, New Zealand, Miss Bowden took up war work in May, 1915, and nursed for three months at the Prince of Wales' General Hospital, Tottenham ; in August of the same year, she joined the staff of No. 2 New Zealand General Hospital, Walton-on-Thames, where she still works (1918) as a New Zealand " War Probationer."

MISS ELIZABETH ANNIE BUDGETT.

THIS is another lady, who, before the war, had fully qualified in the nursing profession, having trained at the West Suffolk General Hospital. From 1914, Miss Budgett performed valuable war work as Sister-in-Charge at Guy's Cliffe Hospital, Warwick, for eighteen months, and in 1918 was attached to the private staff of Westminster Hospital, London. At Warwick, Guy's Cliffe Hospital had thirty-five beds, all usually occupied, most of the cases being surgical, with operations almost daily, splendid work being performed by the V.A.D. nurses ; whilst the patients had much to interest them in the extensive grounds, and at nearly all the concerts and games arranged for the men's recreation Miss Budgett gave a display of Indian clubs, always greatly appreciated. It is interesting also to mention that the men being often too ill or helpless, Miss Budgett frequently had to shave them herself.

MISS EDITH BROWN.

MISS E. BROWN has been a V.A.D. nurse at Albion House Red Cross Hospital, Newbury, Berks, also at Bannow Hospital, St. Leonards-on-Sea.

Lady Magdalen Bulkeley

Miss E. Brown

Miss A. Birrell

Miss E. A. Budgett

The Late C. W. Bartholomew, Esq.

Mrs. Bartholomew

MRS. C. W. BARTHOLOMEW.

ON 21st November, 1914, the late C. W. Bartholomew, Esq., of Blakesley Hall, near Towcester, opened a hospital for wounded soldiers at Blakesley, where he rented a house for that purpose. The institution, which was the first to be established in the neighbourhood, was equipped with 17 beds, and except that the inadequate maintenance grant of 3s. 3d. per occupied bed per diem was drawn, Mr. Bartholomew bore the full cost of equipment and maintenance.

Mrs. Bartholomew rendered great assistance in the Hospital, of which she had entire charge as regards catering, etc., and the welfare of the patients and the staff.

Between November, 1914, and 1st January, 1919, when the building was closed, 581 patients had been treated, and that without a single fatality.

THE LADY MAGDALEN BULKELEY.

THE LADY MAGDALEN BULKELEY'S public work began long before the out-break of the war. For fifteen years her Ladyship has been President of the Anglesea branch of the Red Cross Society, and is herself a trained masseuse. The wounded in Bodlondeb received the benefit of her skill, for her Ladyship massaged them in the Red Cross Hospital there.

The Lady Magdalen Bulkeley is also the president of the Soldiers' and Sailors' Family Association, and her name is on the Roll of Honourable Service. She has also received a certificate from the Soldiers' and Sailors' Family Association and the Long Service Red Cross Medal, and two certificates.

The Lady Magdalen Bulkeley, daughter of the Earl of Hardwicke, is the wife of Commodore Sir Richard Williams-Bulkeley, Bart.

Her Ladyship is a Guide Commissioner; and her recreations are riding, golfing, swimming and painting.

THE DUCHESS OF BEDFORD, F.L.S., R.R.C.

IT was given to some to realise almost at the outset of the struggle the supreme necessity for women's work and ministration. Quietly and without ostentation they took their places as pioneers in the ranks of the war-workers, and bore the burden and heat of the day without complaint or slackening of effort until the return of peace brought them the " well done " of a grateful country.

Among these was the Duchess of Bedford, who in September, 1914, opened a military hospital (with 102 beds) for rank and file, the cases being received by convoy direct from the battle fronts. During the last three years of the war only surgical cases were admitted, and in June, 1918, it was recognised as one of the special Surgical Military Hospitals.

On the signing of the Armistice, the Duchess of Bedford's hospital was authorised by the Ministry of Pensions as an institution for the reception of Pensioners requiring further surgical treatment, and is still open for that purpose (January, 1920), being entirely privately supported by the owner, and having received no Government grant whatever.

Nor did the Duchess confine her beneficent work to conducting and supporting her own Hospital. In her personal ministrations she was untiringly assiduous, and during the five years of the war did not leave her hospital for one night. For the last three years she was responsible for all the operating theatre sister's work, and also undertook the whole of the official correspondence, book-keeping and returns of the hospital.

She is the daughter of the Ven. W. H. Tribe, late Archdeacon of Lahore, and married in January, 1888, Herbrand, 11th Duke of Bedford.

Her recreations are yachting, shooting and fishing, and she is a keen student of natural history, particularly ornithology.

Clubs : Alexandra, Halcyon, Bath.

LADY MURIEL VERE BERTIE.

LADY MURIEL VERE BERTIE, daughter of the Earl of Lindsey, has, during the war, performed excellent patriotic service, tending the wounded in Guy's Hospital, the 2nd London General Hospital, and elsewhere. She drove a car in France for some months, worked in a Y.M.C.A. Canteen at Calais from November, 1917, to July, 1918, and also worked for the French Wounded Emergency Fund.

The Duchess of Bedford

MISS EVELYN BYRDE.

AN enthusiastic Art Student before the war, on the outbreak of hostilities Miss Evelyn Byrde laid aside her other interests to fill the post of Assistant Quartermaster, Section III, Exeter War Hospitals (Oct., 1914, to March, 1915) and later that of Quartermaster, Section V, Exeter War Hospitals. She was a member of Detachment V.A. Devon 24 from October, 1910, and Quartermaster of the same from 1911. She is a daughter of the late Rev. R. A. Bryde, M.A., Headmaster of Allhallows School, Honiton, Devon, and Rector of Widworthy, Devon.

MRS. CHARLES BROOK.

FROM 1915 to the close of 1918 Mrs. Charles Brook acted as Commandant of the private hospital for soldiers, which she and her husband, Colonel Brook, established at their Scottish home of Kinmount, and during this period she was also Convenor of the Red Cross Work Party held regularly at Kinmount Hospital. She is Vice President of the Dumfriesshire Branch of the British Red Cross Society.

Mrs. Brook leads a quiet country life in her Dumfriesshire home, spending much time in the gardens. All work of a philanthropic nature, particularly local, finds in her a warm, practical supporter, and her interest in the cottagers and tenants on her husband's estate is greatly appreciated by them.

She is a daughter of William Brook, of Healey House, Huddersfield, Yorks, and in 1892 married Lieut.-Colonel Charles Brook of Durker Roods, Huddersfield, and Kinmount, Dumfriesshire, N.B.

Clubs: The New Empress Club, London.

MRS. HERBERT H. BURNEY.

IN the course of her valuable and extensive war-work, Mrs. Burney served as a V.A.D. nurse in the Red Cross Hospital, Alton, Hants (October, 1914, to May, 1915); Auxiliary Hospital No. 16, French Croix Rouge (October to December, 1915); V.A.D. Hospital, 18, Grosvenor Crescent, S.W. (4 weeks, August, 1916); and Freemasons' War Hospital, Fulham Road, S.W. (September to

c

November, 1916). She also did duty as a masseuse at Barton Court Military Hospital, Hungerford, Berks (October and November, 1917) and Rhode Hill Hospital, Uplyme, Devon (September, October and November, 1918).

Mrs. Burney is the daughter of the late Major-General J. Talbot Coke, of Trusley Manor, Etwall, Derby, and wife of Brig.-General H. H. Burney, C.B., C.B.E., of Ensleigh House, Lansdown, Bath.

Her recreations are hunting and riding.

Clubs : Ladies' County Club, Bath.

MISS BOTTOMLEY.

IN the Report of Voluntary Aid Work carried out in Dorset from August, 1914, to June, 1919, the Honorary County Director, Brigadier-General Balguy, says :

" Grata Quies Hospital was a privately managed Auxiliary Military Hospital till 1918, when it was included in the Roll of Red Cross Auxiliary Hospitals, and we appointed Miss Bottomley, its Q.M., a member of Dorset/66 as Hon. Commandant. The Hospital was largely staffed by V.A.Ds. and was beautifully run."

This appreciation of Miss Bottomley's powers of organisation was thoroughly well deserved, and further recognition came to her in the form of the bestowal of the Medaille de la Reine Elizabeth. In final recognition of her highly efficient work at Grata Quies Hospital, the compliment has since been paid her of making her an Honorary Life Governor of the Cornelia Hospital, Longfleet. Miss Bottomley resides at Valley House, Lilliput.

MISS ETHEL BRIDSON.

FOR approximately a year, dating from July, 1915, Miss Ethel Bridson was Hon. Secretary for the Petersfield Branch of the National Land Council which found employment for women land workers, and in 1916 became District Representative for the Petersfield District of the Hants and Winchester Committee for providing war work for women on the land under Lord Selborne's Scheme.

Lady Caillard, O.B.E.

Miss E. Caillard
(now Mrs. Harola Warnes Fry, R.F.C.)

Miss Bridson was Hon. Secretary both for the Petersfield and District War Weapons Week, 1918, and for the Petersfield and District Victory Week in 1919. She was also Joint Hon. Secretary for the Petersfield and District Farmers' National Union " Jumble Sale " for the relief of the Agricultural Allies, and a member of the Petersfield Urban Food Control Committee for the duration of the war.

Miss Ethel Bridson is the daughter of the late J. R. Bridson, Esq., J.P., of Bryerswood, Windermere.

Club : The Ladies' Empire Club, 69, Grosvenor Street, London, W.

LADY CAILLARD, O.B.E.

Lady of Grace of the Order of St. John of Jerusalem and holder of the Grand Cross of the Order of the Shefkat.

THE daughter of the late Captain John Hanham, of Dean's Court, Wimborne, Dorset, and his wife, Amy Hanham (née Copland), Lady Caillard was married to Sir Vincent H. Penalver Caillard, of Wingfield House, Trowbridge, Wiltshire, in the year 1881. Lady Caillard's elder brother, Sir John Alexander Hanham, succeeded in 1877 his uncle, the 8th Baronet.

Lady Caillard's father, the late Captain John Hanham, was distinguished for his conduct in the Sutlej Campaign. The Hanhams came originally from Gloucestershire, taking their name from a place called Hanham in that county, but their association with Dorset dates from Elizabethan times, when Sir Thomas Hanham, of Wimborne, whose father had married an heiress of that town, was Sergeant-at-Law, and Member of Parliament for Melcombe Regis. His grandson, Sir William Hanham, who married a niece of the 1st Earl of Shaftesbury, was the 1st Baronet of Dean's Court, that dignity being conferred upon him in 1667.

From October 9th, 1914, Wingfield House was opened as a military auxiliary hospital by Sir Vincent and Lady Caillard, and was not closed until February, 1919, when over 500 patients had passed through the wards.

Every possible comfort was at the disposal of the wounded patients at Wingfield House, and the Hospital possessed an admirable operating theatre, day rooms, etc. Lady Caillard was herself Commandant, and her daughter, Miss Esmah Caillard, Staff Sister. There was also a staff of a Matron, three Sisters, two Nurses, and four V.A.Ds., with a doctor in constant attendance. So severe were the demands upon Lady Caillard's energies and patriotism that the seventeen beds, with which the Hospital was originally opened, very shortly were doubled in number, and ultimately totalled 40.

From October, 1914, to February, 1915, sixty English and Belgian patients are recorded to have passed through the institution, and from February, 1915, to July, 1916, the number (including officers) reached 160, a total of over 500 patients being ultimately reached with the last drafts of wounded. After January, 1915, Wingfield House Red Cross Hospital was attached to the Second Southern General Hospital, Bristol.

Lady Caillard was presented with the Order of the British Empire in January, 1918, and made a Lady of Grace of the Order of St. John of Jerusalem in August of the same year.

Before the war, among the varied pursuits, activities and recreations of this lady may be mentioned :—Farming, gardening, embroidery, riding, boating, tennis, reading.

Lady Caillard's Club is the Ladies' Empire, Grosvenor Street, London, S.W.1., and her address is Wingfield House, Trowbridge, Wiltshire.

MISS ESMAH M. CAILLARD, R.R.C.

(Now Mrs. HAROLD WARNES FRY).

WHEN Wingfield House, her parents' home, was thrown open as a military hospital in October, 1914, by Sir Vincent and Lady Caillard, Miss Esmah M. Caillard took up the duties of Staff Sister, and only relinquished them in the month of October, 1918. During that anxious period she fulfilled her self-imposed task with the same thoroughness and zeal which had characterised her pursuits and recreations in the peaceful days before the great cloud burst.

Miss Caillard was awarded the 2nd Class of the Royal Red Cross in 1919.

Before the war Miss Caillard was devoted to golf and skating, in addition to being a keen horsewoman, while her more restful moments were occupied in music, reading, or embroidery. She has travelled a good deal.

MISS KATHLEEN CAMBRIDGE, R.R.C.

IT is not alone the martyr's crown that marks the heroine. The truth of this is apparent in the testimony of the nurses who worked under Edith Cavell. Among these none has given her warmer praise than Sister Kathleen Cambridge, who was one of her staff for three years.

Miss Kathleen Cambridge always intended to be a nurse, and finally took her training at the North Infirmary and City of Cork General Hospital. Then in 1911 she went to Brussels and joined Miss Edith Cavell's private nursing staff. From this work she passed on to private nursing, and in August, 1914, when war was declared, she was in charge of a case at Mons. With the true instinct of the capable nurse she decided to offer her services where experience tells in the alleviation of suffering humanity. She joined the Belgian Red Cross and helped to tend Belgians coming from Liége.

Following swiftly on the heels of the Fall of Liége came the terrible Retreat from Mons, and about three miles from that city, between Casteau and Maisieres, Nurse Cambridge was living in the house of a Belgian family. On August 21st, 1914, she saw German Uhlans pass the house, and about an hour later, going to Mons by car, she encountered some British Troops at the Bridge of Nimy. The 4th Royal Fusiliers, the 4th Middlesex, 2nd Royal Irish were guarding the Canal further down to the left of Nimy and Obourg. She met on her way back from Mons the 4th Dragoon Guards. The following day she saw a conflict between the 4th Dragoon Guards and the Uhlans and German prisoners taken. The next day, August 23rd, was the Battle of Mons.

Nurse Cambridge, helped by her mother, who was in Belgium at the time, and the loyal Belgians at whose house she was living, set about preparing the house as a hospital, so far as it was possible, and within a few hours she was busy tending the wounded from the battle area. Swiftly the sad procession increased, and finally she saw some British prisoners being escorted past the house, tired, wounded, pitifully helpless. Just as they came abreast of her window, she saw two of them drop to the ground. Heedless of what her reception might be by their German captors, she rushed out and begged that the lads might be given into her charge.

So earnest was her plea, so forceful her personality, that a German doctor standing by offered to help her to carry the exhausted British soldiers indoors. There they were swiftly attended to, and as a token of her gratitude on behalf of her wounded countrymen,

Nurse Cambridge later attended to some German wounded with just the same tender care that she gave to the British boys so bravely bearing their pain.

To a certain extent, she was at this time a prisoner in the hands of the Germans, but later she was allowed to go out and visit our men in the different hospitals and houses near by. To many of the British lads, delirious with pain and hunger, she came as a veritable Angel of Mons, and pitiful indeed were some of the tales of suffering poured into her sympathetic ears. To all she ministered sympathetically and tenderly, and it is probable that the full extent of her energies will never be completely known.

In December, 1915, when at last she was free to leave Belgium, she returned to England, but not to idleness. Almost immediately she joined Queen Alexandra's Military Nursing Reserve, and was eventually sent to Egypt, where she did further noble work as an army sister. Her steadfast courage and her cheerful capacity will ever remain in the minds of those who worked with her, as well as the wounded whom she tended.

It is interesting to note that her grandfather, Daniel Cambridge, won the V.C. at the Crimea. Who shall say that there is not a heritage of bravery, just as there is of physical appearance ? Nurse Cambridge is a woman of whom the nation is proud because of the noble work she did in the war areas during the time of the Great Strife of 1914–1918, just as the nation is also proud of the gallant gentleman who won his V.C. in the wars of long ago.

MRS. CAMPBELL OF BORLAND.

THIS lady is the daughter of the late W. E. Brinckman, R.N. (son of Sir Theodore H. L. Brinckman, Bart.) and the widow of Major-General Charles Wm. Campbell of Borland (whom she married in 1888, who died in 1894—he had commanded the 2nd Bengal Cavalry and was a Mutiny Veteran) ; and before the war, joined the V.A. Detachment of Denbigh 8, at its formation in 1912, finding her recreation in the usual pursuits of country life, especially gardening and taking an active interest in G.F.S. work, in addition at other times to travelling a great deal abroad. After the Auxiliary Military Hospital, Ystrad, Isaf, Denbigh, was opened in February, 1915, Mrs. Campbell worked there almost continuously, principally as night nurse ; and was " mentioned " in 1917. Her son is Major Charles W. Campbell, R.F.A., M.C., who was wounded in September, 1914.

Miss C. E. Campbell

Mrs. Campbell of Borland

Miss M. A. Campbell

Miss M. Campbell

MISS COLINA E. CAMPBELL.

MISS COLINA E. CAMPBELL, is the eldest daughter of the late Major-General C. W. Campbell of Borland and Mrs. Campbell ; and before the outbreak of hostilities, hunting, tennis and motoring were her favourite recreations. In 1912, with her mother and sisters, she joined the V.A.D. Denbigh 8 ; and since 1915 has worked keenly, nursing at the Auxiliary Military Hospital, Ystrad, Isaf, Denbigh, also at the Beaulieu Auxiliary Hospital, Harrogate, then at the Russian Hospital in London. Miss Campbell was Quarter Master at Beaulieu, Harrogate, and in 1918 was in France driving a motor for the Y.M.C.A. till July, 1919. She has since married Capt. T. Macdonald Hussey.

MISS MARGARET A. CAMPBELL.

MISS MARGARET A. CAMPBELL, is the third daughter of the late Major-General C. W. Campbell of Borland ; and like her mother and sisters, has been an indefatigable and thoroughly zealous war worker since the end of 1914, when she went as Probationer for four months to the Denbighshire Infirmary ; then nursed at the Auxiliary Military Hospital, Ystrad, Isaf, Denbigh ; afterwards offering her whole time to the Red Cross Society, and was sent to the Military Hospital, Fazakerley, for seven months ; and in 1918 was helping her country in its dire hour of need by working on the land—a patriotic contrast to a young lady's pre-war enjoyment of country pursuits, when she was able to devote much of her time to tennis and motoring. She joined, with her mother and sisters, the V.A. Detachment, Denbigh 8 on its formation in 1912.

MISS MARY G. CAMPBELL, M.M.

THE second daughter of the late Major-General C. W. Campbell, of Borland, Miss Mary Campbell, before the war, was devoted in recreation hours to gardening and tennis ; and in 1912, with her mother and sisters, she joined the V.A. Detachment, Denbigh 8, on its formation. In February, 1915, Miss Mary Campbell also entered enthusiastically into war work, nursing at the Auxiliary Military Hospital, Ystrad, Isaf, Denbigh. She volunteered for whole time service and the B.R.C.S. sent her in October, 1916, to France, where she continued her nursing duties. Her work was very arduous and often performed under most trying conditions. Her experiences included many air-raids on hospitals (the last occasion being the very serious one which provoked world-wide indignation), and she was fittingly awarded the Military Medal for her splendid conduct during the night air attack on the hospital at Etaples.

MRS. R. M. CAULFEILD.

THE outbreak of the world-wide war evoked a magnificent response from the women of the land. Vast numbers offered their services in the factories and workshops of the country, and others undertook work of equal national importance.

Included in this category is Mrs. Reginald M. Caulfeild, of Broadhanger, Petersfield, who fulfilled the honorary duties of Registrar for the Women and Girls working on the land in and near the village. Mrs. Caulfeild also supplied fruit and vegetables for the Fleet and local Hospitals, and helped in many other ways.

MRS. J. HUBERT CHARLESWORTH.

WHEN in August, 1914, Germany delivered her fatal challenge to the civilised world, the British nation with one accord arose, and casting aside all class and political prejudices, devoted an undivided energy to the gigantic task of shattering an evil power, once and for all.

And while the " flower of our manhood " sacrificed everything with a splendid altruism that made the world marvel that human flesh and blood could possibly endure so much on the battle-fields, the women of England rose superior to the conventions of centuries and devoted themselves whole-heartedly to the " backing up " of our war-stained warriors.

Ladies of gentle birth accustomed to an environment of ease and culture, abandoned their privileged mode of life and took up various forms of arduous and rough war work, so that the country

Mrs. Caulfeild

Mrs. Charlesworth

should " carry on " as well as possible during the absence of so many men at the front.

During her husband's two years' tenure of active service, Mrs. J. Hubert Charlesworth personally carried on the farming of his estate in Hampshire.

In addition, Mrs. Charlesworth bore a share of the burden of organizing the women of her district in the making of clothes for the Red Cross Society for the wounded ; and also in the knitting of socks and stockings, providing the materials at her own personal expense.

She started a branch and is President of the Women's Institute in her district, and it is a great success. Toy-making was taken up successfully, and this also proved an excellent means of keeping the women together and happy.

In another sphere, Mrs. Charlesworth was also an indefatigable worker. She conducted a private soup kitchen for children in the district, during the winters of the war ; and, in addition, helped to organize, and was on the committee of "The Land Girls Association," thus, throughout the conflict, exerting herself to mitigate the disastrous effects of the world-wide strife.

For instance, she was (and still is) on the Ladies' Organizing Committee of the Comrades of the Great War, and was one of the joint hostesses in the district of the Americans when their Army was here, and is, indeed, a fine and typical example of the un-tiring war-worker. She is also on the committee as Vice-Chairman of the Constitutional Association for Women in the district, and several other Associations and Committees.

Mrs. Charlesworth is the elder daughter of William Charles-worth, Esq., J.P., of Hawkchurch, Axminster (youngest son of Joseph Charlesworth, Esq., D.L., J.P., of Lofthouse Park, Wakefield, Yorkshire), and was married on December 1st, 1908, at St. Peter's, Eaton Square, to J. Hubert Charlesworth, Esq., late Lieut. Hants Carabineers, who was invalided out of the Army in 1917 on account of neuritis and being blinded in the war. He is the second son of the late Joseph Charlesworth, Esq., of Glenapp Castle, Ayrshire, and Lofthouse Park, Wakefield, Yorkshire.

Before the war Mrs. Charlesworth's many activities and recreations included hunting, and indeed all sports and games, in addition to gardening, tennis, politics, music and art-needlework.

D

MRS. CURRE.

A DEVOTED and efficient band of war workers toiled untiringly at Itton Court, Chepstow, under Mrs. Curre. That lady is the second daughter of the late Mr. Crawshay Bailey, of Maindiff Court, Abergavenny, and married Colonel Curre, D.L., J.P., of Itton Court, Chepstow, who keeps his own pack of fox hounds which he hunts himself ; whilst Mrs. Curre's pre-war favourite recreations were hunting and entertaining shooting parties.

Since the outbreak of the war Colonel and Mrs. Curre have hospitably received at Itton Court over 200 overseas officers.

They have also entertained, for convalescence, usually for a month or two at a time, wounded soldiers from Roehampton to the number of over 100, who have lost their limbs in the war ; and for the benefit of these maimed heroes have kept a masseuse or nurse.

They also provided generously for a Belgian family for nearly two years, in addition to performing a great deal of valuable war work at the Grosvenor Square and the Belgravia depôts. A house belonging to Mrs. Curre, Maindiff Court, near Abergavenny, was patriotically lent as a Red Cross Hospital, where as many as 700 patients have been received, Colonel and Mrs. Curre also helping substantially with the expenses and necessary upkeep of the establishment.

MRS. LAURENCE CURRIE.

FROM September, 1915, to December, 1918, Mrs. Laurence Currie carried out thoroughly and sympathetically the responsible duties of Commandant and Lady Superintendent of the Minley Military Auxiliary Hospital, of which she was also Hon. Secretary, personally attending to all the accounts, and latterly filling in all the papers.

On June 8th, 1918, H.M. Queen Mary, accompanied by Princess Mary and H.R.H. Prince Henry, visited the institution and expressed themselves as entirely pleased with all the arrangements, and signed the visitors' book. Her Majesty also honoured this Hospital, in the spring of 1916, with the gift of a canary, a distinction quite unique, as this was the only Hospital in Great Britain so favoured.

Long before the outbreak of the European War, Mrs. Laurence Currie had devoted herself to the public welfare, especially around her own neighbourhood in Hampshire. She is President of the Yateley Cottage Hospital, a member of the Ladies' Committee of the

Mrs. Curre

Mrs. Laurence Currie

Hartley-Wintney workhouse, a member of the Committee of the District Council Schools, and was President of the North Hants N.L.O.W.S. In addition, she was known as a successful breeder of Berkshire pigs, and of Blue Bedlington terriors, and she superintended a cattery of White Persians for her son.

Mrs. Currie is a daughter of a well-known and highly respected Parliamentarian, the late Right Honourable George Henry Finch, of Burley-on-the Hill, Rutlandshire, who sat for that County from 1867 until 1907, and at the time of his death was the Father of the House of Commons.

She married, February 23rd, 1895, Laurence Currie, Esq., M.A., J.P. for Hants, partner in Messrs. Glyn, Mills, Currie & Co., who has also discharged important war duties for the Government. Mr. Currie, who was a member of the Council of India 1911-18, and a member of the Royal Commission on University Education in London 1909-12, is a Public Works Loan Commissioner, and Chairman of the Committee of London Clearing Bankers, 1919.

MISS MARGARET CRICHTON-NEATE.

THE only daughter of Reginald Crichton-Neate, staff paymaster, R.N.R., and chief superintendent of the Board of Trade for the Bristol Channel District, Miss Margaret Crichton-Neate, before the war, evinced a zest for just those pursuits and studies which to-day befit the valuable and indispensable war worker. Previous to 1914, as a masseuse and student of physical culture, she had made her mark, as a mistress and lecturer of anatomy, hygiene, physical training, etc.

Outdoor pursuits, hockey, boating, motoring, etc., frequently engaged her attention. So when the war occurred, she was highly qualified as a type of the British young lady ready to take up Red Cross work, and was appointed Commandant of the V.A.D. 24 Glam., August, 1914. In the following February she became the voluntary masseuse at the 3rd Western Gen. Hospital, Cardiff, and in November, 1915, she was received on the staff and became Head Masseuse, A.P.M.N.C. From May to November, 1917, she was in France, driving an ambulance for the F.A.N.Y. Corps. She returned to the 3rd Western Gen. Hospital in November, 1917, and at the time of writing (April, 1918) was still there. She also acts as Consulting Masseuse to the Red Cross Aux. Hospital, Cardiff, Div. 1. Miss Crichton-Neate was " mentioned " in Dispatches October, 1917, for valuable work.

MRS. J. CAUSTON, M.B.E.

MRS. J. CAUSTON, M.B.E., organised the Pinner V.A.D. Hospital (43 beds), which was opened in February, 1915, and was Commandant until it closed in February, 1919.

Mrs. Causton is the daughter of William F. Paul, Esq., O.B.E., J.P., of Orwell Lodge, Belstead Road, Ipswich, and on July 3rd, 1902, married Joseph Causton, Esq., now Lt.-Colonel J. Causton.

She has always been very interested in all parish work ; and she is Commandant of St. John V.A.D. (started in May, 1913). Her favourite recreations are painting and needlework.

MISS D. COLLINS.

MISS D. COLLINS is the only daughter of Frederick Charles Collins, Esq., and Mrs. Collins, of The Hills, Bingley.

After completing her education at Fulneck College, she engaged actively in philanthropic work, largely in the interests of children ; and following the necessary training received her ambulance certificate.

Needlework and music are her favourite subjects of recreation. Her war record shows that she has been a V.A.D. nurse at Morton Banks Military Hospital, nr. Keighley, Yorks, where she became attached as nurse in 1916 ; and at the time of the first preparation of this book (1918) she had had several months' experience in the operating theatre, where she was still serving in the sacred duty of aiding the amelioration of the sufferings of our brave wounded heroes.

She is thoroughly devoted to her work, and holds splendid credentials from the Matron and Medical staff.

MISS BLANCHE CHICHESTER-CONSTABLE.

MISS CHICHESTER-CONSTABLE, eldest daughter of Colonel and Mrs. Chichester-Constable, of Burton Constable, East Yorkshire, has been a V.A.D. nurse at the Kensington Infirmary, Marloes Road, Earl's Court ; also at the Hon. Mrs. Guest's Hospital for officers, Aldford House, Park Lane ; and at The Lady Inchcape's Hospital for officers, 7, Seamore Place, Park Lane, London. Miss Chichester-Constable is a member of the Ladies' United Service Club, Curzon Street, Mayfair, W.

Miss B. Chichester-Constable

Miss D. Collins

Mrs. E. Curwen's Hospital

The Viscountess Cowdray

MRS. E. CHALONER CURWEN.

AT Christmas, 1915, Mrs. E. Chaloner Curwen's house, Shorne Hill, Totton, Hants, was generously offered and gratefully accepted by the authorities as a private hospital for soldiers, and was opened March 18th, 1915 (24 beds). It remained open during exactly four years, closing in March, 1919, and a total of 604 patients passed through the institution. Its high situation and south aspect made it especially adapted for the purpose of a hospital, and enabled Mrs. Curwen to nurse some very difficult and critical cases.

Everything proceeded smoothly at Shorne Hill, where very gratifying success attended this lady's self-denying war services.

Mrs. Curwen, the daughter of General Sir William Gordon Cameron, G.C.B., is the widow of Chaloner Frederick Hastings Curwen, Esq., of Withdeane Court, Brighton.

Mrs. Curwen is a member of the Ladies' Park Club, Knightsbridge, S.W.

MISS EVELYN CARLISLE.

MISS EVELYN CARLISLE is the daughter of E. J. Carlisle, Esq., and Mrs. Carlisle, of Clysbarton, Cheadle Hulme, Cheshire. At the outbreak of war, she had passed some months, after leaving school, studying in Paris.

Miss Carlisle has been a zealous war worker. Her record includes V.A.D. probationer for one year, and V.A.D. staff nurse for two years at Rock Bank Hospital, Bollington, nr. Macclesfield.

THE VISCOUNTESS COWDRAY.

WHEN the crash of arms came in August, 1914, and the lurid tragedy of Armageddon fell upon the face of the earth, many thousands representing our best families responded promptly and spontaneously to the call of grim duty ; likewise, the women of the Empire rallied, every one a patriot, to her post. And so we find, in every sphere, those of gentle birth forsaking ease and social amenities, eager to take a part as far as possible in the stress and the turmoil of England's dire hour of trial.

The Viscountess Cowdray (daughter of the late Sir John and Lady Cass and wife of The Viscount Cowdray) has borne an important share of patriotic war work, for her Ladyship, in addition to performing very valuable Red Cross work, is Joint Hon. Treasurer of the Scottish Women's Hospitals for Foreign Service (London Unit), Hon. Treasurer of the British Women's Hospital Star and Garter Building Fund, and also of the Nation's Fund for Nurses and the College of Nursing, which embraces educational advantages, and is chairman of the Women's Emergency Corps.

MRS. COLVILLE-HYDE.

MRS. COLVILLE-HYDE, of The Salterns, Parkstone, was one of those happy spirits who in their war-time activities were able to combine a vigorous energy with the grace and amenity of a charming personality. Inspired by what we can only call feelings of chivalry towards our troops, this lady brought into play every faculty of kindness, tact, generosity and thoughtfulness which could benefit the men with whom she came in contact.

Early in the progress of the war large numbers of men in training were stationed at Wareham and elsewhere in East Dorset, whence in their hours of relaxation they flocked rather aimlessly into Poole. Most of them had exchanged good homes and the care of mothers and wives for the rough-and-ready life of a military camp. Many of them were young and inexperienced—mere boys—and found themselves perhaps for the first time thrown among strangers and strange influences.

Mrs. Colville-Hyde lost no time in securing from the East Dorset Conservative Association—with the sanction of the President, the late Lord Alington—the use of the Shaftesbury Hall, Poole, where for many months she entertained soldiers and sailors every Saturday and Sunday, not only attending to their material needs, but showing a warm personal interest in their affairs and difficulties. She undertook the correspondence of those unable to help themselves in this respect, met confidences with timely advice and assistance, and proved herself a real friend to the fighting men of East Dorset. A silver rose bowl presented in recognition of her splendid work, was the outcome of a penny subscription from over 2,500 soldiers.

Mrs. Colville-Hyde

As time went on, this lady's ready sympathy found fresh channels —in the distribution of " send-off " gifts to the men proceeding overseas, the provision of concert parties for the camps in the neighbourhood, and looking after the interests of the men on the mine-sweepers, whose perilous calling was a special appeal to her. She took a leading part in providing for the furnishing and equipment of the various Red Cross hospitals and convalescent homes as one by one they were called for in the district, and acted as deputy for Lady Dudley. Springfield, the Mount, Branksome Gate were all deeply indebted to her. In the case of the last she had the valuable co-operation of Lord & Lady Alington, Mrs. Vandeleur, the Mayors and Mayoresses of Poole and Bournemouth and others.

Mrs. Colville-Hyde was also one of the leaders and most energetic supporters of the Dorset Guild of Workers.

In the summer of 1915 Mrs. Colville-Hyde entertained at Salterns a number of Indian officers and soldiers then stationed at New Milton and satisfied even their dietetic prejudices of caste and race.

She was also indefatigable in her care for the refugees sent her by the Belgian Refugees Committee in London, and devoted much of her time to receiving and finding homes and employment for these poor people.

We may mention also that—through the instrumentality of the Director-General of Works—all the Dorsets who were Prisoners of War, were fed; no less a sum than £11,000 being spent during the last two years of the War.

After the signing of the Armistice she co-operated with some friends to give a supper in Poole to as many of the returned prisoners as could be gathered together.

Among her other activities we must not lose sight of the splendid organising abilities which enabled her to raise large sums, by means of flag-days, concerts, fairs, etc., for the Red Cross, the Guild and other worthy causes.

At the time of her marriage with Mr. F. M. Colville-Hyde (who served with distinction in the E. Surreys), she was the widow of Captain Butts, who carried the colours of the Middlesex Regt. at the battle of Alma.

Mr. F. W. Colville-Hyde was a member of the senior branch of the family whose nominal head is Lord Clarendon, descendent of the famous Lord Chancellor.

MRS. J. B. CROCKER.

THE daughter of the late S. W. Allen Sly, Esq., of Widworthy, Devon, and married in January, 1885, to J. B. Crocker, Esq., Brookside House, Liegh, Sherborne, Mrs. Crocker before the war, took a deep interest in village nursing, besides finding time to assist in the management of the local free library, and enjoying delightful recreation in gardening.

Soon after the outbreak of hostilities, Mrs. Crocker devoted her knowledge of and skill in nursing to the welfare of the Auxiliary Hospital at Chetnole, taking night duty half of her time during the first two years.

MISS MARY CLARE CAWLEY.

MISS CAWLEY is the daughter of the late John Cawley, Esq., of Northwich, Cheshire; and before the war was trained at the Royal Infirmary, Liverpool, subsequently serving as Sister in the same institution for over twelve years. Since the war, Miss Cawley has done admirable war work for two-and-a-half years (at the time of the first preparation of this volume in 1918) at Myrtle Street Military Hospital, Liverpool.

MRS. R. CROFT.

THE daughter of John Flint, Esq., and Mrs. Flint, of Sunderland, this lady, who was married on March 28th, 1891, to Mr. Ralph Croft, of Sunderland, before the war helped in church work, and found her recreation in cycling and golfing. She quickly applied her abilities and energies to patriotic purposes on the outbreak of hostilities, and in August, 1914, assisted in organising the 11th Durham V.A. Hospital; has acted as Quarter-Master and Deputy Commandant since; is also Lady Superintendent of Detachment 62 S.J.A.B. She was twice " mentioned " in Dispatches, and made an Honorary Serving Sister of the Order of St. John.

Miss Cawley

Mrs. Croft.

Mrs. J. B. Crocker

Mrs. Calverley

Mrs. E. C. Clay

MRS. J. A. ERSKINE CUNINGHAME.

DURING the war Mrs. Cuninghame was appointed Convener of the Culross district to carry on Red Cross Work in connection with Dunfermline, and was instrumental in raising, approximately, £500 by organizing fêtes and sales.

Mrs. Cuninghame also instituted 36 Red Cross flag days in her village producing an average of about £6 per day. Work parties were also organized for knitting various articles for our brave fighting men overseas.

Mrs. Cuninghame was always ready and most energetic in her support of the Y.M.C.A. and the Red Cross in Dunfermline. For her invaluable services she has been the recipient of the Queen Alexandra's medal to the Soldiers' and Sailors' Help Society and of a Long Service Medal for Y.M.C.A. work.

Mrs. Cuninghame has been a member for three years of the War Pensions Committee in the Culross district.

Mrs. Erskine Cuninghame is the daughter of William Carstares Dunlop, Esq., of Gairbraid and Mrs. Wm. Carstares Dunlop, of Wayside, Dormans, Surrey; and married John Alistair Erskine Cuninghame, Esq., of Balgownie, Culross, Fife, in 1901.

Mrs. Cuninghame takes a keen interest in all kinds of sports and games.

MRS. H. CALVERLEY, O.B.E.

MRS. CALVERLEY was the Vice-President of the British Red Cross Society, Harlow (Essex) division. She gave up her own home, Down Hall, as a Hospital from 1915, to February, 1919, and was herself its Commandant. For this valuable and much appreciated war work she was " mentioned " in despatches in 1916. Other honours were conferred upon her, she being made an Officer of the Order of the British Empire, in 1918; also a Lady of Grace of the Order of St. John of Jerusalem, 1919.

Mrs. Calverley, O.B.E., is the daughter of Sir Brydges and Lady Henniker, and married Major Horace Calverley, of Oulton Hall, Leeds, and Down Hall, Harlow, Essex; also of 18, Chesham Place, London.

Before the war Mrs. Calverley employed most of her spare time in gardening, farming, hunting, also motoring in England and on the Continent; and was a member of the Ladies' Automobile Club, Brook Street.

LADY EMMA CRICHTON.

LADY EMMA CRICHTON, daughter of the late Earl of Northbrook and wife of Sir Harry Crichton, A.D.C., K.C.B., has associated herself very largely with war work in Southampton and elsewhere. From 1914 to May 1919 she served in various hospitals in Southampton, besides establishing a Depot of Work for Sir E. Ward for hospitals and hospital ships, and starting a store of garments and comforts for hospital ships. She also founded a Handicrafts Depôt at the Royal Victoria Hospital, Netley, which is still being carried on.

Lady Emma is President of the S.S.F.A., Women's Club and W.N.S. Club (now the Women's Section of the Comrades of the Great War).

Though she spends part of her time at her flat at 3, Buckingham Gate, she is devoted to out-door pursuits—yachting, gardening, etc. She is also a talented artist.

MRS. E. C. CLAY, HOLYHEAD.

MRS. CLAY, daughter of O. Williams, Esq., and wife of Dr. T. W. Clay, J.P., had for some five years before the war helped her husband to form Women's Classes for First Aid and Home Nursing, and these she carried on in addition to her charitable work among the poor. From October 4th, 1914, she was in charge of The Holborn Red Cross Auxiliary Military Hospital, when it was first opened for Belgian Soldiers, and continued in charge until it was closed in June, 1919. She was Assistant Commandant for the Anglesey No. 8 V.A.D. for some years until appointed Commandant, which position she still holds. For over two years she worked under the Red Cross at the Holyhead Station, meeting the Troop Ships and trains and helping to feed and administer comforts to the soldiers, applying her valuable experience to the alleviation of the sufferings of our troops.

Mrs. Clay was " mentioned " in September, 1917, by the Secretary of State for War for valuable services rendered in connection with the war, received the Roll of Honour, 1st Class, February, 1919, and was awarded the A.R.R.C. in 1920.

Mrs. Clay also did work in connection with the Ministry of Agriculture and Fisheries, being the Holyhead District Representative and also Chairman of the Recruiting Committee for the Land Army. In recognition of her services she received the " Certificate of Service " in May, 1920.

Countess of Darnley

Hon. Mrs. Dalgety

THE COUNTESS OF CARNWATH.

THE Countess of Carnwath, who is well known for her sympathies with and invaluable work for the cause of caring for and succouring our brave wounded heroes, and whose war-work in other spheres has been untiring, is the wife of the 13th Earl of Carnwath, and before her marriage (in 1910) was Miss Maude Maitland, the youngest daughter of John Eden Savile, Esq., of St. Martin's, Stamford.

THE HON. MRS. DALGETY.

THE Hon. Mrs. Dalgety, the wife of Capt. F. J. Dalgety, 15th Hussars, of Lockerley Hall, Hants, proved herself a most untiring and invaluable war worker. From October, 1914, to April, 1918, she personally superintended a convalescent home for officers at Lockerley Hall and she drove her own car for the benefit of the officers under her care. Lockerley Hall was recognized as an annexe to King Edward VII Hospital. In addition, Mrs. Dalgety was an active member of the Women's War Agricultural Committee for Hampshire, and acted on local Committees undertaking war work of all kinds.

Her marriage took place on June 10th, 1897. She is the third daughter of Lord Rathdonnell of Lisnavagh, Rathvilly, Ireland.

Club :—Ladies' Athenæum Club, 32, Dover Street.

THE COUNTESS OF DARNLEY, D.B.E.

LADY DARNLEY'S home, Cobham Hall, Kent, was equipped and used as a war Hospital from October, 1914, to December, 1918, and during the first year her Ladyship ran it herself for the benefit of soldiers. In 1916 it became a convalescent hospital for Australian officers. During four years of the war Lady Darnley organized concerts and entertainments at Cobham Hall for the wounded and collected funds for V.A.D. hospitals in Kent.

Her Ladyship also exerted great energies in other directions to aid war charities, and being a gifted artist, used her brush for the benefit of the cause, her own paintings and water colour sketches realising welcome sums to swell the war funds. She also spoke at public meetings and for two years auctioneered at the Farmers' Red Cross Sale, Rochester.

She was President during the war of two Y.W.C.A. huts; one bears her name at Gravesend, and the other is at Chatham. She hopes these huts may go on working as they do so much good and make a centre for girls, giving them healthy interests and education.

Before the great crisis came in 1914, Lady Darnley was in other spheres an indefatigable worker for the public welfare, especially in her own County of Kent, where she was the Dame President of the Primrose League, Gravesend; and is still President of the Girl Guides; President of the Thimble League, St. Bartholomews' Hospital, Chatham; Lady President of the Chatham House of Refuge and Preventive Work; President of the Cobham Arts and Crafts Society. Very fittingly Lady Darnley has been made a D.B.E. in recognition of her invaluable war work. Her versatile accomplishments include authorship, for her Ladyship has written and published (in collaboration) a novel, also children's stories, in addition to a waltz and a song.

The youngest daughter of John Stephen Morphy, Esq., of Kerry, and of Beechworth, Victoria, Australia, she married in 1884 the Hon. Ivo Bligh, second son of the sixth Earl of Darnley, who succeeded his brother in October, 1900.

MISS MARIANNE E. DANN, R.R.C.

A TRAINED and thoroughly qualified nurse before the war, having been Sister-in-Charge of the Welwyn Cottage Hospital for one year and District Superintendent at Plaistow for two years, Miss Marianne E. Dann has since 1914 performed very valuable and thoroughly efficient war work, first as Sister at the Oakley Red Cross Hospital, Bromley Common; then as Night Superintendent at the Endsleigh Palace Hospital for officers; Matron for two years of the British Red Cross Hospital, Reigate, Surrey; afterwards joining the Q.A.I.M.N.S. Reserve. She was awarded the R.R.C., 2nd class, at the completion of her second year as Matron at Reigate.

Miss Dann is a member of the Trained Nurses' Club, Buckingham Street, Strand; also of the Imperial Nurses' Club, Ebury Street, S.W.

Mrs. Duncan
(formerly Mrs. Clark-Neill).

Miss Dashwood

Miss M. E. Dann

Lady Eden

Mrs. S. E. Faith

Sherborne Castle Hospital was opened in a wing of Sherborne Castle lent by Major and Mrs. Wingfield Digby, and here, amid the pleasantest surroundings, men broken in the war were nursed back to health and strength. This hospital was afterwards transferred to a charming house in Sherborne itself, rented, through the generosity of its owner, Major G. R. Ricket, at half its value. Greenhill Hospital, also in this Division, claims the distinction of being one of the first hospitals in Dorset to try the open-air treatment in revolving shelters.

In Dorchester, by December, 1915, there were two V.A. hospitals, Colliton House and Church Street. The Shaftesbury Division had four hospitals—Plank House, Station Road, Mere and The Retreat—and the Weymouth Division four hospitals and two convalescent homes. Four V.A. Hospitals in the Wimborne Division, two in the Poole Division and two in the Wareham Division completed the list.

In 1919 Lady Ilchester became President of the Dorset Branch of the Red Cross Society.

MISS JESSIE ELMS. A.R.R.C.

THE daughter of the late J. P. Elms, Esq., of " Brooklands," Newport, Mon., Miss Jessie Elms was trained in hospital work at Liverpool before the war, and held Sister's posts in the Eye and Ear Hospital there ; also at the Central London Ophthalmic Hospital ; at the Birmingham and Midland Eye Hospital ; the Bradford Eye and Ear Hospital ; and in 1907 was appointed Matron at the Sussex Eye Hospital, where she has since remained. In October, 1914, she received twelve hours' notice for the first convoy of wounded. It is pleasing to record the fact that she has been awarded the Royal Red Cross.

MRS. DOROTHY C. EDMONDES.

MRS. DOROTHY C. EDMONDES was one of many amongst the women of Great Britain who willingly endeavoured to lighten the burdens of others during the five years of the Great Strife.

Mrs. Edmondes was Hon. Secretary of the Soldiers' and Sailors' Families Association for Bridgend and the surrounding districts during 1914-15 ; afterwards becoming President. She was also head of the Soldiers' and Sailors' Help Society for the Cowbridge

District and on the War Pensions Committee for the county of Glamorgan.

In 1916 Mrs. Edmondes received training in massage and Swedish remedial exercises at Dr. Barrie Lambert's College, London, later taking a course of medical electricity.

Mrs. Edmondes voluntarily and energetically gave her services to Red Cross hospitals in Glamorgan in 1917 and early in the following year started the Bridgend Orthopædic Outpatient Clinic under the Ministry of Pensions, working there voluntarily until March, 1919, and after that date indefatigably and efficiently undertaking the duties of head masseuse and administrator.

Mrs. Dorothy Caroline Edmondes, who is the daughter of John Illyd Nicholl, Esq. of Merthyr Mawr, Bridgend, Glamorganshire, is the widow of Charles G. T. Edmondes, Esq., of Cowbridge, Glamorganshire.

Her recreations are hunting and gardening.

MISS S. M. G. EAKIN.

THE daughter of J. H. Eakin, Esq., of Drumcovitt, Londonderry, Miss S. M. G. Eakin has been a zealous and thoroughly efficient member of the Army Nursing Service since the beginning of 1915, and was "mentioned" in October, 1917, for valuable services rendered.

MISS A. M. EVANS.

MISS A. MARJORIE EVANS devoted herself to war hospital work and performed thoroughly efficient and valuable services as V.A.D. nurse at the Oaklands Auxiliary Military Hospital since February, 1915. Miss Evans is the daughter of C. L. Evans, Esq., and of Mrs. Evans, of Norton Hill, Runcorn, Cheshire.

Miss Elms

Miss S. M. G. Eakins

Mrs. Edmondes

MRS. DUNCAN.

SINCE the day Armageddon shattered the peace of the world in July, 1914, it is remarkable beyond all conception how much the women of gentle birth in England quickly and nobly accomplished in the sacred cause of assuaging the anguish, healing the wounds, and brightening the outlook of our intrepid heroes who returned maimed from the firing line.

There have been thousands of Florence Nightingales in our land during the years of war, and one devoted and efficient band worked untiringly at Barra House Auxiliary Hospital, Largs, under their greatly respected Officer-in-charge, Mrs. Duncan. The Hospital was entirely equipped by the late Mr. Clark-Neill and received the first patients on 5th December, 1914. Originally there were 20 beds and these increased later to 40, 15 of which were in a wing of Mrs. Duncan's own house. Barra House was closed on 20th March, 1919, and during its existence, 1304 patients were treated. Massage and electricity were made specialities. The Sister-in-charge was Miss I. M. Beaton, R.R.C.

Mrs. Duncan, daughter of the late Charles G. Ramsay, Esq., of Greenock, was before her maraiage with Mr. Duncan, the widow of James Clark-Neill, Esq., director of Messrs. J. & P. Coats, Ltd. She is a keen sportswoman and especially fond of yachting, golf and tennis.

Clubs : The Scottish Automobile and Kelvin Clubs, Glasgow.

MISS DIANA DASHWOOD.

AMONG the younger women of gentle birth, who so willingly and numerously devoted their whole time and energies to the alleviation of the poignant suffering caused by the war, was Miss Diana Dashwood, who is a member of V.A.D. Hants, 36.

From August, 1914, to January, 1915, Miss Dashwood indefatigably toiled as a nurse at the Red Cross Hospital, provided by the Winchester College Sanatorium for hospital purposes.

In January, 1915, Miss Dashwood undertook whole time nursing at " The Close," a Red Cross hospital at Winchester.

Miss Diana P. Dashwood is the daughter of Edward Vere Dashwood, Esq., of St. Cross Lodge, Winchester.

LADY DALRYMPLE OF NEWHAILES.

LADY DALRYMPLE, during the war, entertained regularly at Newhailes the wounded men from the hospice in Musselburgh, and also Colonial troops from the Overseas Club in Edinburgh, while all her leisure was given to knitting for the soldiers and sailors. She was President of the Y.M.C.A. War Emergency Club in Musselburgh, in which she took the greatest interest, going down to the Club to see the girls personally, and having them up for recreation in the park at Newhailes.

Lady Dalrymple is the daughter of Sir Mark MacTaggart Stewart, Bart., of Southwick, Kirkcudbrightshire, and wife of Lieut.-Commander Sir David Dalrymple, Bart., R.N., of Newhailes, Musselburgh.

She is very fond of gardening, and has done some exquisite pieces of fine silk embroidery.

MRS. WINGFIELD DIGBY.

THROUGHOUT the war Mrs. Wingfield Digby was an untiring worker in connection with the Red Cross Hospitals in Dorset. And scarcely had the British Expeditionary force reached the shores of France in the first days of the Struggle, ere the Dorset Hospitals also—fully equipped, and staffed by the County V.A.Ds.—were ready to receive our wounded soldiers.

In those early days the President of the Red Cross in Dorset was Mrs. Mount-Batten, the Hon. County Director, Brig.-Gen. Balguy, and the results speak for themselves of pronounced organising abilities. By September 2nd—that is, within a month of the outbreak of war—there were 1,200 beds ready and equipped, with complete trained nursing staff and medical attendance.

The County was divided into twelve Red Cross Divisions :—Dorchester, Sherborne, Shaftesbury, Weymouth, Bridport, Cerne, Beaminster, Blandford, Sturminster Newton, Wimborne, Poole and Wareham.

The Sherborne Division was one of the most important, partly owing to the large number of hospitals in it, and partly to the excellent way in which it was arranged. By December, 1915, there were seven Class A Hospitals and two Class B Hospitals.

Lady Dalrymple

LADY EDEN.

FEW (if any) have accomplished more than Lady Eden in the sacred cause of the amelioration of the sufferings of our wounded heroes. Windlestone, Ferry Hill, the country seat of her son, Sir Timothy Eden, who was at that time a prisoner at Ruhleben Camp, in Germany, was equipped and opened May 26th, 1915, as the 19th Durham V.A.D. Hospital, and Lady Eden became the Commandant and Matron, fulfilling those strenuous and important duties until the closing of the hospital, April 23rd, 1919.

In addition, she served during the war as (and still is) President of the Bishop Auckland Soldiers' and Sailors' Help Society ; Chairman of the Bishop Auckland War Pension Committee ; member of the Committee of the Durham Nursing Association ; President of the Lady Eden Hospital, Bishop Auckland ; Vice-President of the Durham Needlework Guild ; President of Bishop Auckland Branch N.S.P.C.C. ; Hon. Secretary of County Branch of R.S.P.C.A. ; and is also greatly interested in all such movements as the Girl Guides, Boy Scouts, Church Lads' Brigade, etc.

Lady Eden felt very deeply for our wounded men, for two of her sons made the Great Sacrifice in the war.

Lady Eden is a daughter of the late Sir William Grey, K.C.S.I., and was born at Government House, Barrachpore, India, in 1867. In 1886 she married Sir William Eden, Bt. (the 7th Baronet), D.L., J.P., co. Durham, who died in 1915.

Her Ladyship also organized the Lady Eden Hospital, Bishop Auckland.

MRS. S. E. FAITH.

AT the outbreak of the war, Mrs. S. E. Faith secured the tenancy of Rothesay, Weyhill, and there established a Red Cross Auxiliary Hospital, with 30 beds. This hospital was open for more than four years and over 1200 sick and wounded heroes passed through the institution. For this work she received the thanks of the Army through the C.O. of the Southern Command at Salisbury, also of the Military Hospital at Tidworth, and the Army Council at Whitehall.

Mrs. Faith has been mentioned in dispatches and has also had the honour of receiving a Diploma from H.M. Queen Alexandra.

F

Mrs. Faith is the daughter of the late Rev. Stephen Browne, the Rector of East Shefford, Berks, and in 1870 married the late Thomas Faith, Esq., of Clanville Lodge, near Andover, Lord of the Manor of Blissimore Hall, Hampshire.

THE LADY FISHER-SMITH.

THE Lady Fisher-Smith, daughter of the late Joseph Fisher, Esq., of Dedham, Massachusetts, U.S.A., and the late Mary Elizabeth Campbell Fisher, of Cherryfield, Maine, in the same country, is the wife of Sir George H. Fisher-Smith, of The Gleddings, Halifax, Yorskhire. They were married on May 7th, 1890.

Like many of her gifted countrywomen she possesses the faculty of gathering into her hands at one time a large number of different threads—philanthropic, political and educational.

The needs of her own town, Halifax, evoke a large measure of her energies, and her sympathies flow into such channels as shall especially benefit members of her own sex.

For a considerable number of years Lady Fisher-Smith had led a life of strenuous effort for the good of others before the war came, and then she enlarged her sphere of activity and applied her organising power to meet the exigencies of the times.

As a lecturer her Ladyship manifests wide and varied interests, embracing temperance, literature and art. She is devoted to music and has travelled much.

Lady Fisher-Smith was Manager and President of a Toy Factory during the years 1914–15–16 for the benefit of dressmakers and milliners out of work owing to the war ; Member of the Executive of the Mayor's Representative Committee ; Vice-Chairman of the Halifax War Savings Committee and organiser of the Women's Branches ; promoted 21 Flag Days during 1915–16–17–18 ; she is President of the Hostel (for the benefit of relatives of the wounded soldiers) at St. Luke's Military Hospital, Halifax ; Hon. Secretary of the West Riding for the French War Emergency Fund and President of a local branch.

Her Ladyship is a Member of the Executive Committee of the Women's Liberal Federation ; a Member of the Executive Committee of the Yorkshire Council of W.L.A.s ; President of the Yorkshire Area of W.L.A.'s ; Secretary of the Halifax W.L. Association. She is also President of the Yorkshire Band of Hope, while for ten years

Lady Fisher-Smith

Miss Agnes Foster

Miss M. A. Fowler

Mrs. C. K. Fanshawe

she was Poor Law Guardian and for a long time Secretary of the Committee for the boarding out of pauper children. Her care for the young also evinces itself in her management of an Infants' Creche ; also her solicitude for the sick, together with the work which she has accomplished on the Executive Committee of the Halifax Nursing Association.

Lady Fisher-Smith is the Divisional Commissioner of the Halifax and District Girl Guides ; President of a Girls' Club and Hostel ; President of the Free Church Girls' Guild ; President of Girl Life Council and Member of the Halifax Vigilance Society with Hostel for Working Girls.

She is also Secretary of the Halifax Branch of the League of Nations Union.

MISS AGNES FOSTER.

MISS AGNES FOSTER is the only daughter of Robert John Foster, Esq., D.L., J.P., and the late Hon. Mrs. Robert Foster, of Stockeld Park, Wetherby, Yorkshire, who was, before her marriage, the Hon. Evelyn Augusta Bateman-Hanbury (d. 1907), the second daughter of the second Lord Bateman.

Miss Foster had passed her examinations before the war and was allowed to form a Detachment and was registered as Commandant of Wetherby-cum-Stockeld Detachment on September 19th, 1913. In July, 1915, she was transferred to No. 2 Harrogate Detachment No. 94 as Commandant and was subsequently asked to take her Detachment to Beaulieu Auxiliary Military Hospital, Harrogate, in turn with the two other Detachments. Mr. and Mrs. Lund, of Becca Hall, Aberford, Yorkshire, are the owners of the house, which they kindly equipped and lent as a hospital. Miss Foster also devoted herself to other war work, acting for a short time as Superintendent of the dining-room at Viscount Furness' Hospital at Harrogate.

MISS MABEL AMY FOWLER.

THIS lady has been " mentioned " in the honours list for valuable war services performed at Yeovil, and has well earned her two white stripes ; for, in addition to her thoroughly efficient work, she is completely devoted to the sacred cause of alleviating the sufferings of our wounded heroes. During two years Miss

Fowler was a voluntary worker at the Yeovil Red Cross Hospital, giving her whole time to nursing from July, 1915, to August, 1917; then, she proceeded to Winchester for a few months, leaving when the small auxiliary hospital was closed in November, 1917, and on December 12th, she was called up for the 4th Northern General Hospital at Lincoln.

MRS. C. K. FANSHAWE.

MRS. FANSHAWE did excellent service as a V.A.D. nurse from January, 1915, first at the Red Cross Hospital, Netley, and subsequently at Craghead Auxiliary Hospital, Manor Road, Bournemouth. She is the wife of Captain R. D. Fanshawe (late Scots Guards).

MISS A. M. B. FISHER.

MISS ALICE MARY BROMFIELD FISHER was actively associated with Red Cross work in the Isle of Wight for some years before the war, being Vice-President of the B.R.C.S., Ventnor, and Commandant of the Hampshire 176, and forming three detachments of Women's V.A.D. and one of men's. On the outbreak of hostilities she assisted in the equipment and opening of the Underwath Red Cross Hospital by the Red Cross organisation. This hospital was accepted in December, 1914, and opened August 1st, 1915, when Miss Fisher gave up her post as Commandant of the Red Cross branch, and became Hon. Commandant and Vice-President, which positions she still holds. From 1915 onwards she was Colonial Visitor for all the Island hospitals.

From November, 1915, Miss Fisher was President and Organiser of the War Hospital Supply Depôt, Ventnor, working under the Belgravia Workrooms, 4, Grosvenor Crescent, London. Four village parties supplied this Depôt, and in 1918 alone the number of garments made was 2,486.

Miss Fisher is a daughter of the late Colonel Charles Edmund Fisher, Bombay Staff Corps, of Oak Alyn, Wrexham, N. Wales.

The Countess Fitzwilliam

Lady Farren

THE COUNTESS FITZWILLIAM.

DURING the war the Countess Fitzwilliam devoted her time and great influence to Y.M.C.A. work and was President for the West Riding area of Yorkshire,, specialising in canteen work for the benefit of munition workers, and did splendidly in this connection. In addition to all this, the Countess found time also to look after Earl Fitzwilliam's Wentworth Hunt, the Hunt stables and breeding establishment.

Countess Fitzwilliam before her marriage was Lady Maud Dundas (second daughter of the Marquess of Zetland), and therefore comes of a great historic family, remarkable for producing a series of men eminently distinguished for their public services in the highest offices in Scotland ; whilst Earl Fitzwilliam, to whom her Ladyship was married on June 24th, 1896, succeeded in 1902 to a long and illustrious line of ancestors who have figured nobly in history.

Her Ladyship is President of Queen Victoria Nurses' Association, Sheffield, President of The Women's Unionist Association for Yorkshire, and her recreations are hunting, racing, yachting, sailing, acting and music.

Club :—Ladies' Imperial.

LADY FARREN.

LADY FARREN was Commandant of the V.A.D. Suffolk 44, and in 1914 worked at the Red Cross Hospital at Ampton Hall, then during 1915 worked at Devonshire House, and for one year was Commandant of the Red Cross Hospital, Foxborough Hall, Suffolk.

Lady Farren worked during 2½ years in the General Inquiries in Hall, for the Central Prisoners of War Committee, 4, Thurloe Place, and was also in charge of a Hostel for V.A.Ds., who worked there.

Her Ladyship is the daughter of the Rev. W. E. Downes, and in 1885 married General Sir Richard Farren, G.C.B.

MISS D. M. FORSTER.

THE elder daughter of the Rev. W. T. Forster, of the Vicarage, Idle, near Bradford, Miss Dorothy Margaret Forster was, before the war, a pupil at Harrogate College, and since 1915 has been working at the St. Luke's War Hospital, Bradford, where she is now a senior war probationer.

THE VISCOUNTESS GALWAY.

MANY are the ladies to whom the British Empire is indebted for whole-hearted and most valuable work during the terrible years of Armageddon. One of these is the Viscountess Galway, of Serlby Hall, Bawtry, Yorks, whose patriotic labours were actively exercised long before the outbreak of war, for in 1900 her hospital was ready, and four years in succession was inspected by the P.M.O. from York. It was offered to and accepted by the Government in August, 1914, and 40 serious cases received the attention of a resident surgeon and staff. Lady Galway personally conducted the hospital until, most unfortunately, the overwork and overstrain caused a breakdown in health; but immediately upon her recovery she organised a factory in Scarborough, where the war output included 100,000 shell bags weekly besides army clothing. During all this strenuous life, her Ladyship also found time to continue her well-known interest in politics.

The readiness displayed by the Viscountess Galway for the great emergencies of 1914 was the natural sequence of pre-war prescience and attention to hospital organisation and visiting, to both of which her Ladyship had long devoted her abilities and energies; for in the tranquil times of peace her devotion to the cause of public welfare and progress took her not only into the political field diligently, but much time was also given to hospital work, nursing and visiting, and to her duties as Lady of Justice of the Order of St. John of Jerusalem; whilst opportunities for recreation were found in the delightful pursuits of gardening and literature.

The Viscountess Galway, who married in 1879, is the only daughter of the late Ellis Gosling, Esq., of Busbridge Hall, Godalming, Surrey.

THE HON. MRS. GRETTON.

THE daughter of the late Lord Ventry, the Hon. Maud de Moleyns was married in 1900 to Colonel John Gretton, M.P., who followed, as Conservative Member for Rutland, the late George Finch, Esq., of Burley, Near Oakham, for many years the unopposed representative, who, in his time, was " The Father of the House."

In June, 1915, Col. and the Hon. Mrs. Gretton opened their beautiful home, Stapleford Park, Melton Mowbray, Leicestershire, as an auxiliary hospital attached to the 1/5th Northern General Hospital, Leicester, and Mrs. Gretton was its Commandant for nearly four years. She is also the President of the Rutland Branch of the B.R.C.S., in addition to being a member of the S. & S.F.A. Committee and Rutland Branch of the Pensions Committee.

Mrs. Gretton is a Member of the Bath Club.

THE LADY ARTHUR GROSVENOR.

THE daughter of the late Sir Robert Sheffield, Normandy Park, Doncaster, Lady Arthur Grosvenor was married to Lord Arthur on April 12th, 1893 ; and her Ladyship's favourite recreations were hunting and caravaning before the darkness of Armageddon fell in 1914. Then every pursuit was put aside for the one engrossing task of helping to win the war.

From November 4th, 1914, to January 15th, 1917, Lady Arthur Grosvenor was Commandant of Eaton Hall V.A.D. Hospital, which, at the latter date was closed to privates and taken over by the Government for officers. Lady Arthur then removed to Oakfield, Upton Heath, Chester, kindly lent by Beresford Jones, Esq., and started there with 50 beds, which in 1918 were augmented by a large hut containing 38 beds, bringing up the total accommodation for patients to 88. Between 60 and 70 of the disabled were supplied with artificial limbs, until the Minister of Pensions intervened. The hospital closed on April 30th, 1919, and throughout the period 1914–19 the same matron and staff worked untiringly and nobly with Lady Arthur Grosvenor.

MISS AGNES GRAHAME.

DURING the war Miss Agnes Grahame, who is the daughter of James Grahame, Esq., of the family of Grahame, of Easter Drumguhassle, Stirlingshire, gave up her peace-time recreations of sketching and golf to work as the Commandant, V.A.D. Inverness 24, Fort Augustus, Scottish Branch, B.R.C.S. ; her assiduity and efficiency winning for her the honour of being " mentioned " for valuable services rendered, February, 1918, as Commandant at the Abbey Auxliary Hospital, Fort Augustus.

Miss Agnes Grahame is a member of the Ladies' Park Club, Parkside, Knightsbridge, S.W.

LADY GRANTLEY.

FROM October, 1914, for three months, Lady Grantley worked as a V.A.D. nurse at Tidmouth ; then from 1914 until Christmas, 1918, at Rothesay Hospital, Andover.

Lady Grantley is the daughter of the Viscount Ranelagh, and in September, 1899, married Lord Grantley. Her Ladyship devotes much of her time to hunting, and is a very successful breeder of pedigree short horns, for which she has taken many prizes at shows.

MISS FLORENCE GILFORD, A.R.R.C.

SISTER FLORENCE GILFORD, A.R.R.C., is one among many who willingly devoted their whole time and energies to the amelioration of suffering during the Great Strife.

Before the war she received her training at St. Thomas' Hospital, London, S.E., afterwards becoming a member of the Nurses Co-operation, of 22, Langham Street, London, W.

Miss Gilford then joined Q.A.I.M.N.S. Reserve, 1909. On August 5th, 1914, she was called up for duty, and six days later was mobilized at Southsea under the present Matron-in-Chief, Miss Beadsmore-Smith, R.R.C. Sister Gilford has performed much beneficent work at the following Hospitals : —The No. 5 General Hospital at Rouen and Angers, France, and No. 7 Stationary Hospital, Boulogne, from August, 1914, to November, 1915 ; No. 15

Lady Grantley

Lady Arthur Grosvenor

Miss Agnes Grahame

Miss Gilford

Viscountess Galway

The Hon. Mrs. Gretton

Crag Head {	Miss Turner, O.B.E. Miss Moss	} 207	4 yrs.	3 months		
Buckland						
Ripers	Mrs. Douglas	27	4 ,,			
Holnest	Lady Lilian Digby, A.R.R.C., M.B.E.	100	3 ,,	9 ,,		
The Convent	Miss Grey	18	3 ,,			
Infirmary	Mrs. Elwes	68	3 ,,	9 ,,		
Plank House	Hon. Mrs. Anstruther	25	4 ,,	3 ,,		
Church St.	Mrs. Acland		1 yr.	6 ,,		
Ryme	Mrs. Watts, O.B.E.	40	4 yrs.	3 ,,		
The Garden	Miss Ferguson	18	3 ,,	3 ,,		
Castle	Mrs. Hardman, O.B.E.	50	4 ,,	4 ,,		

In May, 1916, a County Red Cross Supply Depôt at Kingston Maurward was formed to receive the large output from working parties and—on the lines of a clearing house—distribute the various articles among the Hospitals of Dorset. Mrs. Hanbury was placed in charge, and under the able organisation of the County Director, General Balguy, the Supply Depôt was brought to a high pitch of efficiency and usefulness. In three years the receipts of clothing, linen, blankets, etc., totalled 119,465 articles, besides 92,549 surgical dressings and large quantities of such articles of hospital equipment as bath and spinal chairs, sterilisers and crutches; while during the same period over 17,000 articles of surplus stock were sent to H.Q., B.R.C.S., London, after the needs of the local hospitals had been satisfied.

General Balguy was himself an indefatigable worker. In addition to his duties as Hon. County Director he undertook metal work and carpentry in connection with the production of surgical appliances, and when, in January, 1918, the County Supply Depôt associated itself with the splint-making industry, he proved himself of valuable assistance, doing much of the actual work with his own hands. During that year 498 surgical boots, splints, etc., 121 papier maché baths and 102 peg legs were completed.

In December, 1918, the Depôt was inspected by Major Chappell, head of the Orthopædic Hospital at Brighton, and Inspecting Surgeon for the new Provisional Limb Department organised by the H.Q. of the B.R.C.S., who expressed his unqualified approval of the work in hand, and as a result of this visit Mrs. Hanbury's depôt was, in January, 1919, appointed the Provisional Limb Depôt for the County of Dorset for Soldiers and Discharged Pensioners.

H

Colonel Carroll, O.C., The Military Hospital, Weymouth, under whom Mrs. Hanbury and her helpers worked, placed a ward of that Hospital at their disposal from February, 1919, to June, 1919, during which period 51 legs were completed. And when, on the closing down of the Hospital, these Red Cross Workers were obliged to leave, Mrs. Hanbury received from Colonel Carroll (June 6th, 1919) a glowing tribute to their work at Weymouth. The letter stated that Mrs. Hanbury had made all the plaster pylons for the amputation cases in the Military Hospital, Weymouth, and its affiliated hospitals from February, 1919. Colonel Carroll could not speak too highly of her work, which was carried out to his complete satisfaction. "In her devotion to the interests of the patients," he says, " she has spared neither time nor trouble, and she possesses great mechanical ability and manual dexterity ; the result being that every patient she has dealt with has left the Hospital with a perfectly fitting and excellently made provisional limb, which moreover, she has taught him to use correctly." In recognition of her services Mrs. Hanbury was awarded the O.B.E.

In May, 1919, the Depôt was closed with a credit balance of £236 0s. 10d., which is being applied to the furnishing and equipment of the new Red Cross War Memorial Hospital for Children at Swanage, which is being run entirely by the Depôt.

In addition to the duties specified above, Mrs. Hanbury was appointed Commandant of the Dorset Reserve V.A. Detachment, formed in May, 1917, for the purpose of providing nursing members for duty in Miiltary Hospitals.

MRS. MOUNSEY HEYSHAM.

MRS. MOUNSEY HEYSHAM, soon after the outbreak of war, offered her beautiful woodland residence of Grata Quies, Parkstone, Dorset, as a hospital for English soldiers. This scheme, however, fell through, as did the subsequent plan of turning Grata Quies into a home for Belgian Refugees ; and Mrs. Mounsey Heysham, through the agency of Miss Bottomley, transferred her offer of this charming residence to the Sub-Committee which the Bournemouth War Relief Committee had appointed to help the wounded Belgian soldiers, who were being shipped in large numbers to this country.

Towards the end of 1915 the number of occupied beds had grown so small that it was considered advisable to close the institution

MRS. J. BEAUCHAMP HOUCHEN.

MRS. BEAUCHAMP HOUCHEN is the wife of Lieut. Beauchamp Houchen, whom she married in August, 1917, and is the daughter of Mrs. J. Emery of Downham Market, Norfolk. Before the war she was greatly interested in educational work and out-door sports for girls. She specialized in mathematics. At the Ford Grammar School for Girls she was sports mistress and was the centre half Norfolk County Hockey Champion. On the outbreak of war she took up V.A.D. nursing at the Downham Market Auxiliary Hospital ; and now (April, 1918) Mrs. Beauchamp Houchen is in charge of the Ambulance room at the British Westinghouse Manufacturing Co. at Manchester. She was " mentioned " in the first Honours List of Nurses, October 20th, 1917.

MRS. C. O. HALL.

AS Commandant of 32 East Riding of Yorkshire Red Cross and Head of the Northern Division of Women Workers on the Land, Mrs. Hall has done excellent war-time service to the country.

She is a daughter of W. F. W. Garforth, Esq., of Wiganthorpe, Yorkshire, and wife of Charles O. Hall, Esq., Settrington House, Malton, Yorkshire.

Mrs. Hall finds recreation in all the sporting pursuits of country life.

MISS AMICIA FRANCES HALL.

MISS AMICIA FRANCES HALL performed much valuable and indispensable work for the Kensington Red Cross (Weir) Hospital, toiling as a V.A.D. nurse in its wards from March, 1915, till its close on June 30th, 1919. Previously, Miss Hall willingly undertook the duty of serving in a Y.M.C.A. Canteen at Nuneaton.

Miss Amicia Frances Hall is the daughter of the late Rev. Bracebridge Hall, formerly Rector of Weddington, Near Nuneaton.

THE HON. LADY HULSE.

THE Hon. Lady Hulse, during the war, was a tireless patriotic worker, sparing nothing of her time or strength in the public interest. She was a member of Queen Mary's Needlework Guild, Vice-Chairman of the War Savings Committee and Vice-President of the Fordingbridge Division of the Red Cross. Early in the course of the war she had offered her house as a hospital, but as there was no telephone communication and no medical staff available locally, the Authorities were unable to accept.

Lady Hulse is a daughter of the first Lord Burnham, founder of *The Daily Telegraph*, and widow of Sir Charles Westrow Hulse, the sixth baronet. Her Ladyship's seat is Breamore House, Hants.

MRS. CECIL HANBURY.

MRS. HANBURY, of Kingston Maurward, Dorchester, carried out the duties of Honorary County Secretary of the Dorset Branch of the Red Cross from June, 1918. This energetic and capable organisation—one of the most efficient in the country—comprised twelve Red Cross Divisions : Dorchester, Sherborne, Shaftesbury, Weymouth, Bridport, Cerne, Beaminster, Blandford, Sturminster Newton, Wimborne, Poole and Wareham.

The following is a list of the hospitals administered by the Red Cross in Dorset :—

Hospital.	Commandant.	No. of Beds.	Period Open.
Colliton	Miss Marsden, O.B.E.	200	4 yrs. 5 months
Cluny	Dr. Baiss, O.B.E.	50	4 ,, 3 ,,
St. John's	Mrs. Gordon Steward, M.B.E.	36	4 ,, 3 ,,
Grata Quies	Miss Bottomley	75	4 ,, 3 ,,
Greenhill	Mrs. McAdam, O.B.E.	77	4 ,, 2 ,,
Massandra	Mrs. Fraser, O.B.E.	76	4 ,, 3 ,,
Chetnole	Mrs. Alexander, A.R.R.C.	32	4 ,, 2 ,,
Newton	{ Miss Wavell, A.R.R.C. / Mrs. Parke }	40	4 ,,
Mere	Mrs. White, O.B.E.	50	4 ,, 5 ,,
Compton	Mrs. Goodden, O.B.E.	23	3 ,, 9 ,,
Beaucroft	Miss Carr-Glyn, O.B.E.	56	4 ,, 3 ,,
Station Rd.	Miss Leatham	62	4 ,, 4 ,,

The Hon. Lady Hulse

was the Government Department at that time responsible for all surgical appliances supplied to men invalided from the Army, an International Limb Exhibition was arranged at Roehampton which was most helpful in securing the supply of the most efficient and up-to-date appliances.

Limb-making as a science had never been very seriously considered in England. It was soon found that it was necessary to have on the premises workshops where limbs could be made and fitted for the men. The work in this respect has increased by leaps and bounds, the output of artificial limbs being now over 150 a week. There are working at Roehampton not only two big American firms, but several of our leading English limb-makers.

There are now in the Limb Shops at Roehampton also a number of the discharged patients themselves wearing artificial limbs. Seeing these comrades in the Limb Shops gives great help and encouragement to all new patients passing through the institution.

At first it was never realised how great would be the number of men who would lose their limbs, and how vast would be the work which the hospital would be called upon to undertake.

It was at one time hoped that an affiliated branch of the Roehampton hospital for limbless men would be opened in different centres in England, Ireland, Scotland and Wales. This, however, owing to personal opposition, was found impossible, and Scotland has now two limbless hospitals—one at Erskine House, near Glasgow, and Eden Hall, Kelso ; Ireland also has two—one at Belfast and the other at Bray ; Wales has another at Cardiff named after His Royal Highness The Prince of Wales. These hospitals supply the needs of the men drawn from those districts.

The magnitude of the work is also indicated by the following figures relating to its finance :—Collected from Private Sources (approximately), £120,000 ; National Relief Fund, £10,000 ; Promised, and also from same Fund for the purchase of Roehampton House, £20,000 ; The British Red Cross and Order of St. John, £11,000 ; Pensions Ministry (promised), £10,000.

MRS. J. HENDERSON, O.B.E.

MRS. HENDERSON organised the Red Cross work in the Leatherhead Division, Surrey Branch, B.R.C.S. The Red House Auxiliary Hospital, Leatherhead, was opened soon after the outbreak of the war on October 21st, 1914, and was not closed until February 4th, 1919. The members of Surrey 17 (men) and Surrey 22 (women) acted as orderlies and nurses. This hospital was in class A, and was affiliated to the County of London War Hospital, Horton, Epsom. There were 40 beds ; and a total of 698 patients and 125 out-patients were carefully treated. When Dr. Done was called up, Mrs. Henderson acted as Commandant, with Dr. Von Bergen as Medical Officer in Charge, from September, 1917, until the Hospital was closed in February, 1919.

Five beds were maintained in the B.R.C.S. Hospital at Netley. Flag days and entertainments were organised for " Our Day " and " Surrey Red Cross Week " in the Division.

Mrs. Henderson fittingly received, in recognition of her valuable and untiring services, the O.B.E. in March, 1919.

She is the daughter of the late John Smith, Esq., of 27, Prince's Gate, and Mickleham Hall, Dorking, Surrey, and step-daughter of Sir Dyce Duckworth, Bart, M.D.

In 1881 she married John Henderson, Esq., of Randalls Park, Leatherhead, Surrey.

Mrs. Henderson in the midst of a busy life finds time for her favourite recreations of music, travelling, and all work connected with the Leatherhead Division, Surrey Branch, B.R.C.S., of which she has been Vice-President since its formation in 1911.

Club : The Ladies' Empire.

MISS ELIZABETH HADFIELD.

BEFORE the war, Miss Elizabeth Hadfield (the daughter of Mr. and Mrs. Joseph Hadfield, of Stockport) was on the staff of Queen Victoria's Jubilee Institute for Nurses ; and since the outbreak of hostilities in 1914, her most valuable war record includes the following :—With the Society of Friends in France ; Sister at the Scottish Women's Hospital, Salonica ; Sister-in-Charge, St. John's A.M. Hospital, Rugby ; Sister at the Rust Hall V.A.D. Hospital, Tunbridge Wells ; Sister at Maxillo Facial Hospital, Kennington, London ; Matron, Ickleton V.A.D. Hospital, Gt. Chesterford, Essex ; Sister at the Military Hospital, Arc en Barrois, France.

Mrs. J. Henderson, O.B.E.

Miss E. Hadfield

Mrs. J. Beauchamp Houchen

January, 1915. She explains that one day in that month while walking through the wards at Millbank Military Hospital with the Matron, just after the first exchange of our prisoners of war from Germany, she saw at a table, sitting with a look of unutterable sadness and hopelessness on his face, a man who had lost both arms. In front of him lay what the Government had sent as a substitute for those arms—two leather sockets with hooks attached. She bent down and asked him to tell her his story. He looked up with eyes full of pathos and said : " Is this all my country can do for me ? " This man was Private F. W. Chapman, of the 23rd R.W.F., with a record of over twenty-one years' service, who rejoined his regiment at the very beginning of the war, giving up good employment at the age of forty-six to serve his country once again.

Then and there Mrs. Holford made a vow that she would work for one object—to start a hospital whereby all those who had the misfortune to become disabled in this terrible war could be fitted with the most perfect artificial limbs human science could devise.

In March, 1915, she drew up a scheme out of which grew the present hospital at Roehampton. Her plan was for a convalescent hospital for limbless sailors and soldiers. At that time sailors and soldiers were leaving the hospitals, in many cases, without artificial limbs, which, when ready, were sent on to them, and if they did not fit (frequently the case), a local agent was supposed to adjust them to the patients' requirements. That meant that the artificial limbs never fitted comfortably, and were a source of trouble and pain to the wearer instead of being a comfort.

Mrs. Holford's patriotic aim was to provide an institution where artificial limbs could be properly adjusted and fitted, and where the wearers could be taught how to make the best use of them, before being discharged from the service.

Her scheme was taken up by various influential people, including the Duke of Portland, Lady Falmouth, Mr. Walter Long, Sir George Murray, and Mr. Kenderdine, who gave her his able assistance and became Honorary Secretary and Treasurer, and who has been rewarded by a K.B.E. Within the next three months the hospital opened its doors under the name of Queen Mary's Auxiliary Hospitals for Sailors and Soldiers who have lost their limbs in the war. Premises were secured at Roehampton, the house and grounds being lent by Mr. Kenneth Wilson. At first accommodation was provided for 170 patients, but that was soon found to be inadequate, and it was increased to nine hundred beds, which, however, were wholly inadequate to accommodate the large number of men needing artificial limbs.

Their Majesties the Queen and Queen Alexandra became patronesses.

Before very long it was realised how much greater and more important the work of this hospital was to become, and department after department had to be organised.

Mrs. Holford personally undertook the Limb Office, a work of absorbing interest. It brought her into personal touch with each patient as he passed through the institution, and Mrs. Holford says : " None but those who work among these gallant men can realise their superhuman courage and unselfishness. The greater the disability it seems to me the greater the courage ; never have I heard a word of complaint from these men ; so often they came to me with their troubles and placed in me a child-like confidence and trust, that whatever happens the best would be done for them."

Over thirteen thousand cases have passed through her hands, and several thousands of these have returned a second time for renewals and repairs to their artificial limbs. It is most interesting here to quote from Mrs. Holford's Report :—" I confess there are two things in my life I look back to with pride. One that I was fortunate enough to be the first to put into concrete form some scheme for the supply of artificial limbs to the men who had lost theirs in the service of our country ; the other, that I had the honour of knowing as intimately as I have done, all those splendid fellows, and have been able to give them help and human sympathy,which has, I hope, made their lot more bearable. I am proud of the gratitude and affection which they have given, and I am proud that I had the privilege of being able to help them."

An employment bureau and a technical workshop have been organised representing the first attempt made in England to deal seriously with the all-important question of the men's after-careers while they are still in hospital. Ever since 1915, all the men passing through the hospital have been systematically classified from an industrial stand-point, while their requirements have been considered and dealt with.

Four Sergeant-Majors " themselves wearing artificial limbs " are specially selected by the Commandant to train the patients in the art of using their artificial limbs in the best way possible.

The difficulty was to find limb-makers who were in a position to deal with a problem of such magnitude. With the help of Sir Charles Crutchley, then Lt.-Governor of the Royal Hospital, Chelsea, which

General Hospital, Alexandria, in December, 1915; No. 21 Stationary Hospital, Salonica, from January, 1916, to August, 1916; the Military Hospital, Canterbury, from September to December of 1917, and at the Military Hospital, Newark-on-Trent, from December, 1917, to August, 1919.

Miss Gilford was demobilized on August 5th, 1919. Sister Florence Gilford, A.R.R.C., is the daughter of the late John Meadows Gilford, Esq., of Manor House, Somerby, Oakham, and of his late wife, Mrs. Gilford, of Great Bowden, Market Harborough.

THE HON. MRS. F. E. GUEST.

THE Hon. Mrs. F. E. Guest is the daughter of Henry Phipps, Esq., the Pittsburg Steel Magnate, and wife of Captain the Hon. F. E. Guest, Coalition Whip. Her valuable services during the war included the giving up of her London house—Aldford House, Park Lane—as a hospital for Officers (from 1914 to 1918), and later as an American Naval Hospital. Burley on the Hill was also loaned as a convalescent home.

MRS. LOUIS H. GRUBB.

BEFORE the war Mrs. Louis H. Grubb was keenly interested in Church work, being Diocesan President of the Cashel and Waterford Diocese of the Mother's Union, and Diocesan Secretary of the C.E.Z.M.S., etc.

On the outbreak of war Mrs. Grubb's activities increased, and she became Head Treasurer and Secretary of the Cashel District of the Red Cross, including the W.K.S. Depôt, and the Home Needlework and Egg Depôt.

Mrs. Grubb, the daughter of Col., Alexander Grubb, late R.A. of Elsfield House, Hollingbourne, Kent, formerly of Cahin Abbey, Cahin, co. Tipperary, married Louis H. Grubb, Esq., D.L., of Ardmayle, Cashel, co. Tipperary, in December, 1899.

Her recreations are needlework, reading and tennis.

MRS. GEORGES.

MRS. GEORGES, daughter of George Milne, Esq., of Westwood, Aberdeen, and widow of Captain T. M. Georges, was throughout the war a tireless and energetic worker in the cause of the wounded soldier. In March, 1917, she opened and equipped Pembroke Lodge (formerly the residence of the Rt. Hon. Bonar Law, lent by him for the duration of the war), as an officers' hospital of 23 beds. Besides running the institution she acted as her own Matron.

Mrs. Georges is also Commandant of a V.A. Detachment, London 248, which has nearly 200 members. She joined St. John's Ambulance Association in 1899. She also organised in 1916 a Tommies' hospital, from which she afterwards withdrew.

Club : Ladies' Athenæum Club, 32, Dover Street, W.

NEW WONDERS IN ARTIFICIAL LIMBS.

FOR MEN OF SUPERHUMAN COURAGE AND UNSELFISHNESS.

SENDING TO LIMBO THE OLD SOCKETS AND HOOKS.

MRS. GWYNNE HOLFORD'S WORK AT ROEHAMPTON.

MRS. GWYNNE HOLFORD is the daughter of P. R. Gordon Canning, Esq., of Hartpury, Gloucester, and in 1891 married W. Gwynne Holford, Esq., J.P., of Buckland, Breconshire, and Cilgwyn, Carmarthenshire, who died in February, 1916.

Mrs. Gwynne Holford has performed invaluable war work. To her, indeed, is due the initiation and founding of the great institution at Roehampton for supplying artificial limbs to sailors and soldiers. Mrs. Holford's efforts have accomplished results of priceless value, transforming the crudity of earlier treatment of the disabled into the highly organised department which now provides well-fitting artificial limbs instead of sending to the armless warrior wretched substitutes in the form of two leather sockets with hooks attached, which formerly represented the extent to which the official mind was prepared to meet the needs of this class of the suffering service man.

In her report for the War Museum on the Roehampton Hospital for Limbless Sailors and Soldiers, Mrs. Gwynne Holford has lucidly sketched the history of this noble institution from its inception in

The Hon. Mrs. F. E. Guest

Mrs. Georges

Mrs. C. James, M.B.E.

The Viscountess Jellicoe.

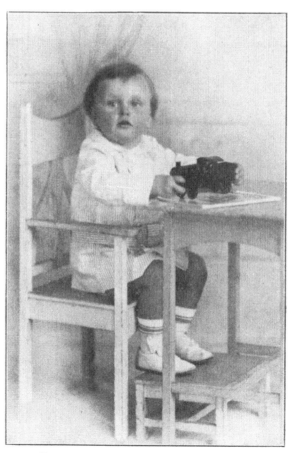

Lord and Lady Jellicoe's " Pat."

as a Belgian Military Hospital, and to offer it to the War Office for use as an Auxiliary Hospital in connection with the Royal Victoria and West Hants Hospital, Boscombe, and the Red Cross Hospital at Crag Head.

The Dorset 66 V.A.D. under Mrs. Pratt continued to staff the Grata Quies Hospital, which was ably supported by the band of ladies and gentlemen who had promoted the original Refugee scheme. The Hospital closed down after the signing of the Armistice.

THE VISCOUNTESS JELLICOE.

AS Admiral of the Fleet, Viscount Jellicoe performed his onerous duties with quiet and masterly skill, and at the same time obtained a wonderful influence over the British sailor, by whom he was regarded as a personal friend as well as a commander.

In each and all of his activities, the Admiral was ably seconded by Viscountess Jellicoe, whose help was naturally confined in certain directions to the silent influence of wifely sympathy. But in addition her Ladyship gave active and vigorous support, which not only helped to increase her husband's influence with the men, but also resulted in practical financial assistance which was of inestimable value.

She never spared herself in attending public functions and becoming a member of numerous committees, and as President of the Women's United Service League, she showed what amazing results a strong personality may achieve. With its surplus funds the Women's United Service League has now opened a Maternity House at Islington for Soldiers' and Sailors' wives, and during the first six months sixty babies have been born. She was also President of the Lady Jellicoe's Comforts Fund for Sailors (Grand Fleet), and her activities were incessant in connection with the Centenary Appeal of the British & Foreign Sailors' Society, when over £200,000 was raised.

The Viscountess Jellicoe is the daughter of the late Sir Charles Cayzer, Bart., of Gartmore, Perthshire, and her marriage to Admiral Viscount Jellicoe took place in 1902. Their heir, little " Pat," was born in 1918.

MRS. C. JAMES, M B.E.

SINCE November 5th, 1915, Mrs. D. James, M.B.E., acted as Commandant of Holeyn Hall Hospital, Wylam-on-Tyne, and the institution was then opened, with 60 beds, for convalescent soldiers, Holeyn Hall being generously lent by Sir Charles Parsons, K.C.B., for that purpose.

Mrs. James is the daughter of De Vere Beauclerk, Esq., and grand-daughter of Lord Charles Beauclerk. She married in January, 1912, Christian James, Esq., of Rudchester, Wylam-on-Tyne.

MRS. FRANK HARDING JONES.

THIS lady, the wife of Frank Harding Jones, Esq., of Housham Tye, Harlow, Essex (niece and adopted daughter of that doughty Parliamentarian, Sir Henry Kimber, Bt.), was a patriotic worker for some years before the outbreak of war ; for in 1910 she joined the V.A.D. Essex, and in 1911 became the Hon. Secretary and Commandant of the Detachment, golf and music being her favourite forms of recreation.

In October, 1914, Detachment Essex 30 became mobilised, and the Hillsborough Red Cross Hospital, Harlow, with 50 beds (later increased to 76), was accepted by the War Office. Mrs. Frank H. Jones conducted this institution most successfully with the co-operation of the Matron, Quarter Master and Medical Officers, together with a small finance committee. She has been twice " mentioned," once in February, 1918, and again in August, 1918.

The devotion to duty of the V.A.D. members was exemplary and evoked the entire commendation of their Commandant, Mrs. Frank H. Jones, whose war work covered five years' service.

Mrs. Jones is a member of the Ladies' Imperial Club, 17, Dover Street.

MRS. ERNEST JOHNSON.

MRS. ERNEST JOHNSON'S name must be included amongst the women of Great Britain who nobly applied themselves to the alleviation of the suffering of our brave heroes.

Immediately upon the outbreak of war Mrs. Johnson, with a sound sense of duty, converted her house, Ashton Hayes, Chester, into a hospital, opening with 20 beds, increasing to 60 beds, in 1916, and closing in January, 1919, with 47.

Mrs. Frank Harding Jones

Mrs. Evelyn de Knoop, M.B.E.

Mrs. Myles Kennedy
*(from a portrait by Pablo de Bejar
painter to the Court of Spain)*

MRS. SALISBURY JONES.

DURING the war Mrs. Salisbury Jones was Commandant V.A.D. Westminster Division, London/62 British Red Cross Society. With the assistance of V.A.D. workers, she also conducted a hospital at her own home at 27, Berkley Square, until March, 1919.

Mrs. Salisbury Jones, daughter of the late Col. Wemyss, of the Seaforth Highlanders, married F. W. Salisbury Jones, Esq., in December, 1895.

Her recreations are travelling and out-door sports, including hunting and golf.

MRS. E. DE KNOOP, M.B.E.

IN August, 1915, when there was an increased demand for hospital beds, Mrs. Jersey de Knoop placed her home, Calveley Hall, Tarporley, Cheshire, at the disposal of the authorities, and it was adapted as an Auxiliary Military Hospital for soldiers, Mrs. de Knoop becoming the Commandant, and during the last year of the war her eldest daughter, Miss Barbara de Knoop, acted as Quarter Master.

Mrs. de Knoop felt very deeply for our wounded heroes and worked very hard for the amelioration of their sufferings, for her husband, Captain Jersey de Knoop (Cheshire Yeomanry and Imperial Camel Corps) himself made the Great Sacrifice on August 7th, 1916, being killed in action in Palestine.

Mrs. de Knoop, whose peace-time pursuits and recreations embraced travelling, hunting, politics, and entertaining, is the daughter of Charles J. Fletcher, Esq., Dale Park, Arundel, Sussex, and she married the late Captain Jersey de Knoop, July 18th, 1898.

MRS. MYLES KENNEDY.

OF the many gifts which cultured women were privileged to devote to the service of their country in war-time, perhaps none had a greater intrinsic and practical value than personality. It is the one quality requisite to inspire and encourage others, to weld conflicting personal elements into a solid unity of aim and effort, to make of any undertaking a real and conspicuous success.

It is this quality of vivid, forceful personality which first appeals to us in the life and work—and especially the war-work—of Mrs. Myles Kennedy, of Stone Cross, Ulverston. Not only did this lady herself work strenuously and tirelessly in the cause of the sick and wounded ; she had the ability to fire others with her zeal and enthusiasm, so that they, in turn, gave of their best to the same righteous cause. Add to this that she possesses in full measure that generous disposition which makes her seek neither praise nor recognition for herself while lavishly bestowing both on those associated with her in her good works.

In a life made full beyond the average by the diversity of her tastes and interests and the versatility of her attainments, she never lost sight of what she considered her first duty—the relief of suffering and the amelioration of the conditions of the poor. Following in the footsteps of her mother, Mrs. Rowley, of Dee Bank, Flintshire, she was to her people a true " Lady Bountiful," while taking an interest in the larger aspect of social questions.

Naturally, when war broke out her activities were diverted into the fresh channels thus created, and in the first week of the war she had opened her house, Stone Cross, as a military hospital, equipped with fifty beds and staffed by a fully qualified matron (Miss Booth) and two trained nurses (Misses Ethel and Winifred Green). This hospital, originally intended for men of the King's Own Royal Lancashire Regiment, who were stationed locally, guarding the Viaduct, the railways, etc., was run entirely at Mrs. Myles Kennedy's own expense. Unfortunately, it had to be closed down towards the end of the year when a serious hunting accident to her daughter called its founder southwards.

Meanwhile (in August, 1914) she had equipped and opened a military hospital at Fair View, the beautiful country seat of her eldest son, Captain Nigel Kennedy, and the old dower house of the Kennedies. This hospital was duly affiliated to the Red Cross Society, and in November, 1914, the first contingent of patients arrived. As the only Red Cross hospital in the district of North Lonsdale or Barrow (with the single exception of that at Grange-over-Sands) the Fair View institution received generous support in the form of subscriptions and presents from the surrounding population, and was run almost entirely on voluntary lines.

It was closed for a time on the retirement of the Commandant, Mrs. Gaisford, but was shortly afterwards re-opened, Mrs. Kennedy seeking the co-operation as president of Lady Moyra Cavendish, who, however, insisted on Mrs. Kennedy presiding over her own hospital. To this Mrs. Kennedy agreed, though with reluctance,

Mrs. Myles Kennedy's Nurses :
Miss H. Hart-Jackson, Mrs. Chapman, Miss Walker,
Miss M. D. Billinge, Miss M. L. Waugh.

Middle Row (left to Right)
Miss F. Stanley, T. Dickson, M. T. L. Waugh, H. Hart-Jackson,
Mrs. Chapman (Cmdt.), Capt. Rowland Thomas (Fusebrill
H. Carlisle), Sister E. Woods (Sister in Charge), Miss A. L. Haines
(Quarter Master), Miss M. D. Billinge, M. Croft, E. Barker, M. Gale.

Back Row
Miss H. Towers, D. Penny, N. Burton, M. Hood, E. Court, E. Case,
Mrs. Burton, Miss P. Harrison, M. Cook, Mrs. Casson, Miss V.
Boddington, Miss F. Coward, M. Petty, S. Croasdell.

being broad-mindedly disinclined to associate herself too personally with an institution so widely supported. Thereafter, she presided at all meetings and bazaars, supervised and organised the hospital, and saw that nothing was lacking which could promote the welfare of the soldier-patients or the staff. The new Commandant was Mrs. Fell, who also took over the secretarial duties, and has since been rewarded with a " mention " and the O.B.E.

Though taking no part in the actual nursing of her hospital, Mrs. Kennedy was very far from being idle in those days. When the men on her husband's estate one by one joined up for the bigger business of fighting, she flung herself into the gap, undertaking strenuous physical tasks which only her indomitable spirit could enable her to carry through.

Yet another of the manifold activities which this talented lady displayed during the war was to raise and maintain (from 1915 to the end of the war) the King's Own Royal Lancashire Ambulance. To this end she visited neighbouring towns and hamlets in her picturesque garb of a Lancashire witch, armed with an Italian organ, a monkey and her familiar big banner, and thus gathered about £1,000. A special appeal was made to the farmers, who made a ready response, presenting her with cattle and sheep, which she publicly auctioned at the Ulverston Cattle Market.

" Our Day " also gave her an excellent opportunity for the organising of raffles, entertainments of various kinds and sales of farm and garden produce, in all of which she was ably assisted by local sympathisers.

Mrs. Myles Kennedy was, and is, the visitor for the Association of Hospital Visitors for Riflemen (King's Royal Rifle Brigade). She has received the Certificate of Honour (National Egg Collection), the Diploma of Voluntary Service in Food Production (Royal Horticultural Society) and a Certificate from the British Red Cross Society and Order of St. John, besides other honours.

She is president of the Lonsdale Women's Unionist Association ; the Ulverston Swimming Association ; the local branches of the Queen Victoria Nursing Association, the League of Pity, the Waifs and Strays, the National Society for the Prevention of Cruelty to Children ; and, with her husband as President, is a lady President of the North Lancashire Branch of the League of Mercy, having been honoured by the King with the Order of Mercy in 1914. She has her own troops of Boys' and Girls' Societies, the girls known locally as her " Lancashire Witches " ; and is president of many boys' football clubs. Not the least part of her public work has been the fighting of consumption for many years in her neighbourhood, where she had wooden revolving shelters made for the use of those requiring outdoor consumptive treatment, and lent freely to all such who applied for them. And these by no means exhaust the list of her activities.

Mrs. Myles Kennedy is a daughter of the late Joseph Rowley, Esq., J.P., of Dee Bank, Flintshire, and of Ann his wife, and married Myles Kennedy, Esq., J.P., of Stone Cross, Ulverston, on February 10th, 1885. They have two sons, Captain Nigel Kennedy, of the Border Regiment, and Captain Hugh Kennedy, of the King's Own Royal Lancashire Regiment; and two daughters—Marguerite, who married, February, 1916, Herbert Goldsmith Squiers (eldest son of the Hon. Herbert G. Squiers, who was the United States Minister to Panama and Cuba); and Guinevere, who married, June, 1916, Colonel James Ogilvy-Dalgleish, R.N. (only son of Captain James Ogilvy-Dalgleish, of Glebelands, Fife).

Both Captain Nigel and Captain Hugh Kennedy were badly wounded during the five years they served in the War, and Mrs. Kennedy lost many relatives on the battlefield; but the poignancy of her own domestic sorrows seemed but to increase her solicitude and compassion for the trials and sufferings of others.

We have already touched on this lady's remarkable versatility. She is an artist, a musician, a littérateur, a practical gardener and forester, a student of theosophy, cheirology, astrology, a pioneer of the women's movement, and a devotée of riding, motoring and all outdoor sports. She has travelled extensively in Europe, Asia, Africa, North and South America, and, indeed, has visited most of the countries of the world.

She is a member of the Ladies' Athenæum Club, and (among other interesting societies) of the Theosophist Club.

Mrs. Myles Kennedy won the co-operation of several other noble war-workers, who toiled unremittingly, nursing the sick and wounded, sitting up day and night to attend to their needs, and courageously taking in hand cases, however dangerous and difficult. This band of unselfish nurses included Mrs. Chapman, Miss H. Hart-Jackson, Miss M. L. Waugh, Miss M. D. Billinge and Miss Haines.

Mrs. Chapman nursed at Fair View from 1914 to March, 1919. She is the daughter of Thomas Stephen Price, Esq., and the wife of Charles James Chapman, Esq. Always of a thoughtful turn of mind, she is very keenly interested in politics, and was for many years Secretary to the Lonsdale Women's Unionist Association. She is also interested in outdoor sports, especially golf, so that the sacrifice of her leisure hours to the voluntary task of nursing the wounded heroes of the war was particularly generous. Miss Hilda Hart-

Mrs. Myles Kennedy and Miss Dawson

Mrs. Myles Kennedy with farmers' wives after
offering a Prize Ewe for auction in the North
Lonsdale Auction Market.

Jackson also nursed at Fair View from 1914 to March, 1919. She is the daughter of Stephen Hart-Jackson, Esq., and has always possessed immense vitality and energy. Besides being a sportswoman of merit, playing good games of tennis and golf, she is very musical. The charm of her violin playing helped to entertain and soothe the sick and wounded under her charge.

Miss Marguerita Isabella Lister Waugh is another keen, clever and sympathetic musician, having won her A.R.C.M. diploma for singing at the Royal College of Music.

Miss Mary Dorothea Billinge is one of those who are specially gifted in the direction of artistic handicrafts. In addition to being a clever artist, she has also a unique faculty for caricature drawing. This gift proved invaluable in providing healthy fun for the wounded men in her charge. She also executes most artistic brass work, and is an expert at embroidery and practical needlework in general. She enjoys the distinction of being an expert rifle-shot, and is a keen golfer. She, too, helped at Fair View from 1914 to March, 1919.

Miss Haines, who was " mentioned," was Quarter Master at Fair View from August, 1914, to March, 1919, and sacrificed her whole time to her hospital duties.

The photograph was taken in 1915 to be inserted in a golfing number of " The Gentlewoman," as all five are members of the Ulverston Golf Club Committee and were all nursing at Fair View at that time.

MRS. E. FESTUS KELLY.

CONVALESCENT wounded officers were generously cared for during the war as the result of Mrs. E. Festus Kelly's energetic benevolence in converting a part of her house into a hospital. With the assistance of a trained nurse and a V.A.D., Mrs. Kelly nursed, at Hollington House, Newbury, Berks, many officers back to comparative health and strength. They remained as patients for any length of time, some exceeding three months, and were sent from Lady Ridley's Hospital, 10, Carlton House Terrace, and the 3rd London General Hospital ; also by Georgina, Countess of Dudley ; The British Red Cross ; the Australian and Canadian Red Cross ; by Sir Alfred Fripp and others.

When in London, Mrs. Kelly helped to pack parcels for the troops at the front and supplied, through various means, at least a dozen prisoners with food.

I

Mrs. E. Festus Kelly, the daughter of Major Horatio Edenborough, married Edward Festus Kelly, Esq., on August 28th, 1879 ; and is devoted to all country pursuits, spending a part of each winter in the South of France and the season in London.

Club :—Imperial Club, 17, Dover Street, London, W.

MRS. ARTHUR KERR.

THIS indefatigable worker devoted whole time energies to ameliorating the sufferings of our brave and loyal countrymen whose deeds of heroism revealed the boundless possibilities lying dormant in the men of Britain.

The Red Cross Auxiliary Hospital at Bakewell was opened in November, 1914, and in February of 1915 Mrs. Kerr became Commandant, not relinquishing her position until the closing, in April, 1919. During this time between 1,100 and 1,200 patients received attention.

Mrs. Arthur Kerr, the daughter of Sir James Robert Walker, of Sand Hutton, York, married Arthur Herbert Kerr, Esq., eldest son of Admiral Lord Fredk. Kerr, in 1889.

THE LATE MISS E. M. KENTISH.

IN August, 1916, poignant domestic grief fell upon Mr. and Mrs. Kentish, for four strenuous years (1913–17) the popular Mayor and Mayoress of Poole, in the death of their elder daughter, Miss Enid Margaret Kentish, whose health had broken down under the strain of Red Cross work. She had been a devoted and untiring member of the Parkstone, Poole and Kinson V.A. Detachment. An impressive military funeral, in which the Lord Bishop of Salisbury took part, was a public manifestation of the deepest possible respect for the departed lady, as well as of profound sympathy and regard for her parents and family in their loss of a young life of great promise and many charms, endowed with artistic and musical gifts of a distinctly high order.

Mr. Kentish is a County Alderman for Dorset, a member of Poole Harbour Commission, a Justice of the Peace for the Borough of Poole and a Governor of the Poole Secondary School, while for nearly ten years he has been Chairman of the Poole Education Committee.

Mrs. E. Festus Kelly

Mrs. Locke

Mrs. Locke

Mrs. H. A. Llewellyn

Gen. Sir Richard Ford, D.S.O., D.D.M.S. (Castle Dublin),
Col. Clarke, A.D.M.S. (Castle Dublin), Mrs. Locke (Commandant),
Miss Brennan, (Matron), Dr. Rowland Hudson, Dr. Keelan.

On the outbreak of war he and Mrs. Kentish had many new and onerous duties to perform. In August, 1914, Mr. Kentish successfully established his Mayor's War Distress Fund, which was the means of helping over 800 local sufferers. He was also the pioneer in England of the organised cultivation of waste lands.

In his many activities he had the earnest co-operation of Mrs. Kentish, who was successful in organising various War Funds, including one for the Poole Ambulance, which did good work in France.

MRS. H. A. LLEWELLYN.

MRS. H. A. Llewellyn is a Dep. President of No. 14 Division, Glamorganshire ; Commandant of the V.A.D. 120 Glamorganshire, and was Resident Matron of the Auxiliary Hospital at her own home, Baglan Hall, Briton Ferry.

The daughter of the late W. Blandy, Esq., this lady is now the widow of the late R. W. Llewellyn, Esq., of Cwrt Colman and Baglan Hall, to whom she was married in 1882.

Clubs :—The Ladies' Imperial, Dover Street ; Church Imperial Ladies' Club ; and the Cardiff and County Ladies' Club, Cardiff.

MRS. JOHN LOCKE.

IN December, 1914, Mrs. Locke arrived at the Hopital du Casino, Fécamp (with all the equipment and stores required, in a ship specially chartered by Lady Guernsey), and ran the institution with Lady Guernsey (succeeding Lady McCalmont, who left in the following April) until June, 1916, when all were demobilized.

Mrs. Locke then contemplated accompanying Mme. La Comtesse de la Boissière and Miss Letterman, of the American Embassy, with the Belgian canteen to Calais, but sacrificed this arrangement in order to be free to set up a Red Cross Hospital, May 18th, 1917, at Bloomfield, Mullingar, in which 40 soldiers were well cared for, with the assistance of a matron and medical officer.

This beautiful place, situated on the border of a lake, was given her by Colonel Bury especially for the purpose of the institution, which was altogether a great success. Mrs. Locke fitted it up with electric light, heating apparatus and a water supply, towards the expenses of which the County subscribed most generously ; and when all was finished Mrs. Locke was able to hand them back £1,400 to be devoted to other charities.

Mrs. Locke was very deservingly " mentioned " for her valuable services.

The Hospital was closed on June 1st, 1919.

This lady, the daughter of Robert Edwards, Esq., of Park House, Killarney, co. Kerry, Ireland, married John Locke, Esq., of Brusna House, Killeoggan and Ballinagore, co. Westmeath, Ireland, and has done much travelling and hunting.

MRS. LUND.

EXCELLENT and efficient war service has been rendered by Mr. and Mrs. Lund, of Becca Hall, Aberford, Yorkshire, who, early in the progress of the Great Strife furnished and entirely equipped their house at Harrogate, Beaulieu, as a hospital for soldiers. It was completed in September, 1914, and on October 15th the first patients—Belgians direct from the front—were received. The original equipment of 15 beds was later increased by Mr. and Mrs. Lund to 30 beds, and sleeping accommodation for a staff of 11 was provided.

Until October, 1917, Beaulieu was an Auxiliary Hospital under Becketts Park, 2nd Northern Military Hospital, but from that date it was affiliated to St. Luke's Military Hospital, Bradford.

Both Mr. and Mrs. Lund took a keen interest in their hospital, which was worked under Mrs. Lund's supervision by three V.A. Detachments : Harrogate 2nd, Commandant, Miss Foster ; Borough-bridge, Commandant Miss E. Smith ; Bramham-cum-Thorner, Commandant Miss Hilda Nussey. In all some 700 patients passed through the hospital.

Apart from hospital work, Mrs. Lund has been very interested in the Aberford War Savings Association, and has been its Treasurer since it was first started.

The photograph of the Beaulieu Auxiliary Military Hospital, Harrogate, shows Mr. and Mrs. Lund in the centre, the Medical Officer, Dr. Neville Williams, and some of the Staff of Harrogate 2nd V.A.D., also some of the patients.

THE MARCHIONESS OF LONDONDERRY.

THE wife of the seventh Marquess of Londonderry, the Marchioness has devoted her time, influence and opportunities ungrudgingly in patriotic war work, and is keenly interested in the welfare of our brave men of the services, which is not surprising in the daughter of Viscount Chaplin.

The Marchioness of Londonderry

When the Hon. Edith Chaplin, she was married to the Marquess in 1899. Her mother was a daughter of the third Duke of Sutherland.

THE LATE HON. MRS. RONALD LINDSAY.

THE Hon. Mrs. Ronald Lindsay performed very valuable war services in Egypt, both relief work and nursing, and finally sacrificed her life in the cause of the sick and wounded. Notwithstanding the many duties which fell to her share as the wife of a diplomat, she found time to organise relief work in Egypt for the wives of the French mobilised (September, 1914), and in the following month organised and established canteens in Cairo—probably the first of the War.

When the Gallipoli campaign brought thousands of British wounded to Egypt, the Hon. Mrs. Lindsay organised hospitals and prepared them for the reception of the suffering men. Then she herself became a V.A.D., and in spite of delicate health and adverse climatic conditions continued to nurse in the hospitals until she contracted an infectious disease of which she died in April, 1918. She was " mentioned in dispatches " by Gen. Sir Archibald Murray in July, 1917, and later was officially thanked for her work.

The Hon. Mrs. Lindsay was a daughter of former Senator J. Donald Cameron, of Pennsylvania, U.S.A., and wife of the Hon. Ronald Lindsay, C.V.O., whom she married in 1909.

THE DUCHESS OF LEEDS.

THE DUCHESS OF LEEDS, who throughout the Great Struggle, has exerted herself tirelessly in the national interest, is the daughter of the second Earl of Durham and wife of the 10th Duke of Leeds, and before her marriage was Lady Katherine Francis Lambton.

She is a lady of many accomplishments, and a writer of charm and distinction, while her husband, a large landowner and holder of many ancient titles, is an enthusiastic yachtsman and a member of the Royal Yacht Squadron, Cowes.

Her Grace spends a good deal of time at her town house at 11, Grosvenor Crescent, S.W. 1.

THE COUNTESS OF LYTTON.

IN October, 1914, this talented lady started a small hospital for rank and file, which was subsequently enlarged twice, and finally moved to 37, Charles Street, Mayfair, lent by the Earl of Dartmouth (February, 1917). The hospital, of which the Countess of Lytton was Commandant, was now equipped with 78 beds, and remained open until March, 1919.

The Countess is a daughter of Sir Trevor Chichele-Plowden, K.C.S.I., and wife of the Earl of Lytton.

Club : Bath Club, London, W.

MRS. LAWRENCE.

MRS. LAWRENCE, only daughter of the late William Sumner Rawcliffe, Esq., of Haigh, Lancashire, and wife of Edward Lawrence, Esq., J.P., of Chorley, Lancashire was part Founder and Superintendent (from 1915 to 1919) of the Wigan Comforts Section Workrooms, British Red Cross Society.

MRS. LANGDALE.

MRS. LANGDALE, daughter of Admiral Derriman, C.B., of Uplands, Sussex, and 52, Queen's Gate, London, and wife of Colonel Philip Langdale, O.B.E., of Houghton Hall, Yorkshire, and 7, Green Street, was, during the war, Vice-President of the East Riding Soldiers' and Sailors' Families' Association.

LADY LYNN-THOMAS, R.R.C.

LADY LYNN-THOMAS was much interested in hospital and Red Cross work before the war, being deputy chairman of No. 1 (Cardiff) Division of the Glamorgan Branch of the British Red Cross Society since 1910. She organised a Red Cross hospital at the Old Mansion House, Cardiff, where she acted as Chairman of the Committee from November, 1915, to January, 1917. This Hospital, converted into " The Prince of Wales Hospital for Limbless Sailors and Soldiers " in 1916, was replaced by another Red Cross

Lady Lynn-Thomas, R.R.C.

The Late Hon. Mrs. Ronald Lindsay

Mr. and Mrs. Lund, with some of the soldiers and staff at
Beaulieu Auxilary Military Hospital, Harrogate.

Lady Shaw-Lefevre St. John Mildmay

Robinia Countess Mountgarret

hospital at St. Pierre, Newport Road, Cardiff, and was closed in April, 1919. She also organised and acted as Chairman of the Committee of the Red Cross Hospital for Officers, Clyne House, Cardiff, from July, 1917, to July, 1919; since reorganised and used as a Red Cross hospital with orthopædic clinic for pensioners; was awarded the Royal Red Cross, second class, and has also received two " mentions."

Lady Lynn-Thomas is the only daughter of the late Edward and Emma Jenkins, Cardiff. Married in June, 1892, Sir John Lynn-Thomas, K.B.E., C.B., C.M.G., F.R.C.S., England.

Addresses: Greenlawn, Pen-y-lan, Cardiff; and Stradmore, Cenarth, S.O. Carmarthenshire.

Clubs: Ladies' County Clubs, Cardiff and Carmarthen; Lyceum Club, London.

ROBINIA VISCOUNTESS MOUNTGARRET.

BEFORE the outbreak of the colossal conflict, Lady Mountgarret had devoted much attention to ambulance work under the St. John A.A., being also a devoted supporter of the S.P.G. missionary undertakings and the Girls' Friendly Society. Soon after the outbreak of the greatest war the world has ever seen, her Ladyship's offer was accepted by the War Office of 18, Cadogan Gardens, as a hospital for officers, and in September, 1914, the institution was opened and conducted until August, 1918, nearly 400 patients altogether being received.

Robinia Viscountess Mountgarret, the daughter of Colonel Edward Hanning-Lee, late Commanding 2nd Life Guards, of Old Manor House, Bighton, Alresford, Hants, was married to Henry Edmund (14th) Viscount Mountgarret, on February 5th, 1902, as his second wife (the Viscount died 1912).

MISS MARGARET MILLER.

AT the outbreak of the war in 1914 our country was fortunate in being able to avail itself of the patriotic services of a large number of fully qualified nurses ready for efficient and responsible work in the care of our wounded intrepid heroes. Miss Margaret Miller was one of this experienced and loyal band of workers. She has now been in the nursing profession nearly thirty years.

LADY SHAW-LEFEVRE ST. JOHN MILDMAY.

LADY SHAW-LEFEVRE ST. JOHN MILDMAY, of Dogmersfield Park, Winchfield, accomplished much beneficent work during her wartime activities, being at the beginning of the war Quarter Master at the Red Cross Hospital, Cirencester, near which she then lived. Her Ladyship was a member of the local branch of Queen Mary's Needlework Guild and on succeeding to the family place at Dogmersfield Park, in 1916, started there a branch of that guild which has gained every badge offered for efficiency and regularity.

Lady Shaw-Lefevre St. John Mildmay also successfully inaugurated a Fruit and Vegetable Association there under the Board of Agriculture, to assist in the increase of food supply. Her Ladyship worked in the Y.M.C.A. " Bryant and May Hut " Canteen in Grosvenor Gardens and is now President of the Odiham Girl Guides in addition to being on the Executive Committee of the Hants Nursing Association, the Fleet Cottage Hospital, etc., etc.

Before the war her Ladyship rendered invaluable assistance to the Red Cross Association at Cirencester, under Countess Bathurst, as Commandant and Quarter-master and was decorated at the first official inspection.

Lady Shaw-Lefevre St. John Mildmay is the daughter of the Rev. Arundell St. John Mildmay, and his wife, Hariet Louisa, the daughter of the Hon. and Rev. George Neville Grenville, Dean of Windsor, of Butleigh Court, Somerset.

Her Ladyship is the wife of Gerald Anthony St. John Mildmay, (present Bart.), the second son of the late Sir Henry Bouverie St. John Mildmay, Bart., of Dogmersfield Park, Hants, and she takes a keen interest in hunting, gardening, etc.

Club :—The Ladies' Empire Club, 69, Grosvenor Street.

MISS EVELYN MOUNSEY.

MISS MOUNSEY is the daughter of the late A. H. Mounsey, Esq., of Castletown, Carlisle, Cumberland (late H.M. Minister Plenipotentiary to Santa Fé de Bogota, Colombia), and of Mrs. Mounsey, of The Hill House, Dedham, Essex. Miss Mounsey has been an indefatigable patriotic worker, both before and since the war ; she formed in January, 1911, V.A.D. Essex 8 in Dedham and became its Commandant ; in May, 1915, was appointed Commandant at the Red Cross Hospital, Ardleigh, near Colchester ; and has fulfilled the duties of Matron since August, 1916.

The Countess of Malmesbury

The Lady Monson

THE LADY MONSON.

THE Lady Monson is Vice President of the British Red Cross Society, Lincoln Branch, and during the war was Principal Commandant of V.A.Ds. in Italy (under the Joint War Committee). Whilst at Lincoln in 1915 she organised a committee called "Lady Monson's Committee for Entertaining Wounded Soldiers,"—which entertained over 48,000 men out of its fund.

Her Ladyship is also a member of the Council for the "Edith Cavell Homes of Rest Fund, and has collected for that and also for the "Officers Families' Fund" in Lincolnshire.

A daughter of General Roy Stone, U.S.A., she married Lord Monson in 1903.

Her Ladyship is a Lady of Grace of the Order of St. John of Jerusalem.

THE COUNTESS OF MALMESBURY.

THE Countess of Malmesbury, who, before her marriage in 1905 to the Earl of Malmesbury, was the Hon. Dorothy Gough-Calthorpe, youngest daughter of the 6th Lord Calthorpe, was the Commandant of the Auxiliary Hospital established at Heron Court, Christchurch, the Hampshire seat of Lord and Lady Malmesbury, where very valuable work was carried on for the alleviation of the sufferings of the wounded. Lady Malmesbury is also the Vice-President of the Christchurch Division of the British Red Cross Society, in addition to devoting her energies, skill and experience to furthering the welfare of the Hants Agricultural War Work for Women.

Music is the Countess's favourite recreation.

Club : The Bath Club, Dover Street, Piccadilly.

MISS ROSE BATTISCOMBE MUSTARD, A.R.R.C.

MISS ROSE BATTISCOMBE MUSTARD accomplished much valuable and indispensable work during the period of Germany's unavailing fight for world supremacy.

Before the war Miss Mustard was a fully qualified nurse, at one time holding the positions of Hospital Sister and Matron, and in 1910 becoming a member of the Territorial Force Nursing Service. On the outbreak of war Miss Mustard's activities increased, for on being mobilized she became a nursing sister in the 4th S.G.H., T.F.N.S.,

J

Stobhill, Glasgow, from August 12th, 1914, until April 30th, 1919. For valuable and assiduous services rendered in connection with the war Miss Mustard was " mentioned " on November 17th, 1917, and on April 9th, 1919, received the Royal Red Cross (2nd class).

Miss Rose Battiscombe Mustard is the daughter of the late Wm. Mustard, Esq., and grand-daughter of the late Rev. C. H. Battiscombe, Rector of St. Germaine Church, Blackheath, Kent.

MISS ETHEL ROSALIE FERRIER McCAUL, R.R.C.

MISS ETHEL ROSALIE FERRIER McCAUL, first entered the nursing profession in 1890, trained at the Radcliffe Infirmary, Oxford. Since 1904 she has been a Lady visitor to King Edward VII. Convalescent Home for Officers, Osborne. During the South African war she nursed in a field hospital with Sir Redvers Buller's column, from the battle of Colenso to the Relief of Ladysmith, and was awarded the South African War Medal, Royal Red Cross. Subsequently, she became the Hon. Serving Sister of the Order of St. John of Jerusalem ; and in 1902 founded the Union Jack Club for Soldiers and Sailors.

Miss McCaul was then sent on a mission to inspect the Japanese Red Cross Society's work during the Russo-Japanese War, and was presented with the Japanese Red Cross decorations, also the Russo-Japanese War Medal.

In 1905 Miss McCaul became a member of the Council of the British Red Cross Society ; was the Founder and Hon. Secretary of the Army and Navy Male Nurses Co-operation, also Founder and Hon. Adviser of the Central Depôt of the Surgical Branch of Queen Mary's Needlework Guild, with 200 branches throughout the United Kingdom.

In 1915, this lady organised the despatch of comforts for the relief of the sick and wounded belonging to the Serbian Red Cross. She owned and organised the McCaul Naval and Military Officers' Hospital, London, 60 beds, and was very fittingly " mentioned " on January 29th, 1918.

Miss Ethel McCaul is the second daughter of the Rev. J. B. McCaul, Hon. Canon of Rochester Cathedral, and grand-daughter of the Rev. Alexander McCaul, D.D.

Miss E. McCaul, R.R.C.

Miss R. B. Mustard, A.R.R.C.

The late Countess of Meath

Mrs. Mallalieu

THE LATE COUNTESS OF MEATH.

THE late Countess of Meath, daughter of Thomas, 11th Earl of Lauderdale, Admiral of the Fleet, Thirlestane Castle, Lauder, Scotland, and wife of Reginald, 12th Earl of Meath, performed excellent and valuable war service, for which she received the thanks of the Red Cross Society. During the war she turned her house, Ottermead, Chertsey, into a hospital for wounded soldiers, and personally laboured to relieve the sufferings in the Workhouse near her Surrey home, and in the Workhouses near her two Irish residences in Wicklow.

Her whole life, before as well as during the Great War, might be described as one of continuous war work, for she laboured incessantly for the good of her fellow subjects.

She was the founder of the " Ministering Children's League," for the promotion of kindness, which was instrumental in the founding of some twenty-two institutions in England, Egypt, Germany (before the war), Russia, India, the United States, Australia, New Zealand and Canada.

She also founded the " Brabazon Employment Society," which brightens the lives of the inmates of over 220 workhouses and similar institutions.

The Godalming Home for Epileptics, and the Reigate Home for Incurables, as well as the Hayling Island Home and the Dublin Home for Aged Ladies at Sandymount, all owe their existence to her.

She started an organisation for providing Concerts and Entertainments in Hospitals and Convalescent Homes. She was one of the pioneers of the " Girls' Friendly Society," and at one time was the head of the Sick Department. She was a most munificent supporter of the Church in East and South London, and at one time annually placed £2,000 per annum at the disposal of the ecclesiastical authorities for the building of Churches and Mission Halls, and for the payment of Clergy and Church Workers.

Her Ladyship died at Killruddery, Bray, Ireland, on November 4th, 1918.

MRS. F. W. MALLALIEU.

MRS. MALLALIEU was before the war President and founder of the Delph and Dobcross District Nursing Association, now in its tenth working year ; President of the Colne Valley Council of Women's Liberal Associations ; President of the

Delph Women's Liberal Association ; and Collector in Saddleworth for Oldham Deaf and Dumb Institute for seventeen years.

On the outbreak of war she became President of the Delph Ladies' Working Party for Soldiers' and Sailors' Comforts, under the auspices of which every house in the neighbourhood was regularly visited by an organised Committee. She was also a canvasser for recruits and a member of the West Riding Pensions Committee, and in March, 1919, became a Guardian of the Poor.

Mrs. Mallalieu, whose recreations are tennis, theatricals, dancing, poultry-keeping and Sunday School teaching, is the daughter of Joseph Hardman, Esq., of Waterhead, Oldham, and Delph Lodge, Delph, Yorks, and wife of County Alderman F. W. Mallalieu, M.P. for Colne Valley. Mr. and Mrs. Mallalieu have a family of four sons.

MISS R. GERTRUDE MOSELEY.

FROM 1914-17 Miss R. Gertrude Moseley was Honorary Staff Secretary of the Brook House Hospital at Levenshulme, and was mentioned in despatches on February 2nd, 1918. She was the driver of an ambulance for East Lancs. Branch, B.R.C.S. ; also helped with her sisters in the care of patients in her mother's home, Cringle Hall ; was searcher attached to the Wounded and Missing Dept., and in 1917 went to France as a member of the First Aid Nursing Yeomanry.

From 1917-19 Miss Moseley drove an ambulance in France, receiving the Military Medal for her services during the second battle of the Marne.

From 1918-19 she was Lieutenant in charge of a motor ambulance convoy, consisting of 25 cars, kitchen and workshop lorries.

Miss Moseley, the daughter of the late Joseph Moseley, Esq., spent much of her time before the war hunting and yachting.

Clubs : The Empress Club, Dover Street, London ; The Royal Anglesey Yacht Club, and the Delamere Golf Club.

MRS. WALDYVE MARTIN.

DURING the war W. A. H. Martin, Esq., and Mrs. Waldyve Martin generously lent their home, The Upper Hall, Ledbury, as an Auxiliary Hospital, Mrs. Martin being the Quarter Master and her husband the Officer-in-Charge.

Mrs. Martin is the daughter of Ferdinand Hanbury-Williams, Esq., of Coldbrook Park, Monmouthshire.

Mrs. J. Peel

Mrs. Claud Pease, O.B.E.

The Countess of Onslow

Lady Oranmore

THE COUNTESS OF NORMANTON.

THE Countess of Normanton's principal war work was as Commaudant of the Somerley Auxiliary Hospital during four ardnous years, from November, 1914, to December, 1918, considerably over 600 patients being under her Ladyship's care and supervision.

The Countess of Normanton is the second daughter of the fourth Earl of Strafford, K.C.V.O., C.B., and in 1894 was married to the fourth Earl of Normanton, whose seat is at Somerley, Ringwood, Hants.

The mansion, situated on the banks of the River Avon, is of white brick with Portland stone dressings, and has a handsome stone portico. It contains a very valuable collection of pictures, including some fine examples of Sir Joshua Reynolds' art.

The Earl of Normanton is Lord of the Manor and owner of almost the entire parish of Harbridge, and of the adjoining parishes of Ibsley and Ellingham.

THE DUCHESS OF NORTHUMBERLAND, C.B.E.

THE Duchess of Northumberland, during the war, has taken a most active and energetic part in the National service, and particularly in administrative work in connection with the Red Cross.

She was President of the Morayshire Branch of the Scottish Section of the British Red Cross Society, President of the Gordon Castle Red Cross Auxiliary Hospital, Deputy President of the Middlesex Branch of the British Red Cross Society, Commandant of the Red Cross Detachment, Middlesex 92, and Commandant of Syon V.A.D. Red Cross Auxiliary Hospital (November, 1915, to January, 1919), and for her valuable services received the distinction of Commander of the British Empire.

Her Grace, who married the eighth Duke of Northumberland in 1911, is herself the descendant of a great House, being a daughter of the seventh Duke of Richmond and Gordon, K.G. Before her marriage she was Lady Helen Gordon-Lennox.

LADY ORANMORE.

THROUGHOUT the war Lady Oranmore has taken an active part in patriotic work of various kinds. Thus for eighteen months she worked in a Canteen at London Bridge, and later as a member of the V.A.D. nursed at the University College Hospital. She also greatly interested herself in a branch of Queen Mary's Needlework Guild in Arlington Street.

Lady Oranmore is a daughter of the Earl of Bessborough and wife of Lord Oranmore and Browne.

THE COUNTESS OF ONSLOW.

THE Countess of Onslow is the wife of the fifth Earl of Onslow, to whom she was married in 1906. Before her wedding she was well-known in Society as the Hon. Violet Bampfylde, daughter of the third Baron Poltimore.

Most of the early years of Lady Onslow's married life were spent abroad, as Lord Onslow was in the Diplomatic Service. She is a breeder and fancier of tropical birds.

The Countess of Onslow has been the Commandant of V.A.D. Surrey 86, since 1914; Vice-President Clandon Division B.R.C.S., 1914; Commandant Clandon Park Private Military Hospital, 1914; Commandant Broom House Auxiliary Hospital, Horsley, 1915; Lady of Grace of the Order of St. John of Jerusalem, 1916; "mentioned" in Secretary of State's List, 1918; Royal Red Cross 2nd Class, 1920; holds five War Service Bars,; Red Cross Nursing Certificate of Proficiency, 1915; Red Cross Nursing Proficiency Badge, 1916; two Bars to latter, 1917-1918.

Clandon Park Hospital was a Private First Line Military Hospital of 132 beds, receiving convoys direct from the ports of disembarkation. It had a completely fitted Operating Theatre and X-Ray installation. The total number of patients admitted since the opening was 5,059. In Broom House Hospital, Horsley, the total number of patients since the opening was 1,092,

The Countess of Normanton

The Duchess of Northumberland, C.B.E.

MRS. JOHN PEEL.

MANY of the fairest women of Great Britain willingly sacrificed ease, comfort and lives of luxury in order to tend the wounded fighting men who had crowned themselves with glory overseas. Colshaw Hall, Mrs. John Peel's home at Over Peover, Cheshire, was in February, 1915, offered and gratefully accepted by the Red Cross Society as a Hospital fully equipped and provided for, excepting for the lowest War Office grant.

Starting with 25, the beds were increased to 60, and in 1918 an Open Air Ward was added, also a Shell Shock Ward on the Kemp-Prosser system, the total number of patients (chiefly surgical) passing through the institution being 1,154. Mrs. Peel fulfilled many responsible and onerous duties, for she was the Officer-in-Charge, Matron, Theatre Sister, electrical and X-Ray expert, until the institution was closed in February, 1919.

Mrs. John Peel is the daughter of the late General Horatio Shirley Morant, and on June 22nd, 1899, married John Graham Peel, Esq., of Colshaw Hall, Cheshire.

Before and since the war this lady has been devoted to hunting, shooting, fishing and gardening.

Club :—Albemarle Club, Dover Street, London, W.

MRS. CLAUD PEASE, O.B.E.

ON January 9th, 1915, Mrs. Lucy Victoria Pease, O.B.E., who before the war evinced a deep interest in Red Cross work, and was Commandant of V.A.D. Yorks, 8, opened a hospital at Kirkleatham Hall, near Redcar, Yorks, with 20 beds, increased subsequently to 50 ; and the institution was transferred on September 26th, 1917, to Red Barns, Redcar, the number of beds being again increased to 60 and eventually to 105.

Patients were received from Tees garrison, in addition to all air casualties from the two local aerodromes, besides the wounded from East Leeds War Hospital. The total number of patients admitted was 1392, including 55 officers.

The institution remained open until June 19th, 1919, having been temporarily closed for only two months during the four years and a half of its tenure.

Mrs. Lucy Pease, O.B.E., the daughter of the late William Clayton Browne-Clayton, Esq., of Brownes Hill, Carlow, Ireland, married in December, 1901, Claud Edward Pease, Esq., of Cliff House, Marshe-by-the-Sea, Yorks, and finds recreation in hunting and gardening, of which she is very fond.

MRS. T. PATENALL.

THIS lady, who, in the year of the preparation of this section of this volume (1918) was the Mayoress of Higham Ferrers, Northants, is a Lady Superintendent of the St. John's Nursing Association. She was married in 1884 to Thomas Patenall, Esq., J.P. (Mayor of Higham Ferrers 1918–19). Both their sons served in the war.

The military hospital at Higham Ferrers was opened on Sunday, March 14th, 1915. There were twenty-two beds. The parish rooms were surrendered for the use of the hospital, and its equipment lent by the townspeople.

The work was performed by V.A.D. nurses, one trained nurse and one orderly. The Mayor and Mayoress closed up their own home to enable Mrs. Patenall to devote all her time to the claims of the hospital; in 1917, she had the honour of being " mentioned " by the Secretary of State for War.

MRS. A. W. PERKIN.

MRS. A. W. PERKIN, the daughter of the late Dr. Robert Johnstone, of San Fernando, Trinidad, West Indies, married to A. W. Perkins, Esq., J.P., C.A., April 30th, 1890, was an indefatigable war worker—staff nurse at Southall Auxiliary Hospital since November, 1914 ; Vice-Chairman of the Women's Agricultural Committee for Middlesex ; and Commandant of Middlesex 70 V.A.D.

Her recreations are tennis, croquet, golf and riding.

Mrs. T. Patenall

Mrs. Perkin`

Mrs. W. Pattrick

MRS. W. PATTRICK.

MRS. W. PATTRICK was the Commandant of the V.A.D. Hospital, Prince Edward Home, Hunstanton, Norfolk, also President of the Hunstanton Branch of the Women's War Work Association. She is the daughter of Alexander Goodman, Esq., and on December 1st, 1892, was married to Colonel Pattrick, V.D.

Mrs. Pattrick has always been devoted to hunting, golfing, and croquet, but has spared much time for philanthropic duties, and is the Hon. Secretary for "Missions to Seamen," and collector for the Norfolk Needlework Guild.

MRS. GUY PILKINGTON.

THE Daughter of Walter Frost, Esq., of Almondsbury, Glos., and married on December 13th, 1917, to Major G. R. Pilkington, D.S.O., this lady, who was "mentioned" in the Autumn list of that year for special war work, rendered valuable services in more than one capacity since the outbreak of war, first in December, 1914, as masseuse at the Military Hospital, Almondsbury, and in January, 1916, she became a member of the A.P.M.N.C. and as such worked at (1) Dartford Convalescent Camp ; (2) the Eastern Command Depôt, Shoreham ; (3) as sister of the Electrical and Massage Departments at Pilkington Special Hospital, St. Helens, Lancs.

MISS JENNIE G. PARKES.

MISS JENNIE PARKES received her training at the Middlesex Hospital, London, afterwards taking up private nursing at Bournemouth. In 1915 she joined Queen Alexandra's Imperial Military Nursing Service Reserve, taking charge of the operating theatre at Hursley Park Camp Hospital, near Winchester, for one year. In September of 1916 Miss Parkes undertook the duties of night superintendent at the Royal Victoria Hospital, Netley, until in May, 1918, she went to the 41st General Hospital, Salonica. In addition to these invaluable services rendered for the benefit of Britain's heroes, Miss Parkes has been on ambulance train duty.

She is the daughter of Mr. and Mrs. S. Parkes of Wheatlands, Aldridge, Staffs.

K

MRS. S. T. PARKES.

THE second daughter of the late Samuel Blakemore Allport, Esq., of Moseley, Master of the Proof House, Birmingham, this lady was married in June, 1895, to S. Thomas Hickling Parkes, Esq., and has worked as Quarter Master at the Auxiliary Red Cross Hospital, The Beeches, Bournville, since its opening on December 1st, 1915, having previously fulfilled the duties of Quarter Master of V.A.D. Worc. 22, since the formation of the Detachment in 1912.

She was mentioned in October, 1917, in the List of Commendations for valuable service rendered in connection with the war.

MRS. CHARLES PINNOCK.

FROM 1914 to 1915 Mrs. Pinnock received into her own house and looked after a number of Belgian convalescent soldiers, taking them two or three at a time. In 1915 she raised a small fund, " Happy Hours for our Wounded," and arranged concerts and outings for them.

In April, 1916, Mrs. Pinnock opened the Sholden Lodge Auxiliary Hospital for Imperials, with 52 beds, she herself being the Commandant, and attached to it was a military M.O. and Ambulance.

In December, 1917, they were obliged to move into larger premises at Warden House, Deal, where there were 80–100 beds. This institution was closed on December 31st, 1918.

In addition to this, in December, 1916, she became Commandant of Glack Canadian Convalescent Home (with 45 beds) ; it was closed in March, 1918.

Mrs. Pinnock opened a small Social Club for nurses and workers (the Leisure Hour Club) in 1917 at Deal, Kent.

This Lady is the wife of Charles Pinnock, Esq. They have two sons (the elder holding a Commission) and two daughters.

Mrs. Pinnock's accomplishments and recreations are varied. She is very fond of piano playing and singing, pursues photography, and drives her own motor car ; besides indulging in golf, riding and fishing.

She is a member of the Ladies' Imperial Club, Dover Street, W. ; also the Walmer and Kingsdown Golf Club.

Mrs. Pilkington

Miss Parkes

Mrs. Pinnock

Mrs. J. M. Pyke-Nott

MRS. J. M. PYKE-NOTT.

DURING the War Mrs. Pyke-Nott performed valuable service as Commandant of Dumbleton V.A. Detachment, Gloucester 34. Her war-work was begun in May, 1915, when the Village Hall was opened as a hospital to take twenty patients, the number being subsequently increased to thirty. Patients were at first received from Tewkesbury, but in June Dumbleton joined the Cheltenham group of hospitals and received patients from St. John and St. Martin. The patients were then mainly convalescents, only minor operations being performed, but in 1916 Dumbleton was granted the rank of (A) Hospital, the actual convalescent hospitals being classed as (B). In all 686 patients passed through this small but efficient hospital from May, 1915, to November, 1918, when it closed down.

The outbreak of war found Mrs. Pyke-Nott well prepared for her work of healing, since for some four years prior she had had a Red Cross Detachment of no less than 40 members in the small village of Dumbleton. Apart from her Red Cross work she finds recreation in golf and gardening.

Mrs. Pyke-Nott is a daughter of Bennet Rothes Langton, Esq., of Langton Hall, Langton, Lincolnshire, and wife of John Möels Pyke-Nott, Esq., of North Devon, whom she married in 1894. Both her own family and her husband's are very ancient. The Langtons are, indeed, one of the oldest of English families, the Langton property having been handed down in direct descent from the time of Henry II, while their lineage can be traced back to Henry III, Philip III of France, the Balliol family, kings of Scotland, and even to the Emperor Charlemagne. Mr. Pyke-Nott also comes of a very old North Devon Family.

THE LADY PETRE.

THE Lady Petre, daughter of the Hon. John and Lady Margaret Boscawen, and widow of Lionel, 16th Lord Petre, was an indefatigable war-worker, acting as President of the Essex Women's War Agricultural Association, President of the County Federation of Essex Women's Institutes, Member of the Essex War Pensions Committee, and of a large number of other committees, including the National Federation of Women's Institutes.

MRS. GUY ST. MAUR PALMES.

MRS. GUY ST. MAUR PALMES, of Lingcroft, York, was a member of the British Red Cross Society from February, 1909, and held the Voluntary Workers' Badge and Certificate of the Red Cross and Order of St. John. Since 1901 she has been Hon. Secretary of the Howden Branch of the East Yorks, S.S.F.A.

On the outbreak of war, working parties were organised by Mrs. Palmes' daughter, who subsequently worked as nurse in the Red Cross Hospital at Esorick, near York, and later at the Military Hospital, Endell Street, London. She died in 1919 from influenza while working there. After she left home Mrs. Palmes carried on the working parties until the Red Cross Rooms were opened in York in 1915, where she worked regularly, and also at the Moss Picking Depôt, opened in 1916.

She collected, made and distributed some 1,550 articles of clothing for our own troops and those of our Allies, while she had also a village branch egg collection for the wounded, collecting approximately 1,500 eggs between 1916 and 1918.

Mrs. Palmes, who is the wife of Guy St. Maur Palmes, Esq., J.P., late 14th Hussars and East Riding of Yorks Yeomanry, takes an interest in social work in York, and in the usual pursuits of country house life.

LADY PORTAL.

FOR two years (September, 1914, to September, 1916) Lady Portal was Commandant of a small hospital at her own home, Laverstoke House, and subsequently Commandant of the Laverstoke Red Cross Auxiliary Hospital.

Lady Portal is the daughter of the Hon. St. Leger Richard Glyn, and wife of Sir William Wyndham Portal, Bart.

She has received the Order of Mercy and is a Lady of Grace of St. John of Jerusalem.

Club : Ladies' Automobile Club.

Mrs. Pratt and Group
from Naval Base Hospital, Poole.

MRS. PRATT.

"THE 'Temporary Wards,' as they were called, were entirely equipped, furnished and staffed by the three local Detachments, and in the first instance £750 was contributed out of the Divisional funds towards their erection, substantial collections amounting to over £1,000 were made locally, largely owing to the energy and keenness of Mrs. Pratt, Commandant Dorset /66, whose Detachment was working at the hospital. Being run in connection with an existing civil hospital and being partly under its management, while being entirely staffed by V. A. Detachments under their own Commandants, made this a very difficult institution to conduct, and great thanks and credit are due to Mrs. Pratt for her untiring energy, both in raising funds, entertaining the men, and in arranging classes for the V.A.Ds."

These words of appreciation from the pen of Brigadier-General Balguy, Honorary County Director of the Dorset Branch of the British Red Cross Society, give some idea of the war-time activities of Mrs. Pratt, The Castle, Parkstone, wife of Colonel H. A. Pratt of the Royal Artillery, Inspector of Munitions at Woolwich Arsenal.

She was identified with the V.A.D. organisation at Branksome in 1911 in co-operation with Miss Girdleston and Miss Turner, both of whom when the war broke out went to Bournemouth to carry on similar work with the Dorset V.A.D. at Crag Head.

The remarkable success in collecting funds to which General Balguy referred is all the more noteworthy when one considers the manifold activities in which Mrs. Pratt was then engaged. She was arranging Red Cross lectures, organising and personally conducting courses attended by some two thousand persons during the war.

She also equipped and staffed wards for Belgian soldiers in the Cornelia Hospital, Poole, and when the military camp and hospital at Wareham were first set up, and it was found that our men were in a hopeless condition during wet weather, she organised relief and set about obtaining funds for blankets, sheets, rugs and "oilies" for the men's comfort and protection.

In November, 1914, Mrs. Pratt, who as we have seen, had already organised work depôts on behalf of Belgian refugees and wounded soldiers, co-operated with Lady Wimborne to establish the Dorset Guild of Workers (dealt with elsewhere in this book). With this admirable organisation she maintained a close association, being a Member of the Committee for four years and a half.

From November also, Mrs. Pratt staffed " Grata Quies " Hospital, Branksome, for two years (afterwards when it became a Red Cross Hospital Miss E. Bottomley, Dorset 66, became her Honorary Commandant there), and in the same month she started the Military Wards at the Cornelia Hospital, Poole, which were entirely built and equipped by the Red Cross.

In January, 1915, Mrs. Pratt equipped and staffed the Naval Base Hospital at Poole (for mine-sweepers, and afterwards for Men of the Naval Flying Corps, Sandbanks, and Naval balloons at Lytchett), and in the following year equipped and staffed Forest Holme Hospital, Poole. She also lent Stratford House, Ryde (completely furnished), as an overflow hospital.

Mrs. Pratt's V.A. Detachments (Dorset 66) had four hospitals and more beds and patients than any other in the county—at one time in 1918 Dorset 66 had members in thirty different hospitals. The Poole and Kinson Detachments equipped a ward in the Cornelia Hospital and helped to staff that hospital and Forest Holme. In July, 1916, some thirty members of the Detachment assisted at the Mont Dore War Hospital and received most appreciative thanks from the Commanding Officer, Colonel Clarkson.

Among Mrs. Pratt's further contributions to the good work of the County on behalf of the wounded men must be reckoned the loan of her motor for convoy purposes, both the use of the car and the petrol for driving it being an honorary gift, and used entirely by the wounded. It is interesting, too, to note that Mrs. Pratt designed the first mosquito net for our troops in the East. She sent her design to Lady Lawley, and it was approved and generally adopted for military use.

Among others to whom Mrs. Pratt gives generous thanks for co-operation are the following :—the Misses Pontifex, of Bessingham, Parkstone (Miss E. Pontifex was Mrs. Pratt's Quarter Master since the Cornelia Hospital started, and Miss Helen Pontifex went to one of the war areas to assist Mrs. Watkins, of Lilliput House, with canteen work among the French soldiers, and afterwards organised and financed the Kitchen Gardens Voluntary Work Parties, and supplied each year about £300 worth of vegetables for the Cornelia Hospital) ; and Mrs. Cecil Scott, of Park Road, Parkstone, who supplied during the war by collections £310 worth of eggs for the patients.

Besides General Balguy's letter, quoted above, very numerous letters of appreciation have been received by Mrs. Pratt, including communications from the Army Council ; the Commander-in-Chief, Southern Command (General Sir H. Sclater) ; The Admiralty ;

The Duchess of Rutland

Headquarters, Red Cross; Sir William May, Surgeon-General, R.N. Headquarters, etc., etc.;

Throughout the war, Mrs. Pratt entirely organised and financed all the entertainments and comforts for the soldier-patients of the three Poole hospitals, taking each week all the available men to Bournemouth Theatre or some similar place of amusement and giving them tea. At Christmas time also, she was indefatigable in arranging cheery entertainments, and in the hearts of the men she is remembered as a nurse, a friend, and a good comrade—a wonderful record indeed.

THE DUCHESS OF RUTLAND.

THE Duchess of Rutland provided a Convalescent Hospital for soldiers at Belvoir Castle, Grantham, during the first year of the war; she then converted and equipped the Chateau de Hardelot (near Boulogne, France) into a hospital of 50 beds, but before this institution could be opened the authorities found it necessary to convert it into a School of Instruction for the 1st Army. The beauty and healthiness of the spot made this a great success, and it was only closed during the summer of 1919.

Her Grace's most important war work was the organization of the " Rutland Hospital " at her London house, 16, Arlington Street, for wounded officers straight from France, who were received and succoured during a period of nearly three years. The institution was conducted in a most thoroughly efficient manner, evoking the highest official recognition and commendation. There were 20 beds.

Dr. Donald Hood and Sir Arbuthnot Lane were the chief physician and surgeon; whilst Lady Diana Manners and Lady Elcho acted as nurses; Miss M. Whyte was the matron.

Her Grace the Duchess of Rutland is the second daughter of Col. the Hon. C. H. Lindsay, C.B., brother of the 25th Earl of Crawford and Balcarres; and on November 25th, 1882, married Mr. Henry Manners, now His Grace the 8th Duke of Rutland.

MRS. E. RICKARDS.

WHEN England found herself in dire need at the outbreak of the Great War, her sons from among all classes rallied round the flag in defence of their country's honour.

At home the women of England also placed their lives at the country's service. The spirit of fervent, defiant patriotism quickly ran through the nation.

Among many who toiled assiduously was Mrs. E. Rickards, who from May, 1916, to March, 1919, was the Organizer and President of the Andover Hospital Supply Depot.

In March, 1915, Mrs. Rickards took charge of the clothing of the 4th Dragoon Guards Prisoners of War, until they were repatriated after the signing of the Armistice, having in all the care of eighty prisoners.

Mrs. Rickards is the daughter of Alex Grant Dallas, Esq., J.P., D.L. for Inverness-shire, and formerly Governor of Ruperts Land. On June 16th, 1896, she was married to Major Edward Rickards, of the 4th Dragoon Guards.

MRS. CRADOCK ROYDS.

DURING the period of the war Mrs. Cradock Royds devoted her time to the laborious undertaking of a private hospital, and having been for several years very fond of amateur acting, as well as sports and games, she very appropriately arranged, during each winter, a series of entertainments, the patients themselves being trained to take part in the programmes.

Mrs. Cradock Royds is the daughter of the late Charles Everard, Esq., of Cawthorpe, Bourne, Lincs., and in 1906 was married to the Rev. Charles Cradock Twemlow Royds, of Heysham Rectory, Lancs.

MISS L. J. ROBINSON.

THIS lady is the daughter of the late William Robinson, Esq., of Higher Broughton, Manchester ; and, like so many others who performed highly trained and valuable war hospital services, became fully proficient before the outbreak of hostilities, having fully qualified both for hospital and private nursing and

Mrs. Cradock Royds

Miss Ross, R.R.C. (1st class)

Mrs. R. W. Rix

held the post of Matron at the Belmont Nursing Home and Private Hospital, at Higher Broughton, Manchester. From July, 1916, to August, 1917, Miss Robinson was Sister-in-Charge at the Callerly Castle Convalescent Hospital, Northumberland (17 V.A.D. Hospital, Northumberland) ; and then became Matron of the Dunston Hill After Care Home for Discharged Soldiers, at Dunston-on-Tyne, Northumberland.

MISS MARY ROSS, R.R.C. (FIRST CLASS).

THE daughter of the late James Ross, Esq., and Mrs. Ross, of " Greenfield," Clogher House, Ballymena, Ireland, Miss Mary Ross was fully qualified before the war, having been Matron of the Hope Hospital, Pendleton, since October, 1913, and previously Assistant-Matron of the Nell-lane Hospital, West Didsbury, Manchester ; and in the early months of the great conflict, viz., in May, 1915, she undertook the onerous duties of Matron of the Hope Auxiliary Military Hospital, Pendleton, Manchester, with its 650 beds for wounded and sick soldiers, and how thoroughly efficient was her management is testified by the official record that she was Decorated by King George at Buckingham Palace on the 20th April, 1918, with the Royal Red Cross, 1st Class.

MRS. R. W. RIX.

THE younger daughter of Philip Wagstaff, Esq., of Blendworth, Berkhampstead, Herts, and married to Captain Rowland W. Rix, F.R.C.S., R.A.M.C., February 23rd, 1914, this lady before the war was a student at the London School of Medicine for Women and at the Royal Free Hospital. Soon after the outbreak of hostilities, Mrs. Rix, in August, 1914, assisted in organising the Red Cross Hospital at Sudbury, Suffolk ; and after January, 1916, was its Commandant, in addition to being a member of the Committee of the Red Cross work room at Sudbury.

L

MISS F. WILLCOCK ROSKILLY.

MISS ROSKILLY was appointed, and performed very valuable war services as Staff Nurse in St. Luke's War Hospital, Bradford, since January 1st, 1916, having fully qualified herself before the war. In 1914 she had already rceeived three years' general training in the Royal Albert Hospital, Devonport; subsequently, she acquired a year's experience in private nursing at Colwyn Bay, N. Wales; then, Miss Roskilly proceeded to Birkenhead and was awarded the C.M.B. certificate. She is the daughter of T. Roskilly, Esq., of Nutley, Tavistock, S. Devon.

MRS. C. F. REES.

A LADY who has done yeoman service in the tending of our wounded is Mrs. C. F. Rees, Commandant of Monmouth 12 V.A. Detachment, raised by her in August, 1914. This Detachment did duty at Maindiff Court Red Cross Hospital, Abergavenny, an institution equipped with 60 beds, of which Mrs. Rees was also Honorary Secretary. She is devoted to hunting and all country pursuits. A daughter of the late Colonel G. F. Blair, R.A., and Mrs. Blair of Chiddingfold, Surrey, she married in 1899 Captain R. Powell Rees, 7th Dragoon Guards, who died in 1911.

Clubs: Ladies' Imperial Club, Dover Street, London; County Club, Abergavenny.

MRS. W. G. RIGBY.

THE Commandant of the Llandyrnog B. Red Cross Auxiliary Military Hospital, Mrs. Rigby, wife of W. G. Rigby, Esq., J.P. (only surviving son of the late William Rigby, of Wold House, Hawarden, and Netherfield House, Glasgow, Col. Lanarks Fus., who died in 1863; and grandson of Robert Napier, J.P., D.L., West Shandon, Dumbartonshire), has long been identified with the public interests of North Wales, where her family has been settled for generations.. Mrs. Rigby is the eldest daughter of the late J. I. Purcell-Williams, Capt. 1st., Batt. (P.C.O.) Rifle Brigade, of Pentre Maw, near Denbigh, N. Wales, who went all through the Crimean War, receiving the Crimean Medal and four clasps, also

Miss F. Roskilly

Mrs. de Rougemont

Turkish Medal, and was one of the " undecorated 26," and grand-daughter of late Frederic Penn (Major, Montreal Light Infantry) a descendant of the Admiral Sir William Penn whose portrait hangs in the painted Hall at Greenwich, and of William Penn of Pennsylvania.

Before the war Mrs. Rigby took an active personal share in encouraging the village V.A.Ds. (men's and women's) raised by her in 1911, the latter entirely working the war hospital which was started in July, 1916, in a house lent for the purpose, being the first Detachment registered by the War Office in Denbighshire or Flintshire. The hospital had thirty beds, and all its equipment was either presented or lent to the institution.

MRS. DE ROUGEMONT.

MRS. DE ROUGEMONT is a member of the Executive Committee, Essex Branch, B.R.C.S., and of the Executive Committee, Essex Branch (Women's) Comrades of the Great War Association ; since January, 1910, Commandant of the V.A.D., Essex 18 ; also of the Brentwood Temporary Red Cross Hospital, from August 9th, 1914, until September, 1914.

In October and November, 1914, Mrs. de Rougemont worked as a V.A.D. nurse at the Middlesex Hospital, Clacton-on-Sea, and from November 6th, 1914, to April 1st, 1919, she was Commandant of the Coombe Lodge Primary Auxiliary Military Hospital, Great Warley, Essex.

Mrs. de Rougemont is the daughter of Mr. and Mrs. Evelyn Heseltine of 48, Upper Grosvenor Street, W., and of Goldings, Great Warley, Essex ; and on May 28th, 1914, married Brig.-General de Rougemont (late R.H.A.), C.B., C.M.G., D.S.O., M.V.O.

Club : The " Forum," Grosvenor Gardens, London.

MISS RACHEL REYNARD.

MISS REYNARD, daughter of Captain and Mrs. Frank Reynard, commenced her war-work in 1914 in the Packing Room of the Kensington War Hospital Supply Depôt. In 1915–16 she devoted three days a week to Canteen work in the

Ripon Camp. From 1917 she has been employed at the War Office, serving in the Officers' Casualty Department until June, 1919, and since then in the Honours Department. She was "mentioned in Dispatches" in July, 1919.

Miss Reynard finds recreation in hunting, gardening and reading.

Club : Empress Club, Dover Street.

LADY ROBERTS.

STRATHALLAN CASTLE, the Scottish residence of Sir James Roberts, Bart., was offered by Lady Roberts, at the close of October, 1914, for the purposes of a V.A.D. Hospital. Sir James and Lady Roberts undertook entire responsibility for the equipment of a large wing of the building, for the requirements of a competent nursing staff, and for the provision of all the needs of the patients.

The first soldiers received here were Belgians, some thirty in number, who arrived direct from the trenches before Antwerp, where they received their wounds. They were in a pitiable condition, but made rapid progress to recovery in the peaceful and healthful surroundings of the Castle.

Upon the Belgians being removed to London, their places were taken by various convoys of British soldiers, so that, when the work of the Hospital was concluded, in March 1917, about 400 men had received the hospitality of Strathallan.

The Castle standing at the foot of the Highlands, occupies a carefully sheltered position, whilst its spacious lawns and parks made it a delightful retreat for wounded men as they approached convalescence. In addition to the actual requirements of the Hospital the Billiard Room of the Castle, with reading and writing rooms, were placed at the disposal of the soldiers, and were greatly appreciated.

Lady Roberts, who is the daughter of Wm. Foster, Esq., of Harden, Yorks, is largely interested in charitable objects, and especially in Dr. Barnado's Homes, to which institution she presented the "Roberts Memorial Home" for crippled children, at Harrogate.

The Lady Roberts' Hospital

Mrs. E. L. Rowcliffe, O.B.E.

MRS. EDWARD LEE ROWCLIFFE, O.B.E.

MRS. EDWARD LEE ROWCLIFFE, O.B.E., organised, administrated and was Commandant of the Oaklands Red Cross Hospital, Cranleigh, Surrey (33 beds) for private soldiers and non-commissioned officers. This Institution was open from December, 1915, until October, 1918. She also assisted to organise the Work Depôt in Cranleigh under Queen Mary's Guild for Women Workers and its usefulness continued for four years.

In June, 1910, Mrs. Rowcliffe was appointed Vice-President of the Cranleigh and District Division of the Surrey Branch, B.R.C.S., and a member of the County Committee of that Branch.

On January 1st, 1919, Mrs. Edward Rowcliffe received the O.B.E.

This lady is the daughter of the late General Sir Edward C. S. Williams K.C.I.E., R.E., Colonel Commandant Royal Engineers, and of Clementina Charlotte Bruce, daughter of the late Thomas Bruce of Arnot, Kinrosshire. On January 11th, 1898, she married Edward Lee Rowcliffe, Esq., of Hall Place, Cranleigh, Surrey ; 70, St. James Court, Buckingham Gate, London, S.W.1., also of 1, Bedford Row, London, W.C.1., a partner in the firm of Messrs. Rawle, Johnstone & Co., Solicitors. Mr. and Mrs. Rowcliffe have one son and one daughter.

Before the war Mrs. Rowcliffe took a great interest in all country pursuits, and was one of the first Vice-Presidents appointed on the County Branch of the Surrey B.R.C.S. work ; also Vice-President of the Cranleigh Branch of the Guildford Division of the League of Mercy, and in 1909 was awarded the Order of the League of Mercy.

Clubs : Ladies' Empire Club, Grosvenor Street, London.

MRS. RAWSON-SHAW.

IN 1914 Mrs. Rawson-Shaw became Assistant Commandant of the Auxiliary Military Hospital (A) Littlehampton—two years later becoming Commandant, and continuing to work as such until 1919.

At the same time Mrs. Rawson-Shaw took her part in ameliorating the sufferings of Belgian Refugees, rendered homeless by the German invader.

She had also been engaged some years ago in philanthropic work, being associated with a Girls' Recreation Club, Children's Training Home, Charity Organisation work, Children's Country Holiday and Boarding Out Committees.

MISS C. STELL.

MISS STELL performed valuable war services from July, 1916, as a V.A.D. nurse at Keighley War Hospital. She is the only daughter of J. S. Stell, Esq., and Mrs. Stell, of " Browfield," Keighley, and was mentioned in despatches October, 1917.

MRS. F. N. QUANTOCK SHULDHAM.

COL. F. N. Q. SHULDHAM very generously lent his property, Norton Manor, as a war hospital and Mrs. Quantock Shuldham, who was already Commandant of Somerset 42, W.V.A.D., managed the institution at Norton Manor.

It was opened in October, 1914, for the Belgians, but after April, 1915, the patients admitted were all British. It was finally closed in January, 1919.

When this Hospital was first inaugurated there were only 20 beds, but later the number was increased to 35 and subsequently to 50.

Mrs. Quantock Shuldham is the daughter of the late W. Macalpine Leny, Esq., of Dalswinton, Dumfries, N.B., and Duror, Argyllshire, N.B.

Col. and Mrs. Quantock Shuldham's home is at the Manor, Norton-sub-Hamdon, Somerset.

LADY SCLATER, D.B.E.

FROM August, 1914, to March, 1916, Lady Sclater was Joint President, with the Hon. Mrs. Wilson Fox, of the S.S.F.A. Committee at Central Hackney ; and from April, 1916, to November, 1916, President of the Salisbury Plain Committee, S.S.F.A. In addition, her Ladyship was subsequently President both of the Pensions Committee until June, 1919, and of the Prisoners of War Packing Association at Salisbury, from November, 1916 to November, 1918.

Lady Sclater was also the organizer and President of the War Hospital workrooms at 18, Pont Street, from July, 1915, to February, 1919 ; also the organizer in September, 1914, of a fund (of which she

Lady Sclater, D.B.E.

became President) for the purpose of providing smokes for soldiers and sailors, both at home and abroad. This fund raised and expended a sum of about £200,000, and continued working until June, 1919.

Lady Sclater, who was made a Dame Commander of the British Empire in January, 1918, is the daughter of the Rt. Hon. Colonel Sir Walter B. Barttelot, 1st Baronet, P.C., C.B., M.P., of Stopham, Pulborough, Sussex, and married General Sir Henry Crichton Sclater, G.C.B., G.B.E., etc. (late Royal Artillery), in 1884.

Club : The Ladies' Imperial Club, 17, Dover Street, London.

MRS. M. STRICKLAND-CONSTABLE.

MRS. STRICKLAND-CONSTABLE did excellent service as Commandant of the British Red Cross Society's Hospital for Officers, Brooklands, Hull, between the years 1917 and 1919, having previously had two years' nursing experience as a V.A.D. on the staff of the Hornsea V.A.D. Hospital. Mrs. Strickland-Constable also worked for some months in the Postal Censorship, and did six months' work under the Ministry of Pensions as a Divisional Secretary. She is a Vice-President of the British Red Cross Society, East Riding of Yorkshire branch.

She is a daughter of the late Rear-Admiral the Hon. T. A. Pakenham, and widow of the late Lieut.-Colonel F. C. Strickland-Constable, of Wassand Hall, Hull, who died on active service, December, 1917.

MISS LILIAN M. SOWERBY.

MISS SOWERBY, the daughter of the late Colonel and Mrs. Sowerby, formerly of Putteridge Bury, Herts, devoted herself to war work in October, 1914, and became a V.A.D. nurse at Little Berkhampstead, a convalescent home for Belgian soldiers ; also at St. Paul's Walden and King's Walden Bury Auxiliary Hospital, until it was closed in January, 1917 ; and in March, 1917, with her sister, joined the Women's National Land Service Corps.

MISS VIOLET F. SOWERBY.

MISS VIOLET F. SOWERBY, the sister of Miss Lilian M. Sowerby, also applied herself to war work soon after the outbreak of hostilities, and went in October, 1914, as a V.A.D. nurse to Bragbury, Knebworth (a convalescent hospital for Belgian soldiers) ; in March, 1915, proceeded to King's Walden Bury Auxiliary Hospital until January, 1917, when it was closed ; and in March, 1917, joined the Women's National Land Service Corps, in which Miss Sowerby is still working at the time of writing (1918).

MRS. H. H. SPRINGMAN.

SINCE Armageddon dawned in July, 1914, it is remarkable beyond all conception how much the women of England have quickly and effectively accomplished at home to assuage the anguish, to heal the wounds, of our intrepid heroes returned to us from the firing line, scarred, suffering, and with many sores to soothe.

There are thousands of Florence Nightingales in our land to-day, and one devoted and efficient band of them worked untiringly and cheerfully at the British Red Cross Military Hospital at Ruthin, North Wales, under their greatly respected Commandant, Mrs. H. H. Springman, the eldest daughter of Lieut.-Col. and Mrs. W. Ingersoll-Merritt, and the wife of H. H. Springman, Esq., J.P., of Brynmair, Ruthin.

Detachment Denbigh 20, organized by Mrs. Springman in 1913, was mobilized in 1914. A new hospital built as a workhouse infirmary was lent by the Ruthin Board of Guardians to Mrs. Springman as a Red Cross hospital, and under her supervision it was equipped with the latest improvements and beautifully fitted with baths, operating theatre and X-ray installation. The institution was opened in December, 1915, with twenty beds, the first patients being admitted January 16th, 1916 ; subsequently, the number of beds was increased to 45.

Excellent work was done throughout all departments and the attention to detail by the Detachment was most praiseworthy. The staff consisted of the following :—M.O., Dr. M. Hughes ; Commandant, Mrs. H. H. Springman ; Qr. Master, Mrs. Eyton ; Assistant-Quarter Master, Mrs. Tate ; Hon. Treasurer, H. H. Springman,

Mrs. Springman

Mrs. Strickland-Constable

Mrs. Springman's Hospital

Esq., J.P.; Chairman, J. Stanley Weyman, Esq.; Hon. Secretary, P. W. Brundrit, Esq. Miss Lilla Hughes is Hon. Secretary V.A.D. Denbigh, 20.

Mrs. Springman is President of the Primrose League, Ruthin Branch; Vice-President, B. Red Cross Society, Ruthin Area; and Vice-President, District Nursing Association, Denbighshire.

Mrs. Springman's club is the Sesame, 29, Dover Street, London, W.

MRS. D. L. SHIELD. A.R.R.C. (SECOND CLASS).

BEFORE the war and until her marriage in August, 1914, to Mr. David Lawrie Shield, who afterwards trained for a military commission (being the son of the late Capt. and Mrs. Shield), this lady devoted herself to work as a trained nurse, and was, therefore, highly qualified at the outbreak of hostilities to respond with efficient and valuable services to her country's needs for the performance of expert hospital duty.

Mrs. Shield was asked in May, 1915, to give assistance in opening and starting the 20th Durham V.A. Hospital; and she took up her responsible position as Hon. Nursing Sister on May 24th, 1915; afterwards becoming Assistant-Matron and in 1916 Matron and was awarded the Army Royal Red Cross (second class). Mrs. Shield has also been keenly interested since the war in V.A.D. organization, being Commandant of the 80th Detachment, Durham, and Lady Divisional Superintendent for the Sunderland Nursing (Western) Division of the St. J.A.B. Mrs. Shield is the eldest daughter of J. Huddart, Esq. and Mrs. Huddart, of Sunderland.

MRS. C. D. SIMMONS.

THIS lady, who married Lieut. Commander C. D. Simmons, D.S.O., R.N.R., on March 30th, 1910, is the daughter of Arthur Pottinger, Esq., of Christchurch, New Zealand, and before the war had spent some time travelling, visiting the Colonies, South America, etc.

M

On the outbreak of the war she joined a Red Cross detachment and worked at Lewisham Military Hospital for a few weeks; she was accepted for special service and after training at Woolwich Infirmary, was sent to Sutton Veny Military Hospital, where some of the German prisoners of war were nursed.

"Mentioned" in despatches in October, 1917.

MISS MARY JANE SMART, R.R.C.

SISTER SMART, who worked at No. 4 special hospital for officers, at Latchmere, Ham Common, Surrey, from the date the institution opened on December 1st, 1915, until it closed down, January 1st, 1920, is the daughter of Mr. and Mrs. Gordon Smart, of Sandyhillock, Dufftown, Banffshire.

She was "mentioned" in 1917 for her valuable nursing services, and at the closing of the hospitals was awarded the Royal Red Cross.

Before the war Miss Smart was trained at the Royal Mental Hospital, Aberdeen, where she gained the medico-psychological certificate of Great Britain and Ireland. Miss Smart was also engaged in private nursing; at other times working at the Scottish National Institution, Larbert; and at the Mental Hospital, Haddington.

THE MISSES SHIFFNER.

THE Misses Shiffner performed excellent war-time service as members of the V.A.D. London, 46. All three—the Misses M. B., E. B. G., and D. M. Shiffner—worked at the Hospital for Officers, 24, Park Street, Mayfair, both in the pantry and in the wards, and Miss Mary Shiffner served also at the Stapleton Park V.A.D. Hospital, Yorks, and the Barton Court Hospital, Berks.

They are the daughters of Mr. George Bridger Shiffner, of Rossington Home Farm, Bawtry, Yorks.

Miss M. J. Smart, R.R.C.

Mrs. Simmons

Mrs. D. L. Shield, A.R.R.C.

Mrs. St. John

MRS. ST. JOHN.

FROM December, 1914, to January, 1918, Mrs. St. John worked as a V.A. member under an army Sister at Pembroke Dock Military Hospital. This lady originated and organised the equipment of Cottesmore Red Cross Hospital, Haverford West, which was opened in May, 1915, and worked there as Commandant until her marriage in December, 1916. She then went to Queenstown where she organised work parties from January, 1917, until June, 1917, then finally did duty at Davenport work depôt daily for nine months. Mrs. St. John has been twice "mentioned" in the "Gazette" for her valuable war services.

The daughter of Sir Charles and Lady Philipps, of Picton Castle, Haverfordwest, she married in December, 1916, Brig.-Gen. G. F. W. St. John, C.B.

Before the war, Mrs. St. John was keenly interested in patriotic endeavours, and served as Commandant of the Women's V.A.D., Pembroke 14, since 1912.

MRS. THORLEY SYKES, M.B.E.

THIS lady is the daughter of George March, Esq., of Oaklands, Thorner, near Leeds, and was married in 1883 to Thorley Sykes, Esq., of Croes Howell, Rossett, for several years J.P. of Denbighshire, but who had to retire through failing health (he died in 1908).

Before the war she was energetically interested in public-spirited enterprises, and founded a Patriotic League for Farmers, also organised and held Unionist and National Service meetings for the League. Quickly upon the outbreak of war, Mrs. Sykes applied her energies and abilities to practical war effort, at first in September and October, 1914, holding a series of sewing meetings at her own address, producing 250 articles for the Red Cross.

During these months a number of buildings at Croes Howell (very picturesque and nearly 200 years old, with beautiful old oak rafters and beams) were being converted into a hospital. This was accepted by the War Office in November, 1914, and opened on the 25th of that month as a Red Cross Hospital. The institution was also equipped by Mrs. Sykes,

At first there was only one large ward with twelve beds and two sitting-rooms, but by 1918 Mrs. Sykes had added to the buildings, and there were four wards, two bedrooms for nurses, sitting-room, mess room, recreation room, operating theatre and X-ray room with apparatus ; thirty-two beds in all for men, and four for the nurses,— a truly patriotic war undertaking.

MISS GERTRUDE M. SALE.

BEFORE the war Miss Gertrude M. Sale, the only daughter of H. F. Sale, Esq., and of Mrs. Sale, of Shipston-on-Stour, found delightful and rational recreation both as a keen athlete, enthusiastic tennis player and an accomplished amateur contralto soloist. But when the great clash of arms came, calling for capable, patriotic war work to be done in our hospitals, Miss Sale, who had been a member of the Red Cross Society since 1911, became a V.A.D. nurse in November 1914, at Park House Hospital, and remained there until its close, performing duties with much care and efficiency.

MRS. ARTHUR SHAW.

THIS lady, the daughter of Paul Platt, Esq., of Bolton, and married to Arthur Shaw, Esq., of Manchester, in 1890, was Commandant of the Wibbersley Auxiliary Hospital, Flixton, near Manchester, since October, 1914, when the institution was opened for the Belgian wounded, and Mrs. Shaw was continuously on duty.

She was presented to Her Majesty Queen Mary on the occasion of the Royal visit to Manchester, by Colonel Coates, C.B., A.D.S., chairman of the B.R.C.S.

Mrs. Shaw, who holds the First Aid and Home Nursing proficiency medals, was " mentioned " in 1917 for valuable war services rendered.

Mrs. Thorley Sykes, M.B.E.

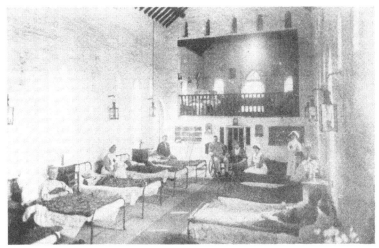

Croes Howell
(Mrs. Thorley Sykes, M.B.E.)

Miss G. M. Sale

Miss E. M. Stein

The Countess of Stradbroke

MISS E. M. STEIN.

THIS lady took up war work enthusiastically and most efficiently at her father's auxiliary hospital since November, 1914.

Miss Stein is the daughter of Charles Stein, Esq., M.D., O.B.E., of Park House, Shipston-on-Stour.

She joined V.A.D. Warwick 34 on its formation in May, 1911, and was fully trained and ready for her duties as V.A. member when war broke out.

In August, 1916, she was appointed Quarter Master at Park House Auxiliary Hospital and energetically worked for the successful enlargement of that hospital from 20 to 60 beds.

Miss Stein in October, 1917, was " mentioned " in the Secretary of State's list for valuable services rendered in connection with the war, and in May, 1918, was admitted a member (for service) of the B.R.C.S.

THE COUNTESS OF STRADBROKE.

THE Countess of Stradbroke devoted her time and home from August 14th, 1914, to the close of the war, to the sacred cause of the amelioration of the sufferings of our brave wounded heroes.

Henham Hall, Wangford, Suffolk, is the seat of the Earl and Countess.

They were married in 1898. Lady Stradbroke is the daughter of General Keith Fraser. The Earl of Stradbroke, C.B., C.V.O., was Colonel, 272 Artillery Brigade on active service in France and Palestine ; is President of the National Artillery Association ; is A.D.C. to the King ; Colonel, 1st Norfolk Royal Garrison Artillery Volunteers, 1888–1908 ; Colonel, 3rd (Howitzer) Brigade, E. Anglian Division, R.F.A. ; Alderman and Chairman East Suffolk County Council ; Chairman County of Suffolk Territorial Army Association.

MISS SOPHIE SCHOFIELD.

MISS SOPHIE SCHOFIELD was a fully trained and certificated masseuse in 1915, being a member of the Incorporated Society of Trained Masseuses, and now she is a member of the A.P.M.N.C. She was appointed Senior Masseuse at Stoke

War Hospital, Newcastle-under-Lyme, a post which she occupied for two years and a half, afterwards taking a training in Medical Electricity at the 2nd Western General Hospital, Ducie Avenue, Manchester. During this time she took lectures privately under Miss Goldsmith, Lime Grove, Manchester, and was successful in passing her final examination.

MISS LAURA W. SANDERS.

WHEN, in August, 1914, England was plunged into the throes of a world-wide struggle, Miss Laura W. Sanders immediately volunteered for Red Cross work only to be rejected on account of her age. This disappointment served only to increase her ardour, for on September 14th, 1914, she began to study nervous diseases at a Mental Hospital until August 23rd, 1916, when she successfully passed her examination. Miss Sanders then offered her services, which were accepted, to Devonshire House, becoming a member of B.R.C.S. 40th London Detachment. In October of 1916 she undertook duties at the 2nd Western General Hospital for officers, and while there received one red stripe for proficiency and valuable service.

Miss Laura W. Sanders is the youngest daughter of Nelson and Mildred Sanders, of Oxhey Bushey, Herts.

MISS MAUDE L. TIDSWELL.

MISS MAUDE L. TIDSWELL has been twice " mentioned " by the Secretary of State for War for valuable nursing services rendered.

In December, 1914, she was appointed Commandant for the R.A.M.C. Military Hospital, 41, Jesmond Road, Newcastle-on-Tyne, and continued until June, 1916, when the hospital was removed to 6, Kensington Terrace and enlarged, with a complement of fifty beds, and attached as an auxiliary to the 1st Northern General Hospital. Miss Tidswell continued voluntary service there until December, 1917.

She is the daughter of the late Thomas Howard Tidswell, Esq., of Long Benton, Northumberland ; and a devotée of all outdoor sports.

Miss Schofield

Miss L. W. Sanders

Miss Maude L. Tidswell

Miss Elsie L. Tunstall

MISS ELSIE A. TUNSTALL.

THE daughter of the late Thomas Tunstall, Esq., and of Mrs. Tunstall, of Grappenhall, Cheshire, this lady, at the outbreak of war, began work at Radden Court V.A.D. Hospital, and since 1916 was at Whitecross Military Hospital, putting in full time as V.A.D. nurse.

LADY DOUGHTY TICHBORNE.

LADY DOUGHTY TICHBORNE, who resides at Tichborne Park, Alresford, Hampshire, has, during the war, performed valuable services in the public interest. She is the daughter of the late Edward Henry Petre, Esq., and widow of the twelfth Baronet.

The Tichbornes are a very old and distinguished Hampshire family, dating from pre-Conquest times. One of its members was the Sir Benjamin de Tichborne who, on the death of Queen Elizabeth, hastened to Winchester to proclaim James VI. of Scotland as King. The family name is taken from the River Itchen.

MISS MATILDA T. TALBOT, M.B.E.

WHEN the hour of England's great ordeal arrived in 1914 Miss Matilda T. Talbot was a certificated teacher of cookery, both plain and advanced.

From October, 1914, to July, 1915, she took charge of the kitchen department at the Coxham V.A.D. Hospital, Wilts. She was also responsible for a family of Belgian Refugees from October, 1914, to January, 1918. In addition, Miss Talbot was engaged in cooking and other duties at La Courneuve, near Paris, with the Croix Rouge Française from January, 1916–April, 1916, and at Bussang, Vosges, France, with the Croix Rouge Française from April, 1917, to September, 1917, between her visits to France, teaching cookery in England.

Miss Talbot joined the Women's Royal Naval Service in February, 1918, and was posted to Cranwell Royal Naval Air Station in March, 1918, where she was Principal in Charge of the W.R.N.S., whose numbers increased from 29 to 380 officers and ratings, including members of the W.R.A.F. She was demobilised in April, 1919.

For her diligent and valuable services she was gazetted M.B.E. Military Division) on January 1st, 1919.

In 1918 Miss Matilda Theresa Talbot took the name of Talbot in lieu of that of Gilchrist Clark. She is the daughter of the late John Gilchrist Clark, Esq., of Speddoch, Dumfriesshire, and niece of the late Charles Henry Talbot, Esq., of Lacock Abbey, Chippenham, Wilts.

Miss Talbot is a keen student and translator of various modern languages.

THE LADY TREDEGAR.

THE Lady Tredegar's war-time activities were very largely directed to the alleviation of the sufferings of our wounded soldiers, and much of her time and sympathy was devoted to helping various military hospitals, especially that which she herself established at her house, 37, Bryanston Square, and which, to a considerable extent, she also maintained.

Her husband, the 3rd Baron Tredegar, served from 1914 to 1918 in the Royal Naval Division, and also fought in the Boer War (1900–1). He is now Hon. Colonel of the 1st Battalion Monmouth Regiment. He also did valuable service in the cause of healing, providing and maintaining the Hospital Yacht *Liberty*, for which he received the distinction of the O.B.E.

The Lady Tredegar herself comes of an old and distinguished family, being a daughter of the 9th Earl of Southesk.

Her recreations are painting and reading.

Club : Ladies' Automobile.

CORNELIA LADY WIMBORNE, O.B.E.

CORNELIA LADY WIMBORNE has taken a very indefatigable share in patriotic service during the war. Her Ladyship is the widow of the first Baron Wimborne, and herself comes of a very distinguished family, being daughter of the seventh Duke of Marlborough. She is a sister of the late Lord Randolph Churchill, Lady de Ramsay, the late Lady Tweedmouth (Lady Fanny Marjoribanks), the Dowager Duchess of Roxburghe, the late Lady Howe and Lady Sarah Wilson, and aunt of Mr. Winston Churchill.

Lady Tredegar

Her husband, the late Lord Wimborne, was an ardent politician, friend of Lord Beaconsfield and Mr. Joseph Chamberlain, besides many other noted statesmen of his day. He contested Poole and twice Bristol in the Conservative interest, and, though unsuccessful on each occasion, was held in much esteem by his Party.

The political traditions of the family are carried on by his sons, the present Viscount Wimborne, who in addition to filling other high offices of state has been Lord Lieut. of Ireland, and Captain the Hon. F. E. Guest, who has for many years sat in Parliament for Poole.

In his lifetime, Cornelia Lady Wimborne was associated with her husband in innumerable works of philanthropy, broadly conceived and generously carried out ; and since his demise her beneficence has never failed the district. Poole Park—forty acres of charming pleasure-ground—is a monumental gift to the town of Poole, and very many other local and county institutions owe their existence and prosperity to Lady Wimborne and her late husband.

Not the least of these is the Cornelia Hospital at Poole (so designated by the first committee of management in honour of Lady Wimborne), which, during the war, ministered abundantly to the needs of the wounded soldiers.

The institution founded in 1907, was the development of a Hospital established at Poole in 1886 by Lady Wimborne and her husband, who supplied the cost of maintenance almost exclusively from that date until 1907.

Then the same generous benefactors gifted to the town the fee simple of about two acres and a half of ground in the Longfleet Road, the conveyance of the mansion and grounds in Market Street, and an accompanying sum of £1,000. With this and the funds resulting from the sale to the Corporation of the Market Street properties, the Trustees built in the Longfleet Road the present Cornelia Hospital, which, it was decided, should be placed upon a public basis, and thereafter upheld by public subscription. Some £3,500 is now required annually for its maintenance.

Before the war the Hospital was equipped with only 17 beds but soon after the outbreak of hostilities a further 65 were provided for the use of wounded soldiers. Two temporary wards were erected, with the necessary annexes, at a cost of £1,200, largely subscribed by the Red Cross (Dorset Branch).

In 1915, Lady Wimborne helped to relieve the congestion at the Hospital by making provision for convalescents at Court House, Canford. The house (furnished and equipped for the accommodation of 23 men) was placed with the services of a matron at the disposal

N

of the Committee. Owing to the closing of Court House and to transport difficulties, the Committee were later obliged to seek other premises, and by a happy arrangement with Mr. Mellersh, the house known as " Forest Holme," Seldown Road, was secured, 26 beds being constantly occupied. The total number of beds was then nominally 100, but with the increase of casualties on the Western Front, the Committee took the responsibility of providing still more beds with the help of the War Office ; and in 1917 five marquees, kitchens and other necessary buildings were found and equipped at a cost of about £700.

During the war period over two thousand military patients were treated at the Cornelia Hospital, these coming direct from the battle fronts.

Between the years 1914 and 1918 a total of 3955 patients (civil and military) were admitted, and the proportion of deaths was infinitesimal. In this period 4241 out-patients also received treatment.

This Hospital, inseparably associated as it is with the name of Cornelia, Lady Wimborne, was by no means her only contribution to the national service. In September, 1914, she inaugurated the Dorset Guild of Workers, in which later she had the co-operation and support of Lady Alington and other earnest ladies.

From slender beginnings this organisation grew and flourished until with ramifications all over the County it was working on a quite magnificent scale.

To the ancient burgh of Poole fell the honour of cradling the emprise. There, at 20, Market Street, an old house lying empty and idle, was taken over by the Guild and speedily transferred into a centre of effective industry. The original purpose of the organisation was to provide socks and other woollen comforts to tide the men over the bitter winter of 1914–15, and even in those early days large quantities of knitted articles were made and dispatched. But the Guild was adaptable and " alive," adjusting itself to the changing conditions and requirements of the troops. Sandbags, mosquito-nets, respirators, hospital requisites, all came within its scope, and each need as it arose was adequately met.

In the autumn of 1915 overtures were made by the War Office with a view to securing the co-operation of the Guild in the official scheme for the direction of Voluntary Organisations, and these having been suitably responded to, the Guild was duly affiliated to the Director-General of Voluntary Organisations. Hitherto it had borne the title of " East Dorset Guild of Workers," henceforth it was to be known as the " Dorset Guild of Workers," and recognised as the centre of Voluntary work in the County. In November, 1915, the Lord Lieut. of the County (the Earl of Shaftesbury) took over the presidency of the Guild from the ladies who had held it jointly— Lady Wimborne and Lady Alington—and they in turn became chairmen of the Executive Committee.

Meanwhile the energies of its members were carefully directed and economically conserved. To ensure thoroughness and prevent overlapping they kept in touch, not only with the Officer Commanding the Depôt Dorset Regiment and the President of the Dorset Territorial Force Association, but also with the Officers Commanding all units stationed in the County. Indeed, the whole record of the Guild shows evidence of excellent organisation and a thoughtful and talented administration unique in the annals of such associations.

In April, 1915, the Guild had found a new outlet for abounding enthusiasm in ministering to the needs of prisoners of War in Germany and elsewhere. The prisoners thus catered for were men of the Dorset Regiment, and in most cases the procedure followed was for one or other of the members to " adopt " a prisoner, for whose food parcels he undertook to provide the money. These food parcels were more or less standardised, and provided excellent fare for men who, in many cases, would have died of starvation were it not for the timely assistance thus rendered. The tremendous task of catering for this huge " family " of over seven hundred prisoners was entrusted to Mrs. C. Trevanion, whose business capabilities stood splendidly the strain thus put upon them. The old house at Poole continued to be the Headquarters of the Guild, where goods were received from the many branches, and parcels packed and dispatched. There huge quantities of provisions were stored, to be sent overseas and as quickly replaced. There was even a " bonded warehouse " for tea and tobacco! Parcels consisting of such varied commodities as tea, cocoa, quaker oats, dripping, tripe and onions, kippered herrings and cigarettes were sent to every prisoner of the Dorsets three times a fortnight. In all, nearly fifty thousand parcels were thus forwarded, and the ultimate expenditure on this item of the Guild's activities was close on £1,000 monthly. It is surely impossible to over estimate the value of such work when one considers how many men have died in the enemy's hand from starvation and bad feeding ; how many more have had their health ruined from the same cause.

A large part of the income of the Guild was derived from subscriptions, but considerable sums were raised from time to time by those means so frequently and effectively resorted to during the war—fêtes, flag days, concerts, bazaars and so on. Here, again, a small army of women gave their time and talents ungrudgingly to the cause they had at heart.

On March 31st, 1919, when the signing of peace was already in sight, the Guild came to an end, the need for its activities being happily passed away.

In the course of a graceful and spirited speech delivered at the closing meeting of the Guild, Cornelia Lady Wimborne remarked that she thought her audience would be surprised, as she was, to note the remarkable amount of work which the Guild had achieved. "As regards the future," she said, " co-operative work must be our motto and object in life. It is by working together for a common cause, such as the work of the Guild has been, that most can be achieved, and the war has taught us there is no happiness in life which does not consist of work. We must have no more of what has been known as the leisured classes, with their amusements and pleasure and indulgence. They are all very well in their way, but they must not be the key-note of life. It must be work, work for our country and the good of others."

THE HON. LADY WHITEHEAD.

THE HON. LADY WHITEHEAD (née the Hon. Marian Cecilia Brodrick) is the youngest daughter of the 8th Viscount Midleton, and wife of Sir Beethom Whitehead, K.C.M.G., of Efford Park, Lymington, Hants. The Brodrick family, which dates back to the time of Queen Elizabeth, has produced many notable English statesmen, among whom may be mentioned the present Earl of Midleton (brother of Lady Whitehead), who was Secretary of State for War 1900–1903 and Secretary of State for India 1903–1905.

During the war Sir Beethom and Lady Whitehead, working in conjunction with Lady Harrowby's scheme, entertained a large number of Colonial Officers as guests at Efford Park for periods varying from three days to fourteen. There, in the pleasant environment of park and pleasure grounds covering about a hundred acres, the overseas officers had a breathing-space before they plunged into the turmoil of battle.

The Hon. Lady Whitehead

Mrs. W. Warde-Aldam

THE VISCOUNTESS WIMBORNE.

LADY WIMBORNE (née the Hon. Alice Katherine Sibell Grosvenor), who was throughout the war an assiduous worker in the cause of Patriotism, is a daughter of the 2nd Baron Ebury, and thus comes of a well-known political family. Her husband, the 1st Viscount Wimborne, is a son of the late Lord Wimborne and Cornelia Lady Wimborne.

Lord Wimborne served with the Dorset Imperial Yeomanry in South Africa in 1900, and since then has had a distinguished parliamentary career. He sat for Plymouth 1900–1906, for Cardiff District 1906–1910 ; was Paymaster-General 1910–1912, and Lord Lieut. of Ireland 1915–1918.

MRS. W. WARDE-ALDAM.

MRS. WARDE-ALDAM'S war-time activities were most numerous and useful. In August, 1914, she lent and fully equipped her house—Hooton Pagnell Hall, Yorkshire—as an Auxiliary Military Hospital, and maintained it as such until March, 1919. During the whole of this time she herself acted as its Commandant, Quarter Master and General Administrator. Very soon the original 16 beds with which the Hospital was equipped increased to 40, and in due course to 100.

Meanwhile Mrs. Warde-Aldam worked as a member of the Red Cross Society, belonging to the " North Riding Reserve, Yorkshire 32." She served under the County Director, West Riding of Yorks (at York) and worked under the No. 3 Base Hospital at Sheffield.

Three " War Working Parties " were, during the whole of the War, conducted by Mrs. Warde-Aldam in three separate villages, for the making of shirts, socks, etc., for the troops. Also she helped with the Belgian Relief Fund in 1915, being Lady President of a local committee.

She is a daughter and co-heiress of the Rev. William Warde of Hooton Pagnell Hall, Yorkshire, and on April 30th, 1878, married William Wright Aldam, D.L., J.P., who, on his marriage assumed the surname of " Warde " in addition to Aldam.

Mrs. Warde-Aldam occupies her leisure with gardening, travelling, and out-door pursuits generally, and with various local public duties.

Club : Albemarle Club, Dover Street.

MISS LUCY D. WISE.

MISS WISE is the daughter of Francis Dickson Wise, Esq., of The Red House, Ripon, Yorks, and before the outbreak of hostilities found much recreation in games, gardening and music, but subsequently to 1915 her time was mainly devoted to war duties as a V.A.D. nurse in H.S.H. the Grand Duchess George of Russia's Hospital, Harrogate.

MRS. T. L. F. WILLOUGHBY.

MRS. WILLOUGHBY'S war-time activities were largely devoted to the interests of soldiers' and sailors' families. In August, 1914, she became Hon. Secretary and Treasurer of the Soldiers' and Sailors' Families Association, Buckrose Parliamentary Division, and in July, 1916, Secretary and Treasurer of the Buckrose War Pensions Committee for Families of Service Men. She was also Vice-Chairman of the East Riding of Yorkshire War Pensions Committee.

She is the daughter of the late Sir Charles W. Strickland, Bart., and wife of Lt.-Colonel the Hon. Tatton L. F. Willoughby.

THE HON. MRS. WILKINSON.

THE Hon. Mrs. Wilkinson, daughter of the 3rd Lord Decies, and wife of Colonel Wilkinson, C.B.E., D.S.O., worked throughout the war, and—as can be recorded of very few ladies of her years—did actual ward work in Hospital in England. In the winters of 1914, 1915 and 1917 she served with the Auxiliary Military Hospitals, Mentone and Monte Carlo, and the Red Cross Hospital, Hyeres ; while in the summers of 1915–16–17–18 she performed part time duty in York Military Hospital.

Before the war the Hon. Mrs. Wilkinson took an active and constructive interest in public affairs, being a member of the Executive Committee of the Yorkshire Ladies' Council of Education and the York branches of the National Society for the Prevention of Cruelty to Children ; the Girl Guides ; the University Extension Society ; the National Council of Women ; and the Charity Organisation Society.

She finds her recreation in gardening and travelling, and is a Fellow of the Royal Geographical Society and a member of the Society of Authors. Club : Lyceum.

Mrs. Welton

Miss Constance M. Wright

Miss L. D. Wise

Mrs. M. E. White-Popham

MRS. MARGARET E. WHITE-POPHAM.

THIS gracious and philanthropic lady during the war interested herself largely in Red Cross Work as President of the Shanklin Red Cross League and Vice-President of the Isle of Wight branch of the Red Cross Society. She is also President of the Isle of Wight Tariff Reform League and Vice-President of the Isle of Wight Unionist Guild, besides owning to numerous other activities of a like nature. Her lively and constructive interest in all good works is well known and much appreciated in the Island. She is a daughter of the Rev. N. Hubbersty and widow of the late F. White-Popham, Esq.

MISS CONSTANCE M. WRIGHT.

IN May, 1915, Miss Constance Wright (the third daughter of George C. Wright, Esq., of Burford-road, Nottingham) began her war services, which proved thoroughly useful and efficient, as a V.A.D. worker at Bagthorpe Infirmary, where she remained for twelve months; proceeding next to the military hospital, Press Heath Camp, Salop, and it is very gratifying to add that Miss Wright was officially " mentioned " in October, 1917, for valuable services rendered, a suitable recognition of her devotion to duty.

MRS. C. H. WELTON.

THE daughter of Joseph Overton Morley, Esq., and married to Charles H. Welton, Esq., October 17th, 1906, this lady before the war qualified and worked as a trained nurse (medical and surgical) from 1899–1902 ; in a private nursing home, 1902–1906 ; and in 1912 enrolled in the B.R.C.S.

In January, 1915, Mrs. Welton as Lady Superintendent, mobilised the Warwick 26 Hillcrest Auxiliary Hospital (20 beds, subsequently increased to 65). Five of the Red Cross nurses were accepted for active service. From January, 1915, to March, 1918, one thousand in-patients passed through the institution ; the local discharged men visited it daily for massage and electrical treatment. On March 19th, 1918, Mrs. Welton transferred to Warwick 70.

MRS. WAILES-FAIRBAIRN.

IN 1914 the ball room at Askham Grange, York, Mrs. Wailes-Fairbairn's home, was converted into a hospital (30 beds). At first only Belgian soldiers were nursed, but subsequently, and until January 4th, 1919 (when it was closed), the patients were all English, the total number received being between 400 and 500. Mrs. Wailes-Fairbairn was herself the Commandant and Acting Matron.

She is the daughter of George Alderson Smith, Esq., J.P., of Wheatcroft Cliff, Scarborough, and on January 14th, 1892, married Major Wailes-Fairbairn, M.A., J.P., D.L.

This lady is devoted to all country pursuits.

LADY WARDE.

LADY WARDE, of Barham Court, Maidstone, is one of the numerous well-born ladies who promptly and ungrudgingly devoted strength, time, and their resources to the amelioration of the sufferings of our brave and intrepid heroes, wounded in the great conflict.

Lady Warde is the daughter of the late Viscount de Stern, and married in 1890 Colonel Charles Warde, M.P., D.L., J.P. (upon whom a Baronetcy was conferred in 1919). He has been the Conservative member for the Mid. Division of Kent since 1892. Colonel Sir Charles Warde is the eldest son of the late General Sir Edward Warde, and served for 23 years in the Cavalry in the 19th and 4th Hussars.

It is not surprising, therefore, that Sir Charles and Lady Warde evince the fullest sympathy with and solicitude for the welfare and comfort of our sufferers from the front.

On the outbreak of war Barham Court was arranged as a hospital with 36 beds for the wounded, and received the first batch of men from the front on 25th September, 1914 ; and since then about 500 have passed through Barham Court under Lady Warde's personal and uninterrupted care. This was not a V.A.D. hospital—all the staff were certificated surgical nurses.

Lady Warde is a member of the Ladies' Imperial Club.

Mrs. Wailes-Fairbairn

Lady Warde

The Duchess of Westminster

THE DUCHESS OF WESTMINSTER.

THE wonderful work which women accomplished in war time for the succouring of our soldiers and the raising of their spirits amid the grim realities of war, reads oftentimes like a romance. Their noble endeavours stand out in high relief and brilliant colours against the sordid setting of the battlefield.

Her Grace the Duchess of Westminster, daughter of the late William Cornwallis West, Esq., of Ruthin Castle, North Wales, was one of those gifted ladies who—happy in the consciousness that they were serving their country and bearing their part in the conflict—spared no personal trouble or expense to heal and help the wounded.

At the beginning of the war—in October, 1914—she equipped and took out to France a hospital for 250 soldier patients, which was definitely opened in the Casino Le Touquet, Paris Plage, in the following month.

In 1915 it was converted into an officers' hospital, and between that year and July, 1918, when the institution was closed, 15,000 officers were treated.

The Duchess of Westminster herself ran the linen room during the first period, and afterwards worked in the X-ray room, and superintended various branches of the hospital work.

Club : Bath Club.

MISS INA WALLACE.

MISS WALLACE, the daughter of Alexander Wallace, Esq., of Woodsdale, Battle, Sussex, performed valuable war services for two years as a night nurse at Normanhurst Hospital, Battle.

MISS G. WARHAM.

MISS G. WARHAM, daughter of the late Edward Warham, Esq., and Mrs. Warham, was, prior to 1914, devoted to the pursuit of nursing, and during the war served efficiently for about three years as Staff Nurse in Northumberland War Hospital, Gosforth, Newcastle-on-Tyne.

o

MRS. HARCOURT WOOD.

DURING the war Mrs. Harcourt Wood was Vice-President of the Breconshire Red Cross Society, representing Builth Wells and district, and worked for some time during 1914 at St. Thomas' Hospital, London.

On Easter Monday, 1915, Mrs. Wood opened the V.A.D. Hospital Builth Wells, where she acted as Commandant for seven months, after which time she had to resign on account of ill-health, family illness, and heavy bereavements.

On leaving the county Mrs. Wood was presented with a medal in recognition of the valuable services she had rendered.

In addition Mrs. Wood helped to form work-parties for providing soldiers' clothing, and later helped supply Lady Smith Dorrien with " treasure bags."

Before the war Mrs. Wood was on many local committees ; was President of the Builth branch of the Breconshire Red Cross ; and about four years previous to the outbreak of war started Red Cross V.A.D's. (including a men's detachment) in her neighbourhood.

Mrs. Harcourt Wood is the eldest daughter of the late Hamon le Strange, Esq., of Hunstanton Hall, Norfolk, and on January 22nd, 1898, married Capt. C. Harcourt Wood (late 15th Hussars) of Carleton Lodge, Pontefract, and of Caer Beris, Builth Wells, Breconshire.

Her recreations are music, gardening and hunting.

MRS. J. WATKINS.

MRS. WATKINS has devoted herself to various forms of national service during the war. For a short time she worked in Shoreditch, arranging Group System Cards, and also at Kensington Court Needlework Red Cross Guild. For two years intermittently she took out blinded soldiers at 2nd London General Hospital, Fulham, and during the same time worked at Queen Alexandra's Field Force Depôt, Brompton Road, under Mrs. Sclayter.

Later she served for six months as V.A.D. at Auxiliary Hospitals " Ashfield " and " Formora " at Malvern, Worcestershire, and at Auxiliary Hospital " Sunnyside," Whalley Range, Manchester.

Mrs. Watkins is a daughter of M. Ffinch, Esq., and wife of Lt.-Col. J. Watkins, late North Stafford Regiment. She is devoted to country life.

Beatrice Eleanor Dormer-Knowles

O.A.S. Sept. 1914 to 1919.

Chevalier de l'Ordre de Leopold
Medaille de la Reine Elisabeth
Medaille de la Reconnaisance Francais
Medaille de la Victoire

MRS. DORMER-KNOWLES

(*nee* BEATRICE ELEANOR DORMER-MAUNDER).

ON April 7th, 1920, Miss Beatrice Dormer-Maunder was married to George Knowles, Esq., of Stockton House, Wiltshire. In the list of British war-workers her name is well-known and greatly respected.

Throughout the colossal conflict practical good war service was her constant aim. She was the pioneer of workers for helping Belgian refugees and wounded in their own country.

At the outbreak of hostilities she went to Ostend, and there established a home for the relief of distressed Belgians, following this up by organising the famous Kursaal which was opened in the first instance for better class refugees, and on the fall of Antwerp was re-organised for the reception of wounded Belgian soldiers. In addition to this, all the British wounded sent from Antwerp were taken to her temporary hospital in the Kursaal which was moved to Dunkirk before the German advance, and then she adopted a Belgian suggestion and established a hospital for Belgian soldiers at Rouen.

Ostend was evacuated October 13th, 1914, and when it was returned Miss Dormer-Maunder was the first British lady to re-enter. She was the organising Directress for Belgian Military Hospitals, 1914-1918.

She has received the following honours :—Chevalier de l'ordre de Leopold, Medaille de la Reine Elizabeth, Medaille de la Reconnaisance Francais, British war and Victory medals.

At her wedding on April 7th, 1920, at the Brompton Parish Church, Miss Dormer-Maunder wore the three decorations awarded by the Belgian Government for her very valuable and untiring devotion to war work in Flanders. The Earl of Athlone was present, also General Mellis, Inspector General of Belgian Military Hospitals, who represented the Belgian Government and referred in grateful and sincere terms to the skilful and gallant services successfully accomplished by the bride during the war as Organising Directress of hospitals under Belgian military control.

Mrs. George Knowles is a daughter of the late George Maunder, Squire of Warleigh, Rangitikei, New Zealand, and for the last 16 years has spent all her time, except nine months, in England.

o*

Before the war as an active Anti-Suffragette, she organised many meetings, and when unavoidably obliged to do so, also fulfilled the rôle of public speaker. As a member of the Eugenic Society she has spent many years in Northern manufacturing towns, giving afternoon and evening talks to women on health and right living, and during dinner hours she devoted her time to talks to women in the factories, often by request of the Directors.

Her favourite recreations are hunting, tennis and dancing. Clubs : The Ladies' Park Club (Hyde Park Corner), London.

THE LADY HOWARD DE WALDEN AND SEAFORD.

IT was given to some to realise almost at the outset of the struggle, the supreme necessity for women's work and ministration. Quietly and without ostentation they took their places as pioneers in the ranks of the war-workers, and bore the burden and heat of the day without complaint or slackening of effort until the return of peace brought them the " well done " of a grateful country.

Among them was the Lady Howard de Walden and Seaford, who ran her own hospital for men, 200 beds, in Alexandria, for a year, 1915–16, during the Gallipoli period, at the same time providing near-by a smaller convalescent hospital for officers, 25 beds.

Her Ladyship also inaugurated in Alexandria a nurses' club which enrolled 300 members. In addition to the strenuous work involved in the administration and supervision of those institutions, Lady Howard de Walden found time to sing at many soldiers' concerts.

From January, 1917, to September, 1919, she ran a maternity home for officers' wives at Albert Road, Regent's Park.

Her Ladyship married the Lord Howard de Walden in 1912, and they have a family of four daughters and one son, including the twins (boy and girl) born in 1912. Lady Howard de Walden is the daughter of the late Charles van Raalte, Esq., of Brownsea Island, Dorset.

The Lady Howard de Walden

Mrs. Hughes-Onslow

MRS. HUGHES-ONSLOW.

PROMPTLY after the declaration of war, the Dorset Hospitals were ready fully equipped and the County V.A.D.'s ready. The excellent organising powers of those in authority, together with the keenness and energy of the workers in the County, combined to bring about this desirable result.

In those early days, the President of the Red Cross Workers in Dorset was Mrs. Mount-Batten, the Hon. County Director, Brig-General Balguy, and the results achieved speak for themselves of pronounced organizing abilities. Within a month of the outbreak of war there were 1,200 beds ready and equipped, together with complete nursing and trained staff and medical attendance. The County Director decided that Dorchester and Weymouth should be the first " Temporary Hospitals " to be made use of if required.

The County was divided into twelve Red Cross Divisions :— Dorchester, Sherborne, Shaftesbury, Weymouth, Bridport, Cerne, Beaminster, Blandford, Sturminster Newton, Wimborne, Poole and Wareham.

Immediately on the outbreak of war, Mrs. Hughes-Onslow, along with her late husband, Major Denzil Hughes-Onslow, engaged in a strenuous campaign for recruits. On 14th August, 1914, they handed over their English residence, Colliton House, Dorchester, to the British Red Cross Society as a Red Cross Auxiliary Hospital. That Hospital (200 beds) was occupied with Belgian wounded in October, 1914, and was not vacated till 1919. She was Commandant of Ayr 50 V.A. Detachment of the Red Cross ; President of the Soldiers' and Sailors' Families Association for the Ballantrae District till it was merged into the Soldiers' and Sailors' Help Association, and the Pensions Committee ; President of Ballantrae War Work Party and President of the District County Committee's Campaign for promoting employment of women on the land. Her husband having in August, 1914, volunteered for foreign service (after declining several home appointments) was attached to the 6th Dorsets and was killed in action in France in 1916. Mrs. Hughes-Onslow then offered to the Scottish Branch of the British Red Cross her residence, Laggan House, Ballantrae, Ayrshire, as a Red Cross Auxiliary Hospital, and it was occupied as such till its close in 1919. It accommodated fifty patients and she acted as Resident Commandant and bore the whole expenses of and connected with the Hospital without Government or other grants.

A second V.A. Hospital at Dorchester was at Church Street, placed at the disposal of the Red Cross Society by Sir Robert Williams, M.P. Much valuable assistance in the transport arrangements of this Division was given by the loan of private cars for meeting convoys.

THE LADY SWAYTHLING.

LADY SWAYTHLING, the wife of Lord Swaythling, of South Stoneham and Townhill Park, is well-known and greatly respected, and nowhere are her public-spirited endeavours more appreciated than in the Southampton district, where she never tires of devoting her time and influence to every phase of good work.

Whilst her husband was busy, day by day and almost hour by hour, in the performance of executive duties of the highest importance, her ladyship was applying herself with unwearied zeal to numerous essential public undertakings at Southampton.

It is astonishing how much the women of England of all classes accomplished during the five fateful years, 1914-19. With one accord they manifested a great womanly compassion for the scarred, the suffering and the dying.

And there was so much to be done suddenly and without ado, calling for supreme organising ability and indefatigable exertion, all requiring the sinews of monetary support in order to attain proficient and prompt results.

In Southampton the sore needs of the times were thoroughly well met. The success of each called for driving force, enthusiasm, and funds.

Lady Swaythling gave threefold in a whole-hearted fashion—her time, her strength, and her resources. Her Ladyship became (and still is) President of the Women's Auxiliary of the Y.M.C.A. (Southampton) ; President of the Women's Emergency Corps in Southampton ; President of the War Hospital Supply Depot, Southampton ; and during the war served on 18 different committees ; indeed there was scarcely a war-time movement of any sort which did not receive her active co-operation.

The Lady Swaythling

One section which appealed very strongly to Lady Swaythling's sympathies was provision for the needs of Belgians, and later the organisation of suitable and adequate hospitality for American soldiers and sailors in respect to whom her efforts were so persistent and benevolent that her Ladyship became known among American naval enlisted men as the " British godmother." She also found time to work on the executive committee of Queen Mary's Governesses' Home in Surrey, and to assist the British Women's Patriotic League.

During the war the Manor House at Allington was converted into a hospital for Belgian consumptive soldiers, and Lady Swaythling, who was chairman of the managing committee, took a deep interest in its welfare, and provided many a cheering hour by singing to the patients.

Her Ladyship since the war has continued to be actively identified with numerous public-spirited movements in Southampton, and is President of the Women's Emergency Corps—of which Mrs. Dashper is Hon. Secretary. Mrs. Dashper is a lady to whom Southampton owes much. She has received the O.B.E. in recognition of her valuable and patriotic work. Lady Swaythling is also President of the Southampton Hostel for Unmarried Mothers (an institution quietly accomplishing sound and practical good results on a considerable scale) ; President of the Southampton branch of the National Society for Combating V.D. ; President of the Southampton branch of the University Extension Lectures movement ; a member of the Travellers' Aid Society ; and chairman of the new conjoint committee of the British Red Cross and St. John's in Southampton.

Her Ladyship's distinctions include the Order of Merit of the Japanese Red Cross (the highest honour in the bestowal of the Japanese and of which there are only four recipients in England) ; also the special medal of the Japanese Red Cross ; the Belgian Medaille de la Reine Elizabeth ; and the silver medal of the British Order of St. John.

At Townhill Park, which Lord and Lady Swaythling love so well, the arts, music and harmony are cultivated, whilst the wonderful gardens are a symphony of colour, and there some one has delicately paid tribute by naming a beautiful new rambler, " The Lady Swaythling," in itself a pretty homage to the hospitable and gracious solicitude which her Ladyship ever shows for the well-being of all who from time to time abide or bivouac within her walls, and where, even as the casual visitor to this charming home may quickly perceive, truth and beauty, peace and love, flourish abundantly.

SUPPLEMENTAL to the foregoing personal tributes to the wartime services of leading and representative British women of all classes, recognition is gladly given of efficient and self-denying patriotic work performed throughout the land by the following ladies for nursing services, all of whom have received from the King the award of the Royal Red Cross Decoration. Each lady is Miss unless otherwise stated.

ALLEN, E. Matron, 2nd Westn. Gen. Hos., Manchester.

ANDERSON, C., Matron, Aux. Hosp., Broughty Ferry.

APPLEYARD, M. L., Matron, 1st London Gen. Hospital.

ARIS, A., A. Matron, Wharncliffe War Hospital, Sheffield.

ACLAND HOOD, MRS., Matron, A. Commdt., Aux. Hos., Norfolk.

ADAMS, E. M., Sister, 1st Southn., Gen. Hos., H.Q. Section.

AKENHEAD, M., Supt. and Matron, Boultham Aux. Hospital.

AKERIGG, H., Matron, Clayton Court Aux. Hospital, Petersfield.

AKRILL, M., A. Nurse, Northd. War. Hospital, Gosforth.

ALCOCK, B., Sister, 5th Southn. Gen. Hospital, Portsmouth.

ALDERMAN, E., Sister, 3rd London General Hospital.

ALDIS, L., Nursing Member, Aux. Hos., Norfolk.

ALEXANDER, C., Matron, Salisbury Isolation Hospital.

ALLOTT, V., Q.M., and Nurse, Aux. Hospital, Essex.

ALTON, MRS., M., Sister, Highbury Aux. Hos., Birmingham.

AMBROSE, E. Supt., Woodlands Aux. Hospital, Wigan.

ANDERSON, B., Matron, Convalescent Hospital, Hornchurch.

ANDERSON, M., Sister, 2nd Eastern General Hospital Division.

ANDERTON, F., Sister, Aux. Hospital, Southampton.

ANGEAR, B., Matron, 19, Park Lane, W.

ANTHONY, L., Matron and Lady Supt., Aux. Hos., Carmarthen.

ANTHONY, E., Staff Nurse, 2nd Northern Gen. Hospital.

ARCHER, Mrs. N., Matron, Bunbury Aux. Hos., Cheshire.

ARKWRIGHT, Mrs. R., Matron, Willersley Aux. Hospital.

ARMSTRONG, E., Sister, 2nd Northern Gen. Hospital, Leeds.

ARNOLD, F., Sister, 3rd Northern Gen. Hospital, Sheffield.

ASHBARRY, E., Sister, 1st Southern Gen. Hospital, H.Q.

ASHBY, H., Comdt. Aux. Hospital, Newbury.

ASTBURY, B., Matron, Aux. Hos., Freshwater, I.O.W.

ATKIN, G., Matron., Aux. Hospital, Theydon Bois, Epping.

ATKINSON, Nurse, Aux. Hospital, Devizes.

BARROW, Mrs., B., Matron, University War Hos., Southampton.

BARROW, L., Matron, N. Evingtn. Exten. of 5th Nthn. Gen. Hos.

BILLING, A., Matron, 3rd Western Gen. Hos., Neath Section.

BOEDDICKER, Mrs., Matron, Aux. Hos., Birmingham.

BOUSTED, I., Sister, Military Hospital, Woking.

BROWN, M. T., Sister, Central Military Hospital, Chatham.

BROWN, S., Matron, Section 5, Reading War Hospital.

BRUNSKILL, E., Sister, Military Hospital, Tidworth.

BAILEY, M., Matron, Aux. Hospital, Aughton, W. Lancs.

BAILEY, T. Sister in Charge, Aux. Hospital, Cheltenam.

BAKER, MRS., J., Matron, Aux. Hospital, Crediton.

BAKER, K., Sister, Military Hospital, Prees Heath Camp.

BAKER, L., Sister, Wool Military Hospital, Dorset.

BAKER, W., Sister, Military Hospital, Tidworth.

BALL, G. L., Sister, King George V. Hospital, Dublin.

BALLINGALL, MRS., Lady Supt. & M., IV. Dur. Aux. Hos., Sunderland.

BARBOUR, MRS., Matron, Aux. Hos., Crawley Down, Sussex.

BARLING, K., Sister, 1st Lond. General Hospital.

BARNES, M., Matron, Hilders Aux. Military Hospital, Hazlemere.

BARRETT, M., Sister, 3rd London General Hospital.

BASKERVYK-GLEGG, Comd., Aux. Hos. Stapeley, Cheshire.

BATEMAN, MRS., S., Sister, University Aux. Hospital, Oxford.

BATHURST, F., Sis. Supt., Downham Market Aux. Hos., Norfolk.

BATSTONE, A. Sis., Aux. Hospital, Weston-Super-Mare.

BATTEN, E., Asst. Matron, R. Free Hospital.

BATTYE, C., Sister, 1st Western Gen. Hospital, Liverpool.

BEATON, MacM., Matron, Barra House Aux. Hospital, Largs.

BEDDOES, M., Sister, Military Hospital, York.

BEDWELL, E., Sister, King Edward VII. Hospital, S.W.1.

BELFIELD, F., Queen Mary's Military Hospital, Whalley.

BELL, E., Late Supt., Beechwood Aux. Hospital, Hereford.

BELL, L., Sister, No. 9 Can. Stationary Hos., Bramshott.

BELLAMY, MRS., Supt. and Ch. Sister, Aux. Hos., Sleaford.

BENNETT, MRS. H., Sister, 4th Southern Gen. Hospital, Plymouth.

BENNETT, MRS. S., Nurse, Horton Aux. Hospital, Glos.

BENT, P., Sister-in-Charge, Aux. Hos., St. Leonards-on-Sea.

BERRY, E., Sister, War Hospital, Sheffield.

BESWICK, M., Sister, No. 2 N.Z. Gen. Hospital, Walton-on-Thames.

BESWICK, S., Sister, Military Hospital, Englefield Green.

BEVAN, A., Matron, No. 1 Aux. Hospital, Melksham, Wilts.

BEVAN, E., Staff Nurse, 4th London General Hospital.

BEVAN, E., Sister, Alexandra Military Hospital, Millbank.

BIGGS, E., Matron, No. 1 Sec., Grouped Hospital, Exeter.

BIRD, L., Sister, No. 2 N.Z. General Hospital, Codford.

BLAKE, P., Matron, Berrington War Hospital, Shrewsbury.

BLAKELOCK, L., Sister, Whalley Range Aux. Hospital, E. Lancs.

BLEWLETT, B., Nursing Sister, C.A.M.G., Kitchener Mil Hos., Brighton

BUNDSTONE, H., S. Nurse, Brookdale Aux. Hospital, Cheshire.

BOLAM, K., Supt., Bilton Hall Aux. Hospital, Warwick.

BOND, MRS. I., Aux. Hospital, Guildford.

BROUGHTON, L., S. Nurse, No. 1 Aust. Aux. Hospital, Harefield.

BOURNE, A., Sister, Military Hospital, Parkhurst, I.O.W.

BOWE, S., Sister, Military Hospital, Magdalen Camp, Winchester.

BOWE, M., Sister, Metrop. Hospital, Kingsland Road, N.E.

BOXALL, W., Sister, Lewisham Military Hospital.

BRAIDWOOD, K., Matron, Infects. Dis. Hos., Colchester.

BREDEN, Matron, Camp. Hill Aux. Hospital, Liverpool.

BRENNAN, C., Sister, Military Hospital, Bangor, N. Wales.

BREWER, G., Supt. De Walden Court, Aux. Hospital, Eastbourne.

BRIDGES, H., Sister, Military Hospital, Fovant.

BRIGG, MRS., F., Supt. and Matron, Aux. Hospital, Northwood.

BROADY, L., Sister, Aux. Hospital, Altrincham, Cheshire.

BROCKLESBURY, A., Matron, Alder Hey, Liverpool.

BRODIE, A., Matron, Seaforth Aux. Hospital, Canon Bridge.

BRODRICK, MRS., Lady Supt. and Matron, Hornsea Hos., E. Yorks.

BROOK, A., Matron, St. John Aux. Hospital, Fareham.

BROTHWELL, K., Sister, Military Hospital, Parkhurst, I.O.W.

BROWN, C., S. Nurse, 4th Northern General Hospital, Lincoln.

BROWN, M., Matron, Keir House Aux. Hospital, Dunblane.

BROWN, M., Sister, 1st Eastern General Hospital.

BRUCE, A., S. Nurse, 1st Northern General Hospital, Newcastle.

BUCK, E., Nurse, Hazlewood, Aux. Hospital, Ryde, I.O.W.

BUCKLEY, T., Sister, Military Hospital, Woking.

BURGESS, A., A. Matron, Crumpsall Infirmary, Manchester.

BURGESS, E., Matron, Gordon Castle, Aux. Hospital, Fochabers.

BURKINSHAW, MRS. M., Theatre Sister, Aux. Hospital, Newmarket.

BURR, E., Comdt., Aux. Hospital, Holyhead.

BURRIDGE, M., Sister, Aux. Hospital, Southend-on-Sea.

BURROUGHS, G., Sister, Alexandra Hospital, Cosham.

BUTTERWORTH, E., Nurse, Aux. Hospital, Bedford.

BUXTON, E., Supt., Aux. Hospital, Theydon Bois, Epping.

BYRNE, M., Matron, Shirley Warren Aux. Hospital, Southampton.

CAMERON, N., A. Matron, C.A.M.C.

CANN, F., Matron, Norfolk and Norwich Hospital.

CHAFFFEY, E., Acting Matron, A.N.S.R.

COOPER, Matron, St. George's Hospital.

CUBITT, M., Matron, Weir Aux. Hospital, Balham.

CADMAN, R., Sister, 4th London General Hospital.

CAIRNS, MRS. A., Matron, Woodford Aux. Hospital, Woodford Green.

CALLANDER, L., Sister, The Lord Derby War Hospital, Warrington.

CALLAWAY, F., Sister, 2nd London General Hospital.

CALTHRON, MRS. L., Comdt., Aux. Hospital, Woodhall Spa.

CAMERON, L., Sister, 1st Birmingham War Hospital.

CAMPBELL, E., N. Sister, Bevan Aux. Hospital, Sandgate.

CANDLER, M., Matron, Aux. Hospital, Campden, Glos.

CARTER, E., Matron, No. 3 Sec., Grouped Hospital, Exeter.

CARTER, F., Matron, 3rd Northern General Hospital, Sheffield.

CATCHESIDE, MRS. F., Comdt. Aux. Hospital, Tynemouth.

CAULCOTT, M., Sister, 1st Birmingham War Hospital.

CAVANAGH, H., A. Matron, Beaufort War Hospital, Bristol.

CHALMER, M., S.-in-Charge, No. 2 N.Z. Gen. Hos., Walton-on-Thames.

CHAPLIN, C., S.-in-Charge, Sherborne Castle Aux. Hospital.

CHAPMAN, Mrs. C., Comdt., Aux. Hospital, Croydon.

CHARLTON, E., Sister, Aux. Hospital, Chelmsford.

CHART, J., Military Hospital, Fort Pitt., Chatham.

CHATER, H., Sister, Aux. Hospital, Westcliff-on-Sea.

CHITHAM, F., Sister, Wharncliffe War Hospital, Sheffield.

CHITTLEBURGH, MRS. L., Sister, Aux. Hospital, Jarrow-on-Tyne.

CHOULER E., Sister, Aux. Hospital, Newmarket.

CHRISP, M., 1st Northern Gen. Hospital, Newcastle-on-Tyne.

CLEGG, MRS. E., Supt. Aux. Hos., Church Accrgntn., E. Lancs.

CLEPHAM, C., Matron, Princes Club Hospital.

CLOUSTON, E., Matron, Drumlanrig Aux. Hospital, Thornhill.

COATES, E., Sister, 2nd Northn. Gen. Hos., E. Leeds War Hospital.

COGGINS, T., Sister, 3rd Westn. Gen. Hospital, Newport Section.

COLEMAN, E., Matron, 3rd Northumberland Aux. Hos., Hexham.

COLLE, G., Welsh Metrop. War Hospital, Nr. Cardiff.

COLLINS, J., Sister, Highfield Hall Aux. Hospital, Southampton.

COLVIN, I., Sister, 4th Scottish General Hospital.

COOK, E., Matron, Reckitt's Aux. Hospital, Hull.

P

COOKE, MRS. F., Matron, Oakwood Aux. Hospital, Chigwell.

COOPER, MRS. E., Matron, Lordswood Aux. Hospital, Birmingham.

COOPER, O., Sister, Welsh Metrop. War Hospital, Whitchurch.

CORBITT, L., Comdt., St. John Amb. Bde. Hospital, Gateshead.

COTESWORTH, M., Comdt., Chailey Aux. Hospital, Sussex.

COURTENAY, M., Matron, Aux. Hos., Mountgreenan, Ayrshire.

COUSINS, MRS. H., Matron, 10, Palace Green, W.

COX, O., Aux. Hospital, Hawarden House, Norfolk.

CRAIG, E., Nurse and Q.M., Writtle Aux. Hospital, Chelmsford.

CRANAGE, N., Mem. 4th Norhtmd. Aux. Hos., Corbridge-on-Tyne.

CRAW, R., Sister, 1st Birmingham War Hospital.

CRAWSHAY, MRS. A., A. Comdt., Aux. Hospital, Diss, Norfolk.

CRYER, E., Lady Supt. Aux. Hospital, Cheshire.

CRYLE, M., S. Nurse, King George Hospital, Stamford Street, S.W.

CUMMINGS, M., N. Sister, Moore Barks. Hospital, Shorncliffe.

CUTHBERTSON, M., Sister, 4th Durham Aux. Hos, Sunderland.

DEANE, M., Matron, E. Suffolk Hospital.

DEWAR, C., Matron, Moray Lodge Hospital.

DAKIN, E., Sister, 4th Northern Gen. Hospital, Lincoln.

DAKIN, S., Sister, Bevan Aux. Hospital, Kent.

DALGLEISH, J., Sister, Netley Aux. Hospital.

DALZIEL, A., Sister, The Lord Derby War Hospital, Warrington.

DAMON, E., S. Nurse, Queen Mary's Hospital, Whalley.

DAVIDSON, A., Matron, Civil Hospital, Gravesend.

DAVIDSON, C., S. Nurse, 4th Scottish Gen. Hospital.

DAVIDSON, K., Sister, 2nd Western Gen. Hospital, Manchester.

DAVIES, A., Sister, Welsh Hospital, Netley.

DAVIES, C., 3rd Western General Hospital.

DAVIES, E. Comdt., Underworth Aux. Hospital, I.O.W.

DAVIES, Mrs. K., Sister, Aux. Hospital, Southall.

DAVIES, M., Matron, Vernon Institute Aux. Hospital, Chester.

DAWSON, MRS. E., Matron, Aux. Hospital, Ashgate.

DEAN, MRS. E., A. S.-in-Charge Aux. Hos., Nr. Birmingham.

DENMAN, M., Sister, University College Hospital.

DENNANT, F., Matron, Aux. Hospital, 6, Third Avenue, Hove.

DERMOTT, A., 1st London General Hospital.

DE VILLE, A., Matron, The Stockport Infirmary.

DIMOND, E., Matron, Holness Aux. Hospital, Sherbourne.

DITCHAM, L., Matron, and Lady Supt., Aux. Hos., Carmarthen.

DOBIE, E., Matron, Infirmary and Dispensary, Bolton.

DOMVILLE, MRS., B., Sister, Women's War Hospital, Paignton.

DONALD, A., Sister, Military Hospital, Curragh.

DONOVAN, MRS. V., N. Sister, No. 1 Can. Gen. Hos., Folkestone.

DOUGLAS, A., Matron, Princess Louise Scottish Ho., Bishopton.

DOWNING, E., S. Nurse, Studley Court Aux. Hospital, Worcs.

DRAPER, E., Nurse, Aux. Hospital, Bicester, Oxon.

DRURY, F., Matron, Aux. Hospital, Attleborough.

DUNLOP, J., Sister, Queen Mary's Hospital, Whalley.

DUNROSE, G., Sister, R. Infirmary, Chester.

EARLE, MRS. E., Overcliff Aux. Hospital, Westcliffe-on-Sea.

EARLE, E., Sister, 5th Southern General Hospital.

ECKERLEY, R., Sister, Bethnal Green Military Hospital.

EDGAR, J., Sister, University War Hospital, Southampton.

ELLIOTT, A., Matron, Wareham Military Hospital.

EDMONDSON, H., Nurse, Aux. Hos., Hanley Castle, Worcs.

EDWARDS, MRS., Sister, 1st Southern Gen. Hospital, Stourbridge.

EDWARDS, J., Matron, Hill Lodge Aux. Hospital, Chipping Norton.

ELDER, M., Matron and Comdt., Dunfermline Aux. Hospital.

ELDRED, A., Woodlands Aux. Hospital, Kilcreggan.

ELDRIDGE, S., Nurse, Hoveton Hall Aux. Hospital, Norwich.

ELLIOTT, D., Matron, Tankerton, Hospital, Whitstable.

ERRINGTON, MRS. I., Supt. and Q.M., Aux. Hospital, Shortley Bge.

ERWIN, M., Sister, Military Hospital, Sutton Veny.

EVANS, H., Sister, King George V. Hospital, Dublin.

EVANS, M., Lady Supt., Aux. Hospital, Latchford.

EVANS, M., 2nd A. Matron, Alder Hey, Liverpool.

EVANS, P., Sur. Nurse, Aux. Hospital, Llanelly.

EVE, J., Sister, Rivercourt Aux. Hospital, Essex.
EYRE, M., Sister, 3rd London General Hospital.

FARLEY, M., Act. Matron, Military Hospital, Fermoy.
FORBES, H., M. Sister, C.A.M.C. Hdqrs., London.
FADDY, G., Sister, Netley Aux. Hospital.
FAGG, M., Sister, Cen. Mil. Hospital, Fort Pitt, Chatham.
FARMER, MRS. M., Comdt., Aux. Hospital, Kettering.
FARNFIELD, MRS. M., Supt. & S.-in-Charge, Aux. Hospital, Gillgm.
FERGUSSON, E., Matron, Aux. Hospital, Budleigh Salterton.
FIDLER, B., 4th London General Hospital.
FIELD, G., S.-in-Charge Aux. Hospital, Ongar, Essex.
FINLAY, MRS. C., Supt., Aux. Hospital, Glos.
FINNIS, F., Sister, 2nd Birmingham War Hospital.
FISHER, E., Matron, Ingestre Hospital, Ashton-upon-Mersey.
FITTON, K., Sister, Wareham Military Hospital.
FITZROY, M., Ward Sister, R. Sussex County Hospital, Brighton.
FLETCHER, M., Matron, Aux. Hospital, Clacton-on-Sea.
FLICK, A., Supt. Nurse, Infirmary, Hartlepool.
FOLEY, Lady, Reading War Hospital.
FORD, J., Matron, Adelaide Street Aux. Hospital, Blackpool.
FOSTER, E., East Leeds War Hospital.
FOTHERGILL, A., Nurse Stramongate Aux. Hospital, Kendal.

FOWLER, G., 2nd Southern General Hospital.

FOX, A., Matron, Clacton Aux. Hospital, Essex.

FRASER, M., Sister and Supt., Aux. Hospital, Codicote.

FRENCH, A., C.A.M.C., Can. Red Cross Hospital, Taplow.

FROST, MRS. C., Matron, Bank Hall Aux. Hospital, Burnley.

FRY, W., 2nd Northern Gen. Hospital, Becketts Park, Leeds.

GARSIDE, E., Matron, Royal Salop Infirmary.

GIRDLESTONE, M., Matron, ret., Manchester.

GOTTS, MRS. G., Matron, Alder Hey, Liverpool.

GREENFIELD, S., Matron, Lewisham Military Hospital.

GAMBLER-PARRY, Hon. MRS., Matron and Supt., Aux. Hos., Goring.

GAMBLIN, A., Sister, Netley Aux. Hospital.

GARFORTH, F., Comdt., Swillington Aux. Hospital, Leeds.

GEM, G., 4th Northern Gen. Hospital, Lincoln.

GIGBS, H., Nurse, Rhydd Court, Aux. Hospital, Hanley Castle.

GIBSON, MRS. C., Lady Supt. and Matron, Aux. Hospital, Coatbridge.

GIBSON, MRS. E., Matron, Bermondsey, Military Hospital.

GIBSON, E., Sister, 5th Northern Gen. Hospital, Leicester.

GILBERT, E., Sister, 1st London General Hospital.

GILBERTSON, N., S. Nurse, 5th Northern Gen. Hospital, Leicester.

GILFILLAN, E., S. Nurse, 2nd Northern General Hospital.

GILLMOR, M., Matron, Castleton Aux. Military Hospital, Rochdale.

GLEAVE, MRS. F., S.-in-Charge, Aux. Hospital, Alderley Edge.

GLOVER, M., S. Nurse, 2nd London General Hospital.

GODBER, MRS. G., Sister, Aux. Hospital, Altrincham.

GOFF, MRS. S., Hill Park Aux. Hospital, Bothwell.

GOOD, E., Charge Sister, Aux. Hospital, Churchfields.

GORE-BROWN, D., Comdt., Aux. Hospital, Holmwood, Nr. Dorking.

GOUGH, MRS. S., Comdt., Aux. Hos., West Herptree, Bristol.

GOUGH, L., Matron, Aux. Hospital, Manchester.

GOURLAT, I., Sister, Military Hospital, Ripon.

GRAHAM, M., Nurs. Mem., Aux. Hospital, Leamington Spa.

GRANT, E., S., King George Hospital, Stamford Street, S.E.

GRAY-MAITLAND, M., Sister, Military Hospital, Bangor, N. Wales.

GREENWOOD, E., Queen Mary's Military Hospital, Whalley.

GREGG, E., Sister, 1st Southern Gen. Hospital, H.Q.

GREHAN, A., Sister, Military Hospital, Mont Dore, Bournemouth.

GRIERSON, E., Sister, Wharncliffe War Hospital, Sheffield.

GRIFFITH, A., Matron, Aux. Hospital, Park Gate, Cheshire.

GRIGOR, M., Sister, No. 2 N.Z., Gen. Hospital, Walton-on-Thames.

GRIMMER, G., Sister, Norfolk War Hospital, Norwich.

GUISE-MOORES, MRS. K., Nurse, Farnborough Court Aux. Hospital.

GURTON, F., Staff Nurse, Q.A. Military Hospital, Millbank.

HARDING, M., Sister, Royal Victoria Hospital, Netley.

HARRISS, M., Matron, 1st Southern Gen. Hospital, Stirchley Section.

HOLDEN, E., Matron, 1st Southern Gen. Hospital, Monyhull Section.

HUGHES, E. A., Matron, 3rd Western Gen. Hospital, Cardiff.

HUSBAND, H., Matron, 4th London General Hospital.

HAIRE, K., Matron, Down Inf. Aux. Hospital, Downpatrick.

HALE, F. S. Nurse (A.-Sister) Mil. Hospital, Canterbury.

HALL, B., Comdt., Raynor Croft Aux. Hospital, Altrincham.

HALL, D., S.N. Fieldend Lodge Aux. Hospital, Eastcote.

HALL, E., Matron, Broadwater Aux. Hospital, Ipswich.

HALL, K., Sister, 2nd Eastern Gen. Hospital, Div. III.

HALLAM, E., S. Nurse, N. Evington Exten. of 5th N. Gen. Hospital.

HALLIDAY, E., Matron, Royal Naval Hospital, Hull.

HAMBLY, M., N. Sister, C.A.M.C., Can. Red Cross Hospital, Taplow.

HANBURY, MRS. F., Princess Christian Hospital, 6, Gros. Place.

HANBY, E., Charge Sister, No. 7 Durh. Aux. Hospital, Durham.

HANCOCK, M., Lady Supt., Aux. Hospital, Bristol.

HAND, MRS. E., Supt., Aux. Hospital, Flixton, E. Lancs.

HANDS, B., Sister, Race Course Aux. Hospital, Cheltenham.

HARBUTT, D., Sister, 3rd Western General Hospital, Cardiff.

HARLOW, E., Sister, Military Hospital, Maghull, Liverpool.

HARRISON, B., Sister, Aux. Hospital, Haslingden, E. Lancs.

HARRISON, M., Nurse, Ramsbury Aux. Hospital, Wilts.

HARRISON, LADY D., Comdt. Aux. Hospital, Cheshire.

HASLEM, M., Nursing Mem., Craghead Aux., Hospital, Bournemouth.

HATCH, E., Sister, 1st Western Gen. Hospital, Liverpool.

HAWKEN, MRS. L., Sister, Taunton Aux. Hospital.

HAWKES, A., Supt. and S.-in-Charge, Aux. Hospital, Weymouth.

HEATON, K., Matron, Aux. Hospital, Bexhill-on-Sea.

HENDERSON, MRS. C., Sister, Aux. Hospital, Westcliff-on-Sea.

HENLEY, LADY. ,Supt., New Court Aux. Hospital, Cheltenham.

HENRY, J., Matron, Cluny Aux. Hospital, Swanage.

HESKETH, Sister, 1st Southern General Hospital.

HEWITT, M., N. Sister, Welsh Hospital, Netley.

HEYWOOD, W., Matron, Aux. Hospital, Warford, Alderley Edge.

HIGGINBOTTOM, A., Sister, 1st Western General Hospital, Liverpool.

HIGGINS, MRS. M., Matron, Aux. Hospital, Erdington, Birmingham.

HIGGS, A., Matron, Bethnal Green Military Hospital.

HIGHAM, J., Supt., Portishead Aux. Hospital, Somerset.

HILL, L., Supt., Leckhampton Aux. Hospital, Cheltenham.

HILL, M., Sister, 1st Northern Gen. Hospital, Newcastle.

HILLING, S., Sister, Welsh Met. War Hospital, Whitchurch.

HILTON, I., Sister, Mil. Hospital, Magdalen Camp, Winchester.

HIRST, D., Huddersfield War Hospital.

HOAR, E. N., Member, Mil. Hospital, Ripon.

HOBBS, S., Nurse, Aux. Hospital, Wolverhampton.

HOBSON, P., Sister, 2nd Southern General Hospital.

Q

HOCQUARD, M., Sister, Queen Mary's Hospital, Whalley.

HODGKINSON, E., Sister, Aux. Hospital, Timberley, Cheshire.

HODGSON, E., Supt. Aux. Hospital, Tunbridge Wells.

HOLLINGWORTH, MRS. J., Sister, Royal Naval Hospital, Hull.

HOLMES, E., Supt., Stroud Aux. Hospital, Gloucester.

HOME, LADY J. D., Eden Hall, Aux. Hospital, Kelso.

HOPWOOD, A., Sister, 2nd Western Gen. Hospital, Manchester.

HORN, M., 2nd A. Matron, Mil. Hospital, West Didsbury, Manchester.

HOWARD, MRS. N., Matron, Aux. Hospital, Moor Park, Preston.

HUGHES, A., N. Member, Beach Aux. Hospital, Holyhead.

HUGHES, C., Matron, Gostwyth, Aux. Hospital, Colchester.

HUGHES, G., Sister, King George V. Hospital, Dublin.

HUGHES, M., Sister, 3rd Northern General Hospital.

HUGHES, W., Sister, Berrington War Hospital, Shrewsbury.

HULLEY, C., Matron, Aux. Hospital, Ashton-under-Lyne, E. Lancs.

HUNPHREYS, Sister, Edmonton Military Hospital, London.

HUNT, F., Matron, Ralston Aux. Hospital, Paisley.

HUNTER, A., Matron, Portissie Aux. Hospital, Buckie.

HUNTER, HON. MRS. L., Aux. Hospital, Llandovery.

HUTCHINSON, R., Matron, Aux. Hospital, Stockport.

HUTTY, R., Matron, No. 2 Section, Grouped Hospital, Exeter.

HUXLEY, Matron, Dublin University Aux. Hospital.

IVEY, A., Sister, C.A.M.C., Officers' Hospital, Hyde Park Place.

JACKSON, B., A.-Sister, Royal Victoria Hospital, Netley.

JACKSON, M., Charge Sister, Aux. Hospital, Daybrook, Notts.

JACKSON, C., The Tower Aux. Hospital, Rainhill, W. Lancs.

JACKSON, E,. Charge Sister, Bowden Aux. Hospital, Notts.

JEFFERY, E., Sister, 2nd Eastern Gen. Hospital, Div. II.

JEFFREY, J., Matron, Stepping Hill Hospital, West Stockport.

JEKYLL, D., Matron, Military Hospital, Huddersfield.

JENNER, K., Supt., Aux. Hospital, 6, Third Avenue, Hove.

JERREMS, G., Matron, Longleat Aux. Hospital, Warminster.

JOHNS, E., Asst. Matron, Lewisham Military Hospital.

JOHNSON, MRS., Comdt., Haigh Lawn Aux. Hospital, Altrincham.

JOHNSON, M., Ulster Vol. Force Aux. Hospital, Belfast.

JOHNSTONE, MRS. G., A. Matron, C.A.M.C., Can Rest Home, Margate.

JONAS, MRS. R., Ickleton Aux. Hospital, Gt. Chesterford.

JONES, J., Supt., Nurse, No. 1, Reading War Hospital.

JONES, K., 3rd Western General Hospital.

JONES, M., Sister, 3rd Western General Hospital, Cardiff.

JONES, MRS. W., Matron, Trafford Hall Aux. Hospital, Manchester.

JORDAN, MRS., Sister and Dep. Matron, Aux. Hospital, Birmingham.

JOYCE, K., Supt. Nurse, No. 1 Reading War Hospital.

KEAVELL, A., Matron, Yeatman Aux. Hospital, Sherborne.

KEITH, M., Matron, Aux. Hospital, Stowmarket.

KELLY, M., S. Nurse, Queen Mary's Hospital, Whalley.

KEMP, L., Sister, Dartford War Hospital, Kent.

KENNEDY, M., Sister, Salford Union Infirmary, Manchester.

KIDD, MRS., Matron, Caird Rest, Red Cross Aux. Hospital, Dundee.

KING, L., Matron, Tesdale Aux. Hospital, Abingdon.

KING, MRS. N., Comdt., Clayton Aux Hospital, Wakefield.

KING, J., Sister, 2nd Western General Hospital.

KIRBY, E., Sister, 5th Southern General Hospital.

KIPPAX, C., S. 4th Southern Gen. Hospital, Salsby-road, Plymouth.

KIRKMAN, Matron, Springfield War Hospital.

KREMER, Sister, No. 1 Reading War Hospital.

KING, MRS. D., Matron, Highfield Hall Aux. Hos., Southampton.

LACEY, Sister, St. Gerard's Aux. Hospital, Coleshill.

LAIDLAW, S., C.-Sister, Clifford St. Aux. Hospital, York.

LANCASTER, E., S.-Nurse, 2nd Western General Hospital.

LANG, M., Commdt. Aux. Hospital, St. Ann's, Lewes, Sussex.

LANGHORN, O., Matron, Harborne Hall Aux. Hospital, Birmingham.

LANGLEY, MRS. E., S.-Nurse, Cornelia Aux. Hospital, Poole.

LAPHAM, D., A.-Sister, No. 1 Reading War Hospital.

LATIMER, M., Matron, Upperton Aux. Hospital, Eastbourne.

LAVINGTON, R., Nurse, Marlborough Aux. Hospital, Wilts.

LAVER, MRS. M., Sister, Hawkstone Aux. Hospital, Fareham.

LAWES, A., Matron, Struan House Aux. Hospital, Reading.

LAWRENCE, MRS. M., Sister, Military Hospital, Endell-St., W.C.

LAWRIE, A., Sister, Gen. Military Hospital, Colchester.

LAY, H., Matron, Milton Hill Aux. Hospital, Steventon, Berks.

LEARK, G., 1st Southern General Hospital.

LEECH, D., Sister, 2nd Western Gen. Hospital, Manchester.

LEES, G., N. Sister and S.-in-Charge, St. John's Hospital, Lewisham.

LEIGH, C., Matron, Endsleigh Palaces Hospital.

LERMITTE, MRS. I., Commdt., Woodhouse Aux. Hospital, Essex.

LESLIE, E., Graylingwell Military Hospital, Chichester.

L'ESTRANGE, E., Matron, Arnsbrae Red Cross Aux. Hos., Alloa.

LIGHTFOOT, F., Matron, Fishmongers Hall Hospital.

LITTLEWOOD, N., Sister, Military Hospital, West Didsbury.

LLOYD, F., 2nd London General Hospital.

LOCKHEAD, H., Nurse, 2nd Eastern General Hospital, Div. I.

LORRIMER, C., Asst. Matron, Queen Mary's Mil. Hospital, Whalley.

LOUGHLIN, M., Sister, 1st Eastern General Hospital.

LOW, B., Sister, Northumberland War Hospital, Gosforth.

LOWE, B., Acting Matron, Birch Hill Hospital, Dearsley.

LUSTED, E., Sister, 4th London General Hospital.

LAMBERT, S., Ngt. Supt., Aux. Hospital, Netley.

LAWRENCE, I., Matron, Star and Garter Aux. Hospital, Richmond.
LEWIS, D., Matron, Military Hospital, Ripon.
LIVESEY, E., Matron, Military Hospital, Woburn.

MACER, M., Sister, 3rd Northern General Hospital, Sheffield.
MACLEAN, H., Matron-in-Chief.
MATHER, S., Matron, Aux. Military Hospital, Ilkley, Yorks.
MATHESON, A., Sister, Royal Victoria Hospital, Netley.
MATHEWS, C., Matron, Natn. Children's & Aux. Mil. Hos., Dublin.
McARDLE, N., Matron, Dublin Castle Aux. Hospital.
McCAFFERTY, E., A.-Matron, Can. Red Cross Hospital, Ramsgate.
MERRY, G., A. Matron, 2nd Southern General Hospital.
MILNE, H., Matron, Cornelia Hospital, Poole.
MUGGRIDGE, L., Matron, Brighowgate Mil. Hospital, Grimsby.
MULDREW, G., N. Sister, Officers' Hospital, Crowborough.
MULLINER, MRS. A., Cmdt. and Matron, Sunnyside, Whalley Range.
MUNN, A., Matron, Roehampton Aux. Hospital.
MURPHY, A., Matron, Military Hospital, Cannock Chase.
MACAULAY, S., Sister, 4th Southern General Hospital, Ford Section.
MACDIARMID, J., Sister, 2nd London General Hospital.
MACDONALD, M., Supt. Nurse, Wareham Military Hospital.
MACDONALD, H., N. Sister, C.A.M.C., Moore Bks. Hos., Shorncliffe.
MACINTOSH, M., Sister, Bermondsey Military Hospital.

MacKay, B., N. Sister, C.A.M.C., Ontario Mil. Hospital, Orpington.

Mackertich, J., Sister, Military Hospital, Sutton Veny.

Mackintosh, D., Sister, 2nd Southern General Hospital.

Mackintosh, I., Matron, Empire Hospital, London.

MacLaren, G., Matron, Red Cross Aux. Hospital, Monifieth.

MacNaughton-Jones, M., Qmstr. Aux. Hospital, Dereham.

Macpherson, A., Matron, Aux. Hospital, Plympton.

MacQueen, J., Asst. Matron, Military Hospital, Bogthorpe.

Magee, G., M., St. John's V.A.D. Hos., Strabane, Londonderry Dis.

Mair, A., Supt. Nurse, Alexandra Hospital, Cosham.

Manning, E., 4th Southern General Hospital.

Mansfield, Mrs. L., Comdt. & Supt., Aux. Hospital, Sevenoaks.

Mansfield, M., Sister, Univer. War Hospital, Southampton.

Marriott, Mrs. M., Supt., Aux. Hospital, Nr. Leicester.

Marsh, A., Sister, Military Hospital, Huddersfield.

Marshall, E., Matron, Aux. Hospital, Brighton.

Martin, Mrs. L., Comdt. Stroud Aux. Hospital, Glos.

Martin, Mrs. M., S.-in-Charge, Red Cross Aux. Hospital, Montrose.

Maskew, M., Lady Supt., Amb. Col., London District.

Masters, L., 1st Eastern General Hospital, Cambridge.

Mathewson, M., Matron., Aux. Hospital, Tynemouth.

Mathews, M., Sister, Great Northern Cen. Hospital.

Maxwell, M., Asst. Matron, Tooting Military Hospital.

MAY, E., Sister, Military Hospital, Endell St., W.C.

MAY, M., Sister, Graylingwell Mil. Hospital, Chichester.

McCALLUM, M., Sister, 3rd Scottish Gen. Hospital.

McCAMMOND, M., Sister, U.V.F., Hospital, Ireland.

McCLEW, M., Spec. Prob., Attd. Gen. Mil. Hospital, Colchester.

McCLINTOCK, MRS. L., Comdt., Aux. Hospital, Loddon.

McDONALD, E., Sister, Military Hospital, Ripon.

McGEE, C., Matron, Aux. Hos., Heaton Mersey, Manchester.

McGEOWN, R., Sister, King George V. Hospital, Dublin.

McGRATH, K., Matron, Hoole Bank Aux. Hospital, Chester.

McINNES, M., Sister, 4th London General Hospital.

McRAE, I., S. &. A. Matron, No. 2 N.Z. Gen. Hos., Walton-on-Thames

MEIKLEJOHN, N., N. Sister, C.A.M.C., Kitchener Mil. Hos., Brighton.

MEREDITH, J., S. Nurse, 5th Northern Gen. Hos., Evington Section.

METHERELL, G., No. 2 N.Z. Gen. Hospital, Walton-on-Thames.

MIDGLEY, MRS. A., Matron, Blair Aux. Hospital, Bolton.

MILLAR, MRS. M., C. Sister, 1st Durh. Aux. Hospital, Gateshead.

MILLARD, L., Sister, 1st Southern Gen. Hospital, Dudley Road.

MILLER, E., Supt., Woodford Aux. Hospital, Essex.

MILLAR, M., Asst. Matron, Salford Union Infirmary, Manchester.

MILLMAY, E., Sister, Queen Mary's Hospital, Whalley.

MILNE, G., Supt., S.-in-Charge, Aux. Hospital, Cheshire.

MINSHULL, M., Nurse, 3rd Northern Gen. Hospital, Sheffield.

MITCHELL, S., 2nd Eastern Gen. Hospital, Brighton.

MOATE, MRS. M., A. Sis., De Walden Court Aux. Hos., Eastbourne.

MOLESWORTH, N., Brookfield House, Cheshire.

MONK, B., Asst. Matron., The London Hospital.

MONTGOMERY, O., 2nd Western Gen. Hospital, Manchester.

MOON, C., Sis. & Actg. Mtrn., Aux. Hos., Normanton, Brks., Derby.

MOOR, A., Sister, 3rd London General Hospital.

MORRIS, E. Matron, The Lady Forester Hospital, Broseley.

MORRISON, J., Sister, 2nd Western Gen. Hospital, Manchester.

MOTHERSOLE, MRS. S., Matron, Watermillock Aux. Hos., Bolton.

MOUISON, M., S. Nurse, 2nd London Gen. Hospital.

MOWBRAY, C., N. Sister, C.A.M.G., Officer's Hos., 1, Hyde Park, P.

MUIR, MRS., Supt., Fairfield Aux. Hospital, Broadstairs.

MUMFORD, A., Comdt., Aux. Hospital, Sandgate.

MUNN, E., Matron, Dover House Aux. Hospital, Roehampton.

MURCH, MRS. E., Sister, 2nd London General Hospital

MURGATROYD, A., Sister, 2nd Northern General Hospital, Leeds.

MURPHY, K., Supt., Nurse, Military Hospital, Sutton Veny.

MURPHY, B., Sister, Aux. Hospital, Lady's Close, Watford.

MURRAY, J., Asst. Matron, Welsh Metrop. War Hospital, Cardiff.

MURRAY, MRS. M., Supt. & Matron, Aux. Hospital, Cheshire.

NORRIS, MRS. E., Supt. Aux. Hospital, Gloucester.

R

NAWTON, H., Sister, Lady Evelyn Mason's Hospital, London, W.

NAZER, E., Sister, Netley Aux. Hospital.

NELSON, H., N. Sister, C.A.M.C. Moore Bks. Hos., Shorncliffe.

NESBITT, B., Sister, Mrs. Dashwood's Priv. Aux. Hos., Ipswich.

NEVILE, E., Matron, W. London Hospital, Hammersmith.

NEWMAN, D., Supt., Ampthill Camp Aux. Hospital, Bedford.

NIBLETT, M., Nurse, Aux. Hospital, Norton-sub-Hemdon.

NICHOLSON, B., Nurse, Cony Home, Westgate-on-Sea.

NICHOLSON, G., Matron, Countess of Radnor's Hospital, Salsby.

NIXON, K., Sis.-in-Charge, Beaucroft Aux. Hospital, Wimborne.

NODAL, A., Matron, Royal Hospital, Salford.

NORTHERN, D., 1st Eastern General Hospital, Cambridge.

O'CONNELL, E., Sister, Dublin Castle Aux. Hospital.

OGILVY, E., Sis.-in-Charge, Bromburgh Aux. Hos., Cheshire.

OLDFIELD, H., Matron, No. 16 Northumberland Aux. Hos., Morpath.

O'NEIL, I., Aux. Hos., Burnham-on-Sea.

ORME, MRS. K., Comdt., Barraclough Aux. Hospital, Clitheroe.

ORR, MRS. M., Matron, Ashbridge Aux. Hospital, Berkhampstead.

OVERSTALL, E., Sister, 2nd Western Gen. Hospital, Manchester.

OWEN, MRS. M., Matron, Aux. Hospital, Merioneth.

OWEN, MRS. J., S.-in-Charge, Aux. Hospital, Warwicks.

OWEN, M., S.-Nurse, Ashton Hayes Aux. Hospital, Nr. Chester.

OWEN, N., Nurse, Aux. Hospital, Harborne, Birmingham.

PICKETT, F., A. Matron, 2nd Western Gen. Hospital.

PULLIN, G., Sister, Mil. Hospital, Tidworth.

PURCELL, M., A.R.R.C., Matron, South African Mil. Hospital.

PALMER, A., Matron, Aux. Hospital, Honiton, Devon.

PALMER, G., Aux. Hospital, Seafield, Gt. Yarmouth.

PANTON, MRS. E., Sister, Northmbld. War Hos., Gosforth.

PARKER, M., S.-in-Charge, Aux. Hospital, Peterborough.

PARKS, M., N. Sister, C.A.M.C., Mil. Hospital, Orpington.

PAFF, A., N. Member, Foye House, Aux. Hospital, Bristol.

PARRY, K., Matron, Aux. Hospital, Cawston.

PARRY, L., Sister, Croes Howell Aux. Hospital, Rossett.

PARSONS, E., Sister, A. Evngtn. Extn. of 5th Northern Gen. Hos.

PATERSON, L., Sister, Royal Victoria Hospital, Netley.

PATTERSON, B., Sister, Military Hospital.

PEARSE, Asst. Nurse, Cleve Hill Aux. Hospital, Bristol.

PEARSE, C., Sister, Sec. 5, Reading War Hospital.

PEARSON, H., 2nd Birmingham War Hospital, Northfield.

PEECH, MRS. E., Matron and Cmdt., Aux. Hospital, Sheffield.

PEILE, I., Sister, Cirencester Aux. Hospital, Glos.

PENGELLY, Sister, N.Z.A.N.S., No. 3 N.Z., Gen. Hos., Codford.

PEPPER, E., Matron, Partington House Aux. Hospital, Glossop.

PERRIER, J., Sister, Military Hospital, Norwich.

PERRY, H., Sister, Beaufort War Hospital, Bristol.

PETERS, R., Supt., Race Course Aux. Hospital, Cheltenham.

PHILLIPS, F., Matron, Newton Don Aux. Hos., Kelso.

PICTON, MRS., Supt., Aux. Hospital, Cheshire.

PILKINGTON, C., Comdt., Rhyl Dis. Aux. Hospital,

PINCHARD, S., Matron, Princess Christian Aux. Hospital, S.E.

POLEHUNT, M. Matron, St. Bartholomew's, Rochester.

POLLOCK, L., Matron, Gifford House Aux. Hospital, Roehampton.

POLSON, A., Matron, Tardebigge Aux. Hospital, Hewell.

POMEROY, K., Sister, 3rd London General Hospital.

POPKIN, B., Matron, Comdt. Holly Park Aux. Hospital.

POPPLEWELL, E., Sister, No. 2 N.Z., Gen. Hos., Walton-on-Thames.

PORTER, J., Asst. Matron, Mil. Hospital, Kinmel Park.

POWELL, E., N. Member, Craghead Aux. Hospital, Bournemouth.

PRATER, C., Nurse, Aux. Hospital, Warwicks.

PRESSLEY, A., Sister, Military Hospital, Norwich.

PRICE, A., Sister, 1st Birmingham War Hospital.

PRICHARDS, M., Edmonton Military Hospital, N.

PROUT, G., S. (A. as M.), 2nd Southern Gen. Hos., Bishop's Knoll Sec.

PUGH, L., Matron, Woodfield Aux. Hospital, Oldham.

QUIRK, E., S. Nurse, 1st Western Gen. Hospital, Liverpool.

RAYNES, Matron, Welsh Metrop. War Hospital, Cardiff.

ROSS, C., Matron, Salford Infirmary, Manchester.

RAMSAY, E., Sister, Military Hospital, Huddersfield.

RANDS, E., Sister, Gen. Military Hospital, Colchester.

RASTALL, Matron, Cameron Hospital, W. Hartlepool.

RICHARDSON, M., Sister, War Hospital, Nottingham.

RICHMOND, E., Nurse, Aux. Hospital, Burnham-on-Crouch.

REDEAL, G., N. Member, Moorfield Aux. Hospital, Glossop.

ROBERTS, MRS. M., Cmdt. Aux. Hos., Parish Hall, Nantwich.

ROBINSON, E., Assylum 2nd Chief Nrs., War Hospital, Sheffield.

ROBINSON, E., Sister, Urmston Aux. Hospital, Eastbourne.

ROBINSON, J., Supt. Nurse, Northumberland War Hos., Gosforth.

ROBINSON, H., Matron, Mil. Hos., Farnsworth, Nr. Bolton.

ROBOTHAM, E., Sister, Charing Cross Hospital.

ROBSON, MRS. M., Matron, Southwood Aux. Hospital, Stirling.

ROGERS, MRS. E., Nur. Mem., 11th Durh. Aux. Hos., Sunderland.

ROOKE, L., Comdt., Hazlewood Aux. Hospital, Ryde.

ROSE, M., Matron, 1st Southern Gen. Hospital.

ROSE, P., N.-Sis., C.A.M.C., Shorncliffe Military Hospital.

ROSS, H., Charge Sister, Loversal Hall Aux. Hospital, Doncaster.

ROUNDEL, M., S. Nurse, 1st London General Hospital.

ROWE, MRS. S., Matron, Moss Side Hospital, Manchester.

ROWSON, MRS. M., Qrmr. and Nurse, Aux. Hospital, Wainfleet.

RUSHWORTH, MRS. E., Matron, Hillsburgh Aux. Hospital, Harlow.

RUTHERFORD, A., Sister, 1st Western General Hospital.

RUTLEDGE, Supt., Wareham Military Hospital.

SANDIFER, I., Matron, 1st Northern Gen. Hospital, Newcastle.

SEYMOUR, E., Matron, 1st Eastern Gen. Hospital.

SILLIFANT, M., Matron, The Mount Aux. Hospital, Torquay.

SMELLIE, L., N. Sister (A. Matron), Moore Bks., Hos., Shorncliffe.

SMITH, M., Matron, Military Hospital, W. Didsbury.

SOLOMON, S., Asst. Matron, 4th London General Hospital.

SPENSER, M., Asst. Matron, 3rd Western Gen. Hospital.

STOREY, M., Asst. Matron, 2nd Northern Gen. Hospital.

SUTCLIFFE, M., Matron, Infirmary, Derby.

SYMONDS, Sister, Evangelist, Matron, Hos. of St. John.

SADD, MRS. A., Qrmr. & Nurse, Aux. Hospital, Loddon.

SANDERS, E., Nurse, Gostwych Aux. Hospital, Colchester.

SANKEY, B., Nght. Supt., Wingfield Aux. Hospital, Oxon.

SAWTELL, M., Military Hospital, Tidworth.

SCOTT, J., S.-in-Charge, No. 2 Sec. of No. 1 N.Z. Gen. Hos., Brockenhurst.

SCHLEGEL, E., Matron, E. Sussex County Hospital, Hastings.

SEABROOKE, E., Sister, The Castle Aux. Hospital, Ryde.

SEARLEY, D., Nurse, Aux. Hsopital, Henley-on-Thames.

SEATON, M., Sister, Cen. Military Hospital, Fort Pitt.

SELBY, A., Nght. Sister, Hillcrest Aux. Hospital, Coventry.

SEWELL, C., Actg. Comdt., Aux. Hospital, Watford.

SEYMOUR-URE, Sister, 2nd London General Hospital.

SHARPE, MRS. B., Matron River Court Aux. Hospital, Essex.

SHAW, MRS. E., Sister, Dunlop House Aux. Hospital.

SHAW-STEWART, M., Nurse, Tisbury Aux. Hospital, Wilts.

SHEPPARD, A., Sister, 3rd Northern Gen. Hospital, Sheffield.

SHORT, L., Matron Aux. Hospital, Golder's Green.:

SIMONS, MRS. E., Nurse, Aux. Hospital, Altricham.

SIMPSON, A., S.-in-Charge, Aux. Hospital, Cheshire.

SIMPSON, A., Sister, Queen Mary's Hospital, Whalley.

SINTON, MRS. A., Sister, Mil. Hospital, Park Hill Camp, Oswestry.

SINZININEX, C., Matron, Queen Alexandra's Hospital, Highgate.

SKINNER, H., Sister, 3rd Western General Hospital.

SKIPWORTH, R., Matron, Aux. Hospital, Richmond.

SLOCOCK, MRS., R. Sister, Aux. Hospital, Spilsby.

SMITH, A., Matron, Gen. Hospital, Tunbridge Wells.

SMITH, E., Matron, Westminster Hospital.

SMITH, H., Sister, 3rd London General Hospital.

SMITH, MRS., J., Asst. Matron, Moore Park Aux. Hospital, Preston.

SMITH, F., A. Sister, Sect. 3 Reading War Hospital.

SMITH, MRS. R., Aux. Hospital, Blackwell, Worcs.

SMITH, MRS. R., Matron, Seaham Conval. Home, Durham.

SMITH, J., Sister, Aust. Aux. Hospital, Harefield.

SOANS, M., Comdt., Flounders Col. Aux. Hospital, Pontefract.

SPENCE, MRS. B., Matron Aux. Hospital, Manor Hill, Birkenhead.

SPINKS, M., Sister, 4th Northern Gen. Hospital, Lincoln.

SPITTALL, M. de H., Mt., Charnwood Aux. Hospital, Nr. Loughboro.

SPONG, A., Sister, Netley Aux. Hospital.

SPURGIN, E., Sen. Nurse, Aux. Hospital, Isleworth.

SQUIRE, L., N. Sis., C.A.M.C. Kitchnr. Mil. Hos., Brighton.

STANLEY, M., Matron, Monkstown House Aux. Hos., Co. Dublin.

STAY, C., N. Member, Aux. Hospital, Sherborne.

STAYNER, MRS. E., Matron, Aux. Hospital, Salisbury.

STEEDMAN, M., Matron, Brook House Aux. Hospital, Manchester.

STELLING, M., Sister, Aux. Hospital, Norfolk.

STEPHENS, MRS. E., Comdt., Northlands Aux. Hos., Emsworth.

STEVENSON, A., Matron, Hartlepools Hospital.

STEWART, A., Sister, 2nd Birmingham War Hospital.

STEWART, E., Matron, Ascot Aux. Hospital.

STEWART, M., Sister, Mil. Hospital, Britannia Park, Norwich.

STODDART, A., S. Nurse, 2nd Western Gen. Hospital.

STODDART, C., 1st, Western Gen. Hospital, Fazakerly, Liverpool.

STRATTON, MRS. E., Matron, Aux. Hospital, Pewsey, Wilts.

STRUDWICK, H., S. Nurse, 4th Northern Gen. Hospital, Lincoln.

STUART, J., A. Sister, Gen. Military Hospital, Colchester.

STUBBS, M., Nurse, Aux. Hospital, Kineton.

SULLIVAN, B., Sister, Dublin Castle Aux. Hospital.

SULMAN, H., Comdt., Kempston Aux. Hospital, Eastbourne.

SUMMERHILL, O., S. Nurse, 1st Southern Gen. Hospital.

SUTTON, W., Nurse, Aux. Hospital, Cheshire.

SWAN, Mrs. A., Matron, The Glen Aux. Hospital, Southend-on-Sea.

SWITHINBANK, G., Sister, Aux. Hospital, Southall.

THOMAS, MRS. F., Supt., Aux. Hospital, Gloucester.

THOMPSON, G., Matron, Mil. Hospital, Liverpool.

TATE, M., Sister, 2nd Birmingham War Hospital.

TAYLOR, E., Nurse Aux. Hospital, Cromer.

TAYLOR, M., Matron, Royal Hospital, Weymouth.

THEOBALD, M., 5th Southern Gen. Hospital, Plymouth.

THOMAS, MRS. M., Sister, Q.A. Mil. Hospital, Millbank.

THOMPSON, G., Sister, 1st London Gen. Hospital.

THOMSON, M., Supt. Nurse, Mil. Hospital, Fargo.

THOMSON, M., Nurse, Ampthill Road Aux. Hos., Bedford.

THURKETTLE, A., S. Nurse, 2nd Eastern Gen. Hospital, Div. II.

TIPLADY, M., Sister, Bradford War Hospital.

TOWER, M., 2nd Eastern Gen. Hospital, Brighton.

TOWNSEND, M., Sister, N.S.R., Beaufort War Hospital, Bristol.

s

TRACEY, C., Matron, Parkfield House Aux. Hospital, Crumpsall.

TREGASKIS, R., Matron, Aux. Hospital, Devon.

TURNER, J., Sister, 3rd Northern Gen. Hospital, Sheffield.

TWEEDALE, MRS. E., Comdt., St. John Aux. Hospital, Rochdale.

TWITE, M., Matron, Rosemeath Aux. Hospital, Wrexham.

UNSWORTH, A., S. Nurse, 5th Northern Gen. Hospital, Leicester.

UNSWORTH, E., Matron, Aux. Hos., Newton Abbot.

URQUHART, E., Nght. Supt., Crumpsall Inf., Manchester.

VALLER, E., Charge Sister, Aux. Red Cross Hospital, Burton-on-Trent

VAREY, M., Nurse, Aux. Hospital, Hull.

VAUGHAN, MRS. L., Supt., Aux. Hospital, Norfolk.

VEACOCK, A., Sister, Royal Victoria Hos., Netley.

VIBART, A., Matron, Aux. Hospital, Ryde.

VIGO, S., 4th London Gen. Hospital.

VYNER, F. M., Sister, Dartford War Hospital, Kent.

VAUGHAN, MRS. M., Matron-in-Charge, Woolton Aux. Hospital.

VEZEY, E., Matron, 5th London Gen. Hospital.

WARTER F., Matron, 2nd Eastern Gen. Hospital Div. II.

WATSON, M., Matron, Mil. Hospital, Yorks.

WILLIAMS, Matron, 2nd Eastern Gen. Hospital, Div. III.

WOODHOUSE, A. Matron, 2nd Western Gen. Hospital, Manchester.

WADELL, C., Sister and Supt., Aux. Hospital, Bristol.

WADDINGHAM, G., Matron, Royal Nat. Orthopædic Hospital.

WAINWRIGHT, MRS. L., Matron, Henley Aux. Hospital, Oxford.

WHITE, R., Nurse, 2nd London Gen. Hospital, Wakefield.

WAKEFIELD, Nurse, Aux. Hospital, Kendal.

WAKEFIELD, J., Sister, 1st Eastern Gen. Hospital.

WALKER, A., Matron, Moss Brge. Aux. Hos., E. Lancs.

WALKER, E., S. Nurse, 4th Northern Gen. Hospital, Lincoln.

WALKER, E., 3rd London Gen. Hospital.

WALKER, M., Sister, Ralston Aux. Hospital, Paisley.

WALKER, F., Sister, Lord Derby War Hospital, Warrington.

WALKER, MRS., Comdt., 18th Durham Aux. Hospital.

WALLACE, C., Matron, 3rd Durh. Aux. Hospital, Sunderland.

WALLACE, I., Sister, Military Hospital, Fovant.

WALLACE, M., Sister, St. Mary's Hospital, Paddington, W.

WALLACE, MRS. W., Matron, Aux. Hospital, Pollokshaw.

WALLEY, M., Sister, 2nd Western Gen. Hospital, Manchester.

WALLIS, K., S. Nurse, 1st London Gen. Hospital.

WALTON-WILSON, A., Comdt., Aux. Hospital, Shortley Bdge.

WARBURTON, M., Sister, 3rd Western Gen. Hospital, Cardiff.

WARNER, Lady Supt., Aux. Hospital, Co. Durham.

WARNOCK, M., 3rd London Gen. Hospital.

WATERS, MRS. E., Sister, Brankesmere, Aux. Hospital, Southsea.

WATSON, I., Nurse, Aux. Hospital, Freshwater, I.O.W.

WATTS, F., S. Nurse, N. Evington Extn. of 5th Northern Gen. Hos.

WAVELL, N., Comdt., Aux. Hospital, Sturminster Newton.

WEBB, M., 1st Asst. Matron, Gen. Hospital, Birmingham.

WEBSTER, M., Matron, Aux. Hospital, Abergavenny.

WENTWORTH-TAYLOR, MRS. C., Southall Aux. Hospital, Middx.

WEST, E., A. Sister, No. 1 Reading War Hospital.

WESTROP, G., Sister, Aux. Hospital, Bristol.

WHISTLER, E., Matron, Heath Lodge Aux. Hospital.

WHITMORE, E., Nurse, Aux. Hospital, Cambridge.

WHITTINGTON, R., Sister, Moray Lodge Hospital, Camden Hill.

WICKER, G., Sister, R. Sussex County Hospital, Brighton.

WILKIN, E., Sister, No. 2 N.Z. Gen. Hospital, Walton-on-Thames.

WILKINSON, M., 2nd, Western Gen. Hospital, Manchester.

WILKINSON, M., Sister, 3rd Southern Gen. Hospital, Oxford.

WILLCOX, M., Asst. Matron, 4th London Gen. Hospital.

WILLIAMS, A., Supt. and S.-in-Charge, Aux. Hospital, Hertford.

WILLIAMS, D., Sur. War Nurses Aux. Hospital, Carmarthen.

WILLIAMS, J., Matron, Common Aux. Hospital, Devon.

WILLIAMS, M., Exeter War Hospital.

WILSON, B., S. Nurse, 2nd Northern Gen. Hospital, Leeds.

WILSON, K., Matron, 3rd Western Gen. Hospital, Newport Section.

WILSON, MRS. L., Comdt., Aux. Hos., Hampton-in-Arden.

WILSON, M., Sister, Stoke-on-Trent War Hospital.

WILSON, M., Sister, Northumberland War Hospital, Gosforth.

WINDEMER, N., Supt., St. Mark's Aux. Hospital, Tunbridge Wells.

WOODS, K., S. Nurse, 1st Eastern Gen. Hospital.

WOOLER, K., Sister, 2nd Southern Gen. Hospital.

WOOLLEY, J., Matron, Oaklands Aux. Hospital, Cheshire.

WOOSNAM, MRS. E., Matron and Supt., Aux. Hospital, Cowes, I.O.W.

WRIGHT, A., Matron, Tillyrie Red Cross Hospital, Kinross.

WRIGHT, K., Sister, No. 2 N.Z. Gen. Hospital, Walton-on-Thames.

WOOLEY, A., S. Nurse, 2nd Northern Gen. Hospital, Leeds.

WYKESMITH, MRS. M., Matron and Supt., No. 5 Dur. Aux. Hospital.

YOUNGE, A. Cheltenham Group Aux. Hospital.

YOUNG, MRS. A., Supt. and Matron, Aux. Hospital, Braintree.

YOUNG, McG. J., Sister Sec. 5, Reading War Hospital.

YOXALL, F., Matron, Aux. Hospital, E. Lancs.

YULE, I., Sister, R. Free Hospital.

THE following is a list of names—principally of women workers in hospitals and institutions throughout the country —brought to the notice of the Secretary of State for valuable services rendered in connection with the war :—

ABBOTT, K., Aux. Hospital, Old Hastings, Hastings, Sussex.

ABELL, M., A.P. Mil. Aus. Cps., Westn. Commd. Dept., Prescott.

ABEL, V., S.-in-Charge, Roehampton Aux. Hospital, Surrey.

ABEL-SMITH, G., Sec. Leader, Aux. Hospital, Hertford.

ABRAHAMS, MRS. E., Beech House Aux. Hospital, London.

ABRAMS, H., Mil. Mas. Cps., Queen Mary's Mil. Hos., Whalley.

ACLAND, A., Comdt., No. 5 Aust. Aux. Hos., Welwyn, Herts.

ACTON, MRS. L., A. Matron, Red Cross Hospital, Torquay.

ADAMS, E., Matron, Met. Ear and Throat Hospital, London, W.

ADCOCK, O., Aux. Hospital, Town Close Lodge, Norfolk.

ADDENBROOK, M., Sec. Leader, Allerton Aux. Hospital, Birmingham.

ADDEY, M., Louth Aux. Hospital, Lincoln.

AINSWORTH, E., Aux. Hospital, Forest Hill, S.E.

AIRTH, D., The Mickie Aux. Hos., Queen's Gate, London.

AITCHESON, K., 25th Dur. Aux. Hospital, Sunderland.

AITKEN, F., Sister, Highfield Aux. Military Hospital, Liverpool.

AKENHEAD, A., Supt. and Matron, Boultham Aux. Hos., Lincoln.

ALDRIDGE, MRS. H., Matron, The Beeches Aux. Hospital, Worcs.

ALEXANDER, H., Sister, St. Luke's War Hospital, Halifax.

ALLAN, MRS. C., Supt., Wells Aux. Hospital, Somerset.

ALLEN, A., Amb. Sister, Amb. Column, London District.

ALLEN, B., Sister, St. Luke's War Hospital, Halifax.

ALLEN, E., Theatre Sister, Borough Hospital, Birkenhead

ALLEN, M., Military Hospital, Endell Street.
ALLETSON, MRS. N., Matron, Mostyn Aux. Hospital, Flint.
ALLNUT, E., Sec. Leader, Swyncombe Aux. Hospital, Henley.
ALLWOOD, MRS. C., Sister, Aux. Hospital, Upton, Nr. Chester.
ALPE, MRS. I., N. Member, Aux. Hospital, Sheringham.
AMBROSE, The Rev. Mother Mary, Matron, St. John's Hos., Limerick.
AMPHLETT, S., Nurse, Hartlebury Aux. Hospital, Worcs.
ANDERSON, MRS. A., Comdt., Aux. Hospital, Farnham.
ANDERSON, E., S. Nurse, 1st Southern Gen. Hospital, Birmingham.
ANDERSON, L., N. Sister, Aux. Hospital, Torquay.
ANDERSON, L., Prob., Queen Mary's Mil. Hospital, Whalley.
ANDERSON, M., Nurse, Aux. Hos., No. 13, Cornhill-on-Tweed.
ANDERSON, R., Nurse, Aux. Hospital, Builth Wells, Brecknock.
ANNEAR, R., Sister, Aux. Hospital, Hampton.
ANTHONY, E., Mil. Hospital, Lichfield, Staffs.
APPLETON, M., Comdt., 23rd Durham Aux. Hos., Eaglescliffe.
APPLEYARD, A., Sister, Fairfield Aux. Hospital, Eastbourne.
ARCHER, F., Aux. Hospital, Earl's Colne, Essex.
ARD, R., Comdt., Rustaal Aux. Hospital, Tunbridge Wells.
ARKWRIGHT, MRS. V., Qrmr., Hillhouse Aux. Hospital, Warwick.
ARMSTRONG, A., Nurs. Mem., Aux. Hospital, Carmarthen.
ARMSTRONG, MRS. E., Matron, Vic. Hospital, Cork.
ARMSTRONG, M., Sister, Royal Vic. Hospital, Belfast.
ARNELL, F., Aux. Hospital, Cowes, Isle of Wight.
ARNEY, A., Nurse, Wool Mil. Hospital, Dorset.
ARNING, C., Comdt., Fallowfield Aux. Hospital, Manchester.
ARNOLD, E., Matron, St. George's Hospital, Harrogate.

ARNOTT, A., Sister, Met. Hospital, Kingsland Road, N.E.

ARROWSMITH, MRS. E., 2nd Dur. Aux. Hospital, Durham.

ARTOM, E., Supt., Marston Green Aux. Hospital, Warwick.

ARTHUR, MRS. E., 2nd Dur. Aux. Hospital, Durham.

ASHDOWN, D., Qrms., Aux. Hospital, Kirstead, Nr. Brooke.

ASHLEY, E., S. Nurse, 1st Southern Gen. Hospital, Birmingham.

ASHMOLE, E., Sister, Ottermead Aux. Hospital, Ottershaw.

ASHTON, E., Nurse, Aux. Hospital, Ellesmere, Salop.

ASKEW, E., Nurse, Royal Naval Hospital, Hull.

ASHWORTH, M., Sister, Birch Hill Hospital, Rochdale.

ASPREY, O., Nurse, 1st Western Gen. Hospital, Liverpool.

ASQUITH, F., 1st Western Gen. Hospital, Liverpool.

ATHERSTONE, P., Sister, Aux. Hospital, Sussex Lodge, Cambridge.

ATKINS, G., Sec. Leader, Allerton Aux. Hospital, Birmingham.

ATKINSON, J., 14th Northd. Aux. Hos., Wylam, Northumberland.

ATLWARD, A., A.P. Mil. Mas. Cps., Mil. Hospital, Grantham.

ATTWOOD, G., Sister, Met. Hospital, Kingsland Road, N.E.

AUBERTIN, MRS. S., Mil. Hospital, Magdalen Camp, Northnts.

AUDLAND, M., Qrmr., Aux. Hospital, Northants.

AVES, A., Nurs. Mem., Mil. Hospital, Ripon.

AWDRY, MRS. E., Actg. Comdt., Aux. Hospital, Stonehouse, Glos.

AYRE, M., Nurse, Royal Naval Hospital, Hull, Yorks.

BABEY, L., Nurse, Gournay Court, Aux. Hospital, Bristol.

BACCHUS, E., Nurse, Howbury Hall Aux. Hospital, Beds.

BACHILDER, E., N. Sister, Wesctliffe Hospital, Folkestone.

BACON, I., Nurse Aux. Hospital, Hendon, Middlesex.

T

BADHAM, C., Sister, Tewkesbury Aux. Hospital, Glos.

BAGALEY, E., N. Mem., Aux. Hospital, Leamington Spa.

BAGLEY, MRS. M., No. 2, N.Z., Gen. Hospital, Walton-on-Thames.

BAGNELL-OAKELEY, B., Supt., Aux. Hospital, Cheltenham.

BAILEY, E., Nurse, Falmouth Military Hospital.

BAILEY, P., Sister, Crumpsall Infirmary, Manchester.

BAILLIE, H., Matron, Bridgnorth and S. Shropshire Infirmary.

BAKER, C., Aux. Hospital, Waldingham, Norfolk.

BAKER, E., Sister, Holnest Aux. Hospital, Sherborne.

BAKER, L., Prob., 2nd Birmingham War Hospital, Northfield.

BAKER, M., Aux. Hospital, Rotherham, Yorks.

BALD, M., The Beeches Aux. Hospital, Birkhamsted.

BALDWIN, S., St. Luke's War Hospital, Halifax.

BALL, K., Sister, Walsall and District Hospital, Walsall.

BALLANCE, M., Sister, 1st Southern Gen. Hospital, Birmingham.

BALLESTE, M., Nurse, Officers' Aux. Hospital, Dublin.

BAMFORTH, L., Prob. Nurse, War Hospital, Sheffield.

BANDFIELD, E., Qrmr., Chard Aux. Hospital, Somerset.

BANNISTER, MRS. H., Matron Aux. Hospital, Cuckfield, Sussex.

BARBER, A., Asst. Nurse, Military Hospital, Fargo.

BARBER, H., S. Nurse, Aux. Hospital, Brooklands, Cheshire.

BARCHARD, E., Nurse, Aux. Hospital, Forest Row, Sussex.

BARENDT, B., Nurse, 26, Park Lane, W.

BARKE, I., 2nd Southern Gen. Hospital, Bristol.

BARKER, MRS. L., The Michie Aux. Hospital, London.

BARKER, M., Aux. Hospital, Middlewich, Cheshire.

BARLOW, E., 1st Western Gen. Hospital, Liverpool.

BARNES, MRS. B., Matron, Aux. Hospital, Blackley, Manchester.

BARNES, F., S. Nurse, Cornelia Hospital, Poole.

BARNES, L., Nurse, Benham Valence Aux. Hospital, Berks.

BARNES, S., Sister, Northumberland, War Hospital, Gosforth.

BARNETT, J., Qrmr., Aux. Hospital, Bracknell, Berks.

BARNEY, E., Prob. Mil. Hospital, Park Hall Camp, Oswestry.

BARRETT, M., Matron, King Edward VII. Mem. Hos., Haywards Hth.

BARRETT, U., A.P., Mil. Mas. Cps. Mil. Con. Hos., Blackpool.

BARRON, D., Sen. Prob. Royal Nat. Orthopædic Hospital, W.

BARROW, U., Nurse, Aux. Hospital, Cooden, Sussex.

BARRY, A., Nurse, Red Cross Hospital, Richmond.

BARTLE, L., S. Nurse, 3rd Western Gen. Hospital, Cardiff.

BARTLETT, M., Sister, Fulham Military Hospital.

BARTON, E., Comdt., Clayton Court Aux. Hos., Petersfield.

BARTON, I., A.P. Mil. Mas. Cps., St. Luke's War Hospital, Halifax.

BARTON, BROWNE, L., Qrmr., Aux. Hos., Burnham-on-Crouch.

BASS, L., N. Mem., Colliton Aux. Hospital, Dorchester.

BASTARD, H., Qrmr., Aux. Hospital, Chigwell, Essex.

BASTARD, W., Nurse, Aux. Hospital, Cheltenham.

BATE, M., Nurse, Mil. Hospital, Grantham.

BATEMAN, D., Nurse, Percy House Aux. Hospital, Middlesex.

BATEMAN, F., Monkstown House Aux. Hospital, Co. Dublin.

BATES, M., Supt., St. John Aux; Hospital, Hastings.

BATHER, MRS. M., Comdt., Aux. Hospital, Shrewsbury.

BATT, W., A.P., Mil. Mas. Cps., Mil. Hospital, Chatham.

BATTEN, I., Sister, Ulster Vol. Force Hospital, Belfast.

BAXTER, J., S. Nurse, Mil. Hospital, Ripon.

BAYFIELD, MRS. A., Lady Supt., Hanover Pk. Hos., Peckham.
BAYNTON, M., Nurse, Aux. Hospital, Wilts.
BEAKBANE, M., A.P. Mil. Mas. Cps., 1st Sth. Gen. Hos. Birmingham.
BEAUMONT, A., Nurse, Wilmslow Aux. Hospital, Cheshire.
BEAUMONT, MRS. E., Sister, Uppingham Aux. Hospital, Rutland.
BEAVER, E., Mil. Prob., 1st Southern Gen. Hos., Birmingham.
BEAVIS, B., Sister, Met. Hospital, London, N.E.
BEDDOE, W., Sister, Aux. Hospital, Rugeley, Staffs.
BEDFORD, DUCHESS OF, Theatre Sister, Woburn Aux. Hospital.
BEDSON, W., Prob., Aux. Hospital, Manchester.
BEECH, JOHNSTON, M., Nurse, Christchurch Aux. Hospital.
BEESON, J., Prob. Nurse, Edmington Mil. Hospital, London.
BEGBIE, E., Sister, St. John Aux. Hospital, Hastings.
BELL, A., Sister, Empire Hospital, London, S.W.
BELL, C., Nurse, Howbury Hall Aux. Hospital, Beds.
BELL, MRS. L., S. Nurse, Aux. Hospital, Hampton.
BELL, M., 4th Northern Gen. Hospital, Lincoln.
BELL, M., King George Mil. Hospital, London.
BELL, N., N. Mem., St. Mark's Aux. Hospital, Tunbridge Wells.
BELLANGER, M., Matron, Waterloo and Dis. Hospital, Lancs.
BELLOW, G., Matron, Wallasey Aux. Hospital, Cheshire.
BELLVILLE, MRS. G., Admstror., The Darell Hospital, St. John's.
BENNETT, E., 2nd Northern Gen. Hospital, Leeds.
BENNETT, J., Sister, Gen. Hospital, Tunbridge Wells.
BENNETT, MRS. M., Nurse, 4th Dur. Aux. Hos., Sunderland.
BENNETT, M., Nurse, Hoole Bank Aux. Hospital, Chester.
BENNETT, R., Sister, Stepping Hill Hospital, Stockport.

BENT, E., Rothesay Hospital, Hants.

BENTHAM, S., Matron, Timberhurst Aux. Hospital, Bury.

BENTLEY, MRS. M., Sister, Furzedown, Limpsfield.

BENWELL, MRS. G., Murrell Hill Aux. Hospital, Carlisle.

BENYON, MRS. E., Comdt., Englefield Aux. Hospital, Reading.

BERKERS, MRS. L., Comdt., Roseneath Aux. Hospital, Wrexham.

BERWICK, MRS. L., Comdt., Aux. Hospital, Bracknell, Berks.

BESWICK, S., Sister, Mil. Hospital, Englefield Green.

BESANT, MRS. A., Lydney Aux. Hospital, Glos.

BETTINGTON, MRS. U., Qrmr., Aux. Hospital, Hereford.

BEVAN, E., Nurse, Aux. Hospital, Cuckfield, Sussex.

BEVAN, E., Sister, Royal Infirmary, Chester.

BIBBY, E., Aux. Hospital, Rhyl.

BICKERSTETH, C., Supt., Bodlondel Aux. Hospital, Anglesey.

BIGGE, M., Comdt., Strood Aux. Hospital, Chatham.

BIGGWITHER, MRS. M., Nurse, Wells Aux. Hospital, Somerset.

BILLINGTON, B., Aux. Hospital, Daventry.

BINNEY, MRS. S., Comdt., Guisnes Aux. Hospital, Essex.

BIRCH, E., Comdt., Aux. Hospital, Newbury, Manchester.

BIRCH, E., Prob., Stoke-on-Trent War Hospital, Newcastle.

BIRD, M., Sister, War Hospital, Bath.

BIRKILL, M., Sister, Edmonton Mil. Hospital, London.

BIRKS, E., Sister, Stepping Hill Hospital, Stockport.

BIRRELL, A., A.P. Mil. Mas. Cps., 3rd Scottish Gen. Hospital, Glasgow

BIRRELL, A., Sister, Lewisham Military Hospital.

BIRRELL, ANTHONY, MRS. N., Qrmr., Thame Aux. Hospital, Oxon.

BIRTLES, E., Comdt., Aux. Hospital, Newbury, Manchester.

BISHOP, F., Corsham Aux. Hospital, Wilts.

BISHOP, L., Nurse, Little Heath Aux. Hospital, Herts.

BISHOP, MRS. P., Comdt., Aux. Hospital, Rainhill, Lancs.

BLACK, J., Sister, Canford Cliffs, Bournemouth.

BLACK, M., Nurse, Aux. Hospital, Forest Row, Sussex.

BLACKWELL, MRS. C., Qrmr., Aux. Hospital, Warwick.

BLAIR, I., Nurse, Aux. Hospital, Carlisle.

BLAGG, M., 1st Western Gen. Hospital, Liverpool.

BLAKELEY, B., Sister, 3rd Northern Gen. Hospital, Sheffield.

BLAUD, M., Sister, Charing Cross Hospital, London.

BLATCH, MRS. K., Matron, Kenilworth Aux. Hospital, Warwick.

BLAYNEY, E., Matron, R. Infirm., Chester.

BLEASE, A., Trowbridge Aux. Hospital, Wilts.

BLENCOW, F., Nurse, Aux. Hospital, Brighton, Sussex.

BLENCOWE, F., S. Nurse, Mil. Hospital, Denbighshire.

BLENNERHASSETT, H., Hospital Ship.

BLENNERHASSETT, V., Hospital Ship.

BLETSOE, MRS. L., Nurse, Upminster Aux. Hospital, Essex.

BLEFIELD, L., Qrmr., Aux. Hospital, St. Gregory, Norfolk.

BLOOD, A., Spec. Prob., R. Herbert Hospital, Woolwich.

BLUNDELL, E., Asst. Nurse, Mil. Hospital, Salop.

BLUNDELL, E., Nurse, Mile End Mil. Hospital.

BLUNDELL, M., Sister, Salford Union Hospital, Manchester.

BLYTH, M., Nurse, Oakhurst Aux. Hospital, Erith.

BODDY, E., S.-in-Charge, Countess Dundonald's Aux. Hospital, W.

BOLE, E., S. Nurse, Scottish Nat. Red Cross Hospital, Scotland.

BOLNS, M., 1st Northern Gen. Hospital, Newcastle-on-Tyne.

BOLTON, K., Matron, Aux. Mil. Hospital, New Brighton.

BONALLO, M., Actg. Sister, Middlesex War Hospital, St. Albans.

BOND, MRS. V., Sister, Lambeth Aux. Hospital, London.

BOORMAN, MRS. G., Sen. Prob., Aux. Hospital, Nr. Guildford.

BOOTH, MRS. I., Qrmr., No. 16, Northd. Aux. Hos., Ashington.

BOOTH, M., Huddersfield War Hospital.

BORRINGLEANE, L., Qrmr., Woodhall Spa Aux. Hospital., Lincoln.

BORTON, E., Matron, Victoria Hospital, Blackpool.

BOSS, A., Supt., Masonic Hall Aux. Hospital, Bromley.

BOSSON, E., 1st Eastern Gen. Hospital, Cambidge.

BOTERILL, L., Netley Aux. Hospital, Hants.

BOTTERILL, A., Sister, 1st Southern Gen. Hospital, Birmingham.

BOULTER, M., R.C. Matron, C.A.M.C., Hdqrs. London.

BOULTON, M., Sister, Aux. Hospital, Moor Park, Preston.

BOURDILLON, D., Netley Aux. Hospital, Hants.

BOURNE, J., Leckhampton Court Hospital, Cheltenham.

BOUTH, M., Nurse, Southport Cottage Hospital.

BOUWENS, H., Nurse, Broxmoor House Aux. Hospital, Herts.

BOWEN, D., Aux. Hospital, Cleve Hill, Glos.

BOWEN, MRS. G., Comdt., Gt. Chesterfield Aux. Hospital, Essex.

BOWEN, M., 2nd Western Gen. Hospital, Manchester.

BOWER, A., Mulmesbury Aux. Hospital, Wilts.

BOWN, E., N. Mem., St. John Aux. Hospital, Weymouth.

BOWRING, F., Nurse, Aux. Hos., Burnham-on-Sea.

BOYCOTT, M., Trnd. Nurse, Aux. Hospital, Hereford.

BOYD, D., N. Mem., Allerton Aux. Hospital, Birmingham.

BOYD, E., Nurse, King Gorge V. Hospital, Dublin.

BOYD, M., St. George's Hill Aux. Hospital, Weybridge.

BRABAZON, M., A.P. Mil. Mas. Cps., Comd. Depot, Ireland.

BRADFORD, MRS. E., N. Mem., Aux. Hospital, Woodbastwick.

BRADFORD, K., Comdt., Aux. Hospital, Golf Club, Brampton.

BRADLEY, E., Sister, St. Andrews Hospital, N.W.

BRADLEY, N., Nurse, Royal Naval Hospital, Hull, York.

BRADSHAW, MRS. S., Aux. Hospital, Bray, Co. Wicklow.

BRAKSPEAR, Nurse, Aux. Hospital, St. Albans.

BRAMELD, L., Actg. S. Nurse, Aux. Hospital, Minehead.

BRAMPTON, A., Prob., Gen. Hospital, Colchester.

BRAND, A., Sister, Southport Infirmary.

BRAY, J., N. Mem., Aux. Hospital, Theydon Bois, Essex.

BREEZE, M., Sister, St. Bartholomew's, Rochester.

BRENAN, E., S. Nurse, Mil. Hospital, Sutton Veny, Wilts.

BRENNAN, A., Wharncliffe War Hospital, Sheffield.

BRERETON, M., S. Nurse, Central Mil. Hospital, Belfast.

BREW, O., Aux. Hospital, Bray, Co. Wicklow.

BRIGHT, E., A.P. Mil. Mas. Cps., Mil. Hospital, London.

BRIGGS, MRS. J., Lady Supt., Aux. Hospital, Lincoln.

BRIMBLE, MRS. M., Nurse, Aux. Hospital, Downend, Glos.

BRINKLEY, M., Aux. Hospital, Rhyl.

BRINKLEY, V., Aux. Hospital, Rhyl, Flints.

BRINTON, L., Nurse, Aux. Hospital, Worcester.

BRISCOE, K., 1st Southern Gen. Hospital, Birmingham.

BREAD, L., S. Nurse, Addington Park War Hospital, Croydon.

BROADLEY, E., Gifford House Aux. Hospital, Roehampton.

BROCK, E., Newlands Corner Aux. Hospital, Merrow Downs.

BRODIE, H., A.P. Mil. Mas. Cps., R. Herbert Hospital, Woolwich.

BRODMAN, H., Nurse, Aux. Hospital, Haywards Heath, Sussex.

BROOKES, D., A.P. Mil. Mas. Cps., Mil. Conv. Hos., Epsom.

BROOKES, MRS. G., Comdt., Aux. Hospital, Harwich.

BROOKS, A., 1st Northern Gen. Hospital, Newcastle-on-Tyne.

BROTHERTON, E., No. 16, Northd., Aux. Hospital, Northumberland.

BROWN, A., Qrmr., Aux. Hospital, Glos.

BROWN, D., Prob., 1st Southern Gen. Hospital, Birmingham.

BROWN, E., S. Nurse, R. Free Hospital, London, W.C.

BROWN, E., Nurse, Albion House Aux. Hospital, Newbury.

BROWN, G., Sister, Aux. Hospital, Wrexham.

BROWN, I., 1st Western Gen. Hospital, Liverpool.

BROWN, J., S. Nurse, No. 3 N.Z., Gen. Hospital, Codford.

BROWN, J., S. Nurse, Stoke-upon-Trent War Hospital.

BROWN, O., 1st Western Gen. Hospital, Liverpool.

BROWN, MRS. M., Aux. Hospital, Berkhamsted, Herts.

BROWN, R., Sister, Graylingwell Military Hospital.

BROWN, S., Sister, Edmonton Military Hospital, London.

BROWN, V., Nurse, Aux. Hospital, Baschurch, Salop.

BROWNE, C., Matron, R. Vic. Hospital, Folkestone.

BROWNE, F., Sister, Officers' Aux. Hospital, London.

BROWNE, M., Sister, Aux. Hospital, Canford Cliffs, Bournemouth.

BROWNE, MRS. S., Comdt., Langfield Aux. Hospital, Warwick.

BROWNE, V., N. Mem., Aux. Hospital, Norfolk.

BROWNLIE, G., Prob., King George Hospital, London, S.E.

BRUCE, E., New Court Aux. Hospital, Cheltenham.

BRUCE-CLARKE, MRS. E., Nurse, Cottenham Aux. Hos., Cambridge.

U

BRUNTON, C., Prob. War Hospital, Newcastle.
BRYANS, M., Nurse, Aux. Hospital, Brecknock.
BRYANT, A., Aux. Hospital, Rhyl, Flints.
BRYCE, E., Comdt., Aux. Hospital, Westmoreland.
BUCK, MRS. M., N.Z. Con. Hospital, Hornchurch.
BUCKLAND, L., Nurse, Aux. Hospital, Hendon, Middlesex.
BUCKLEY, MRS. A., Nurse Mem., Aux. Hospital, Portsmouth.
BUDD, I., Nurse, 2nd London Gen. Hospital, Chelsea.
BUFFARD, D., Matron, Viscountess Ridley's Hospital, W.
BUDGETT, E., Sister, Guys Cliffe Aux. Hospital, Warwick.
BUGLAS, MRS. C., Sister, Aux. Hospital, Manchester.
BULL, K., Nurse, Cottenham Aux. Hospital, Cambridge.
BULLEN, MRS. F., Nurse and Masseuse, Aux. Hospital, Wilts.
BUNCE, O., Supt., Gardenhurst Aux. Hospital, Bexley.
BURBRIDGE, C., S.-in-Charge, Aux. Hospital, Stonehouse, Glos.
BURGESS, A., Sister, Aux. Mil. Hospital, Liverpool.
BURGHALL, M., Nurse, Tranmere Mil. Hospital, Birkenhead.
BURKE, MRS. H., Comdt., Aux. Hospital, Eastbourne.
BURKE, N., S. Nurse, St. Nicholas, Harrogate.
BURN, The HON. MRS., Matron and Comdt., Aux. Hospital, Torquay.
BURNISTON, D., Dispenser, Aux. Hospital, Southampton.
BURNLEY, S., Sister, Ilkley Aux. Hospital, Yorks.
BURROWS, D., A.P. Mil. Mas. Cps., Mil. Hospital, Devonport.
BURROWS, M., 2nd Southern Gen. Hospital, Bristol.
BURTON, E., Nurse, Hilsborough Aux. Hospital, Harlow.
BUTCHER, E., Prob., No. 1 Mil. Hospital, Canterbury.
BUTLER, E., S. Nurse, King George Hospital, S.E.

BUTLER, M., Hd. Sister, 30, Hill Street, Mayfair.

BUTLER, R., Nurse, Brooklands Mil. Hospital, Cheshire.

BUTTERS, M., Cheveley Park Aux. Hospital, Cambridge.

BUXTON, C., Comdt., Hanover House Aux. Hospital, Essex.

BYRDE, A., Qrmr., No. V. Sect. Grouped Hospital, Exeter.

BYRNE, C., A.P. Mil. Mas. Cps., Com. Dpt., Ireland.

BYRON, M., Amb. Sister, Amb. Column, London District.

CAIL-COOK, MRS. K., Comdt., Aux. Hospital, Newcastle-on-Tyne.

CAINES, A., Sister, Aux. Hospital, Park Hall Camp, Oswestry.

CAINS, Nurse Sister, Hdqrs., London.

CALCOTT, M., Hdqrs., A.P. Mil. Mas. Cps.

CAIDER, Sister, G., No. 2 N.Z., Gen. Hospital, Walton-on-Thames.

CALLARD, M., Sister, 1st Southern Gen. Hospital, Birmingham.

CALLAWAY, W., A.P., Mil. Mas. Cps., Southern Com. Dept., Ireland.

CALLINGHAM, M., Nurse, Hylands Aux. Hospital, Nr. Chelmsford.

CAMERON, K., Matron, Vic. Aux. Hospital, Shelford.

CAMERON, M., Sister, Tooting Mil. Hospital.

CAMERON-SMITH, J., Actg. Matron, Can. Con. Hospital, Buxton.

CAMPBELL, A., Sister, Aux. Hospital, Newmarket.

CAMPBELL, C., A.P., Mil. Mas. Cps., East Leeds War Hospital.

CAMPBELL, MRS. G., Nurse, Aux. Hospital, Denbigh.

CAMPBELL, L., Sister, 3rd Aust. Aux. Hospital.

CAMPBELL, M., Nurse, Southport Cottage Hospital.

CAMPBELL, M., Nurse, U.V.F. Hospital, Belfast.

CANDLER, MRS. M., Qrmr., Sandon Aux. Hospital, Thorpe.

CANTY, C., Sister, Mrs. Hall Walker's Hospital, London, N.W.

CAREW, M., Nurse, Taunton Aux. Hospital, Somerset.

CAREY, M., Nurse, Aux. Hospital, Watford, Herts.

CARLISLE, E., S. Nurse, Aux. Hospital, Bollington, Cheshire.

CARLISLE-HEYS, N., S. Nurse, Prees Heath Camp Mil. Hos., Salop.

CARR, Sister, Field House Aux. Hospital, Bradford, Yorks.

CARR-ELLISON, A., Nurse, 17 Aux. Hospital, Northumberland.

CARRICK, M., A.P. Mil. Mas. Cps., Com. Dpt., Nth. Camp, Ripon.

CARRIER, E., Lydney Aux. Hospital, Glos.

CARRUTHERS-LITTLE, M., Actg. Comdt., Aux. Hospital, Glos.

CARSE, F., Nurse, R. Free Hospital, Gray's Inn Road, W.C.

CARTER, MRS. A., Sister, Hoole House Aux. Hospital, Chester.

CARTER, E., 1st Southern Gen. Hospital, Birmingham.

CARSON, S., Nurse, Aux. Hospital, Smethwick, Staffs.

CARSON, C., Qrmr., Aux. Hospital, Brundall, Norwich.

CASHIN, A., A.R.R.C., Acting Matron.

CASSAN, G., Sister, Dobson Relief Hospital, Blackheath.

CATOR, D., Princess Club Hospital, Bermondsey, S.E.

CAWLEY, MRS. A., Nurse, Brooklands Aux. Hospital, Surrey.

CAWLEY, A., Sister, Newnham Paddox, Warwick.

CAWLEY, M., Sister, Myrtle Aux. Hospital, Liverpool.

CHAINEY, F., Sister, Aux. Hospital, Taunton.

CHALLONER, M., Nurse, Aux. Hospital, Abington, Berks.

CHAMBERLAIN, D., Sister, A.P. Mil. Mas. Cps., Bermdsy Mil. Hos.,S.E.

CHAMBERLAIN, H., Sister, Met. Hospital, N.E.

CHAMBERS, E., Supt., Kingsbury Aux. Hospital, Shortlands.

CHANDLER, A., Nurse, St. Anne's Aux. Hospital, Caversham.

CHAPLIN, A., 1st Borough Aux. Hospital, Cambridge.

CHAPMAN, C., 4th Northern Gen. Hospital, Lincoln.

CHAPMAN, M., 1st Western Gen. Hospital, Liverpool.

CHAPMAN, N., S. Nurse, 2nd Birmingham War Hospital, Northfield.

CHARLESWORTH, A., Nurse, The Coulter Hospital, London, W.

CHARLESWORTH, M., Nurse, The Coulter Hospital, London, W.

CHARLETON, MRS. E., Lady Supt., 23rd Durham Aux. Hospital.

CHATFIELD, W., Netley Aux. Hospital, Hants.

CHEETHAM, MRS. E., Comdt., and Matron, Aux. Hospital, Norfolk.

CHILTON, M., S. Nurse, 2nd Western Gen. Hospital, Manchester.

CHOLOMONDELEY, H., Aux. Nurse, Aux. Hospital, Thame.

CHORLTON, E., Prob., Aux. Hospital, Manchester.

CHRISP, M., N. Mem., 1st Northern Gen. Hos., Newcastle-on-Tyne

CHRISTIAN, A., Sister, R. Southm. Hospital, Liverpool.

CHRYSTAL, E., S.-in-Charge, Aux. Hospital, Roehampton.

CHUBB, E., Aux. Hospital, Wilts.

CHUCK, S., A.P., Mil. Orthopædic Hospital.

CHURCHILL, M., Nurse, Cyngfield, Shrewsbury.

CLARK, D., Mem., Soldiers Aux. Hospital, Royston.

CLARK, N., Nurse, 2nd Birmingham War Hospital, Northfield.

CLARKE, A., Nurse, W.V.F. Hospital, Belfast.

CLARKE, E., Sister, R. Free Hospital, Gray's Inn Road, W.C.

CLARKE, E., 2nd Southern Gen. Hospital, Bristol.

CLARKE, MRS. M., A.P., Mil. Mas. Cps., Irish Com. Dpt., Tippery.

CLAXTON, MRS. N., Nurse Mem., Aux. Hos., Northwood, Middlesex.

CLAY, MRS. E., A. Comdt., Aux. Hos., Holyhead, Anglesey.

CLAYDEN, M., Qrmr., Aux. Hospital, Essex.

CLAYTON, MRS. C., Supt., Aux. Hospital, Willesden.

CLAYTON, M., Nurse, Aux. Hospital, Surrey.
CLAYTON, M., 3rd London Gen. Hospital, Wandsworth.
CLAYWORTH, M., Nurse, Aux. Hospital, Lincoln.
CLEMENTE, A., Qrmr., Aux. Hospital, Seaford.
CLEMENTS, K., Aux. Hospital, Burton-on-Trent.
CLEPHAM, D., Mil. Hospital, Endell Street.
CLEVERLEY, H., N. Mem., Mil. Hospital, Sutton Veny.
CLIFT, E., Nurse, Ware Aux. Hospital, Herts.
CLINCH, J., 1st Western Gen. Hospital, Liverpool.
CLOAKE, F., Sister, 1st Southern Gen. Hospital, Birmingham.
COAD, E., Comdt., Aux. Hospital, Bromley.
COATHAM, Sister, Aux. Hospital, Abergavenny.
COATES, E., Sister, Aux. Hospital, Sussex.
COBB, M., Nurse, Aux. Hospital, Wall Hall, Watford.
COBBAN, M., Nurse, Aux. Hospital, Liverpool.
COCHRANE, K., Sister, Royal Infirmary, Halifax.
COCHRANE, L., N. Mem., St. John Aux. Hospital, Durham.
COCKTON, A., Mil. Hospital, Kinmel, Denbighshire.
COFFEY, E., Matron, Barrington's Hospital, Limerick.
COLE, A., 4th Northern Gen. Hospital.
COLE, B., Actg. Sister, Caterham Hospital, Surrey.
COLES, A., Nurse, Portishead Aux. Hospital, Somerset.
COLES, B., Nurse, Aux. Hospital, Downend, Glos.
COLES, H., Nurse, 3rd London Gen. Hospital, Wandsworth.
COLEY, MRS. A., Filsham Aux. Hospital, St. Leonards-on-Sea.
COLGRAVE, MRS., Lady Supt., Princess Christian's Hos., Norwood.
COLLARD, M., Nurse, Myrtle Aux. Hospital, Liverpool.

COLLINGS, C., Sister, London Hospital, Whitechapel.

COLLINS, MRS. A., Sister, Met. Hospital, London.

COLLINS, D., Prob. War Hospital, Keighley, Yorks.

COLLINS, F., Sister, Fulham Military Hospital.

COLLINS, N., Sister, Edmonton Military Hospital, London.

COLLYER, A., Ickleton Aux. Hospital, Gt. Chesterfield.

COMBER, H., Prob., Priv. Aux. Hospital, Cheshire.

COMMINGTON, MRS. E., Comdt., Bilton Hall Aux. Hospital, Warwick.

CONALTY, M., Sister, 10, Place Green, W.

CONDI, A., S. Nurse, Univ. Col. Hospital, W.C.

CONNELL, MRS. J., Comdt., Myrtle Aux. Hospital, Liverpool.

COOK, D., Nurse, Little Heath Aux. Hospital, Herts.

COOK, E., Matron, Reckitts Hospital, Hull.

COOKE, A., Aux. Hospital, Cheshire.

COOKE, MRS. E., Nurse, Hammersmith.

COOKE, M., Nurse, Aux. Hospital, Olton, Warwick.

COOPER, A., Nurse, Section 3, Reading War Hospital.

COOPER, K., Nurse, Aux. Hospital, Cheshire.

COOPER, K., Matron, Dist. Infirmary, Ashton-under-Lyne.

COOPER, M., African Hospital, Richmond Park.

COPELAND, MRS. A., Nurse, The Darrell Hospital, London, W.

COPSON, M., A.P., Mil. Mas. Cps., Croydon War Hospital.

CORNELL, F., A.P. Mil. Mas. Cps., Mil. Hospital, Nottingham.

CORNES, M., Acting Sister, Military Hospital, Notts.

CORRIGAN, F., Sister, Mil. Hospital, Nell Lane, Manchester.

COREY, L., S. Nurse, Aux. Hospital, Nr. Guildford.

CORY, V., N. Mem., Aux. Hospital, Dereham, Norfolk.

COTTER, F., Aux. Hospital, Brecondale, Norwich.
COULCHER, M., Comdt., Broadwater Aux. Hospital, Ipswich.
COULDREY, MRS. M., Qrmr., Aux. Hospital, Abingdon.
COUNSELLOR, A., Qrmr., Aux. Hospital, Weymouth.
COUPLAND, S., Sister, Bathurst House Aux. Hospital, S.W.
COURSE, M., Prob., 1st Birmingham War Hospital.
COURTAULD, MRS. E., Nurse Comdt., Aux. Mil. Hospital, Essex.
COUSONS, M., S. Nurse, Aux. Hospital, Suffolk.
COWAN, M., Asst. Nurse, Northd. War Hospital, Gosforth.
COWE, E., Fulham Military Hospital.
COX, J., Sister, Vic. Hospital, Blackpool.
COX, MRS. M., Qrmr., Aux. Hospital, Hove, Sussex.
COXALL, Nurse. Sister, Hdqrs., London.
CRAIG, MRS. E., Hon. Lady Supt., Con. Hospital, Hereford.
CRAIG, MRS. G., Comdt., Hillingdon Aux. Hospital, Middlesex.
CRAIG-CRAWFORD, J., Asst. Comdt., Aux. Hospital, Highams.
CRAIGIE, MRS., X-Ray, Asst. War Hospital, Bath.
CRAMP, M., Sister, Endsleigh Palace Hospital, N.W.
CRAWFORD, G., Matron, Aux. Hospital, Pontefract, Yorks.
CRAWFORD, MRS. K., Matron, American Hos. for English Soldiers, N.
CRAWLEY, MRS. C., Comdt., No 7, Durham Aux. Hospital.
CRICHTON-NEATE, M., M. Mas. Cps., 3rd Westn. Gen. Hos., Cardiff.
CROCKER, MRS. F., N. Mem., Chetnole Aux. Hospital.
CROFT, MRS. M., Qrmr., 11th Durham Aux. Hospital, Sunderland.
CROFTON, D., Aux. Hospital, Sunderland.
CROFTON, K., Nurse, Hoole Bank Aux. Hospital, Chester.
CROFTON, L., Dublin Castle Aux. Hospital, Dublin.

CROLL, J., Matron, St. Nicholas, Harrogate.
CROMBIE, J., Matron, Aux. Hospital, Hampstead Heath, N.W.
CROOK, J., Rosemeath Aux. Hospital, Middlesex.
CROOK, M., Edmonton Mil. Hospital, London.
CROOKSTON, M., Edmonton Military Hospital, London.
CROOKSTON, B., Sister, Stoke-on-Trent Hospital.
CROOT, G., N. Member, Military Hospital, Ripon.
CROSBIE, A., Prob., Queen Mary's Military Hospital, Whalley.
CROSLAND, M., Huddersfield War Hospital.
CROSLAND, M., Nurse, Aux. Hospital, Aberford, Yorks.
CROSS, A., Sister, Shirley Warren Aux. Hospital.
CROSS, C., Sister, Walsall and District, Aux. Hospital, Staffs.
CROSS, D., Qrmr., Red Cross Hospital, Middlesex.
CROSS, E., Nurse, Brook House Aux. Hospital, Manchester.
CROSS, E., Nurse, Aux. Hospital, Bury St. Edmunds.
CROSS, M,. N. Mem., Aux. Hospital, Sturminster Newton.
CROSSKILL, A., Asst. Matron, R. Salop Infirmary, Shrewsbury.
CROWE, D., Nurse, Aux. Hospital, Weston-super-Mare.
CROWTHER, MRS. B., Sister, Aux. Hospital, Southampton.
CROXFORD, J., Sister, 37, Eaton Square, S.W.
CULHAM, C., Prob. Nurse, Wharncliffe War Hospital, Sheffield.
CULLEY, G., Nurse, Gostwich Aux. Hospital, Colchester.
CULLEY, K., Nurse, Gostwich Aux. Hospital, Colchester.
CULLINAN, A., Sister-in-Charge, Aux. Hospital, Northampton.
CULLWICK, F., Sister, 1st Southern Gen. Hospital, Birmingham.
CUME, E., Sister, Military Hospital, Sutton Veny, Wilts.
CUMMINGS, S., S. Nurse, 4th London Gen. Hospital, Chelsea.

v

CUNNINGHAM, A., Actg. Qrmr. Aux. Hospital, Burnham-on-Sea.
CUNNINGHAM, E., M. Mas. Cps., 4th Northern Gen. Hos., Lincoln.
CURLEY, M., Qrmr., 14th Northd. Aux. Hospital, Wylzam.
CURRY, G., Nurse, Henham Hall, Suffolk.
CURTIN, P., Matron, Mater Infirmorum Hospital, Belfast.
CURTIS, G., Heatherdene, Harrogate.
CURTIS, S., Sister, King Edward VII. Hospital, London, S.W.
CURTIS, W., S. Nurse, St. Mary's Hospital.

DADSON, M., Qrmr., Aux. Hospital, Roehampton.
DADSON, S., Comdt., Aux. Hospital, Roehampton.
DAKERS, M., N. Mem., Mil. Hospital, Canterbury.
DAKIN, A., Sen. Nurse, Aux. Hospital, Isleworth.
DALE, C., Sister, Asst. Comdt., Aux. Hospital, Kent.
DALLOW, M., Sister, Mrs. Hall-Walker's Hospital, London, N.W.
DALTON, Sister, Linden Conv. Aux. Hospital, Co. Dublin.
DALTON, M., Sister, Dobson Relief Hos., Blackheath.
DALY, G., Sister, St. George's Hospital, London, S.W.
DAMBRILL, A., Nurse, Aux. Hospital, Ryde, Isle of Wight.
DAMS, M., Sister, Charing Cross Hospital, London.
DANGER, MRS. W., N. Mem., Aux. Hospital, Bristol.
DANIELS, MRS. A., Qrmr., 2nd Durham Aux. Hospital, South Shields.
DANIELS, G., Sister, Alder Hey Aux. Hospital, Liverpool.
DARBYSHIRE, MRS. E., Nurse, Pav. Aux. Hospital, E. Lancs.
DARLINGTON, M., Nurse, Southport Cottage Hospital.
DARLINGTON, M., Nurse, Aux. Hospital, Southport, Lancs.
DARVIL-SMITH, MRS. K., County of Middx. Enq. for Mis. Dept.

DAVENPORT, J., Nurse, Naunton Aux. Hospital, Cheltenham.

DAVEY, D., Prob., Worcester Infirmary.

DAVIDSON, E., Sister, Mil. Hospital, Lichfield.

DAVIES, MRS. F., Qrmr., Aux. Hospital, Lincoln.

DAVIES, F., 3rd Western Gen. Hospital, Cardiff.

DAVIES, MRS. G., Comdt., Aux. Hospital, Anglesey.

DAVIES, K., Sister, 3rd Western Gen. Hospital, Cardiff.

DAVIES, K., S. Nurse, 1st Southern Gen. Hospital, Birmingham.

DAVIES, M., Palace Aux. Hospital, Glos.

DAVIES, M., Prob. Nurse, Welsh Met. Hospital, Nr. Cardiff.

DAVIES, R., Matron, Aux. Hospital, Cirencester.

DAVIES, R., S.-in-Charge, Aux. Hospital, Brettenham.

DAVIS, F., Nurse, Limpsfield.

DAVIS, MRS. F., Matron, Paddington Aux. Hospital, London.

DAVIS, H., Nurse, Maidenhead Aux. Hospital, Berks.

DAVIS, M., Nurse, 2, Alexandra's Hospital, Highgate.

DAVY, H., S. Officer, Grouped Hospital, Exeter.

DAWE, A., Sister, Mil. Hospital, Ripon.

DAWES, MRS. L., Qrmr., Aux. Hospital, Northampton.

DAWSON, A., Supt. Nurse, Liverpool.

DAWSON, A., Sister, Lewisham Mil. Hospital, SE.

DAY, E., Sister, War Hospital, Bath.

DAY, F., Qrmr., Banbury Aux. Hospital, Oxon.

DEACON, G., Actg. S. Nurse, The Norfolk War Hospital.

DEAN, E., Sister, Oak Dene Aux. Hospital, Lancs.

DEAN, MRS. E., Sandon Aux. Hospital, Stafford.

DEANS, MRS. P., Comdt., Aux. Hospital, Beds.

DEARDEN, A., A.P. Mil. Mas. Cps., 1st London Gen. Hos., Chelsea.
DENISON, G., S. Nurse, 1st Southern Gen. Hos., Birmingham.
DENNIS, E., 1st Southern Gen. Hospital, Birmingham.
DENNIS, O., 1st Southern Gen. Hospital, Birmingham.
DENNY, C., Qrmr., Christchurch Aux. Hospital.
DENT, MRS. M., N. Mem., Aux. Hospital, Norfolk.
DENTON, M., Nurse, Clifford Str. Aux. Hospital, York.
DE SEGUNDO, MRS. G., Matron, 4, Lyndhurst Gardens, N.W.
DESART, DOWAGER COUNTESS, Red Cross Hospital, Co. Kilkenny.
DE STOECKL, Z, St. Nicholas, Harrogate.
DEUCHFIELD, W., N. Evington War Hospital.
DEWBERRY, A., Nurse, St. Chad's Aux. Hospital, Cambridge.
DEWING, M., N. Mem., Aux. Hospital, Norfolk.
DICEY, F., N. Mem., Red Cross, Hospital, Torquay.
DICK, MRS. H., Joint Comdt., Aux. Hospital, London.
DICKE, E. Prob., 2nd Birmingham War Hospital.
DICKENSON, E., Matron, Aux. Hospital, Anglesey.
DICKSON, MRS. L., Sister, Southport Infirmary.
DICKSON, MRS. M., Sister, Aux. Hospital, Middlesex.
DILLON, HON. MISS E., Prob. Princess Club Hospital, S.E.
DIMMOCK, L., A.P. Mil. Mas. Cps., Holborn Mil. Hospital.
DIMSDALE, M., Qrmr., Amb. Col. London Dist.
DIXON, MRS. M., Asst. Comdt., Aux. Hospital, Worcs.
DOBBIE, J., Qrmr. and N. Mem., Aux. Hos., Nr. Reading.
DODD, E., Prob., 1st Southern Gen. Hospital, Birmingham.
DODD, MRS. N., N. Sister, Aux. Hospital, Cheshire.
DODGSON, G., Supt., Aux. Hospital, Canterbury.

DODGSON, L., Mil. Mas. Cps., Mil. Con. Hos., Epsom.
DOIG, H., Sister, Aux. Hospital, St. Leonards-on-Sea.
DONALD, J., N. Mem. and Masseuse, Aux. Hospital, Warwick.
DONALD, M., Sister, 1st Southern Gen. Hospital, Birmingham.
DONNELLY, M., Sister, 34, Gros. St., London, W.
DONNISON, E., 1st Eastern Gen. Hospital, Cambridge.
DONOVAN, M., Asst. Matron, St. John's Hospital, Southport.
DOUDNEY, MRS. A., Lady Supt., Aux. Hospital, Wainfleet.
DOUGALL, M., Qrmr., Kidderminster Aux. Hospital, Worcs.
DOUGHERTY, S., S. Nurse, 4th Sec. Gen. Hospital, Glasgow.
DOUGLAS, MRS. M., Nurse, Aux. Hospital, S. Norwood Hill, London.
DOWNES, S., Nurse, St. John's Aux. Hospital, London Rd., Salop.
DOWNISON, E., 1st Eastern Gen. Hospital, Cambridge.
DOWNS, G., Spec. Prob. R. Victoria Hospital, Netley.
DOWSE, E., Matron, Lakenham Mil. Hospital, Norwich.
DOWSON, MRS. A., N. Sister, St. John Hospital, Cheltenham.
DRANE, E., Comdt., Aux. Hospital, Guilsborough, Northants.
DREWE, A., Prob., 2nd Birmingham War Hospital, Northfield.
DREWITT, L., Matron, Gen. Infirmary, Cheshire.
DREWRY, A., Sister and Actg. Supt., Aux. Hospital, Somerset.
DROWER, V., Sister, Kensington Aux. Hospital, Surrey.
DE CROZ, E., Nurse, Brooklands Mil. Hospital.
DUFF, N., Nurse, Falmouth Mil. Hospital.
DUGDALE, MRS. E., Matron & Comdt., Eggington Hall Aux. Hos.
DUGGLEBY, E., Nurse, Aux. Hospital, York.
DUKA, MRS. J., Sister, Paddington Aux. Hospital, London.
DULMAGE, Matron, No. 10, Can. Stat. Hospital, Eastbourne.

Dumble, J., 2nd Asst. Matron, Welsh Met. War Hos., Nr. Cardiff.
Duncan, E., S. Nurse, 3rd Sco. Gen. Hospital, Glasgow.
Duncombe, E., A. Qrmr., Aux. Hospital, Herefordshire.
Dunell, Mrs. M., Matron, Aux. Hospital, Norfolk.
Dunford, C., Spec. Prob., R. Herbert Hospital, Woolwich.
Dunlop, A., Comdt., Aux. Hospital, Berks.
Dunlop, M., 2nd Southern Gen. Hospital, Bristol.
Dunlop, R., W. Sister, Mill Road, Liverpool.
Dunn, V., Supt. St. John's Aux. Hospital, Sevenoaks, Kent.
Dunning, J., Sister, 2nd Western Gen. Hospital, Manchester.
Dunning, H., N. Mem., Aux. Hospital, Emsworth, Hants.
Dunthorne, I., N. Mem., Aux. Hospital, Norfolk.
Durler, Mrs. N., Comdt., Wardown Aux. Hospital, Bedford.

Eakin, G., N. Sister, Univ. War Hospital, Southampton.
Earnshaw, K., Nurse, Aux. Hospital, Northants.
Eastwood, Mrs. J., Matron, Aux. Hospital, Cumberland.
Eborn, J., Mil. Hospital, Lichfield, Staffs.
Edden, A., Comdt., Wier Hospital, Balham, London.
Edden, E., Nurse, War Hospital, Balham.
Eden, E., Woodhall Park Aux. Hospital, Hertford.
Edmurdson, E., Mil. Hospital, London.
Edwardes, E., Matron, Llandaff House.
Edwards, G., Nurse, Red Cross Hospital, Richmond.
Egerton, D., Nurse and Qrmr., Richmond Military Hospital.
Eggins, F., Matron, Skipton and District Hospital.
Elcho, Lady V., Nurse, Rutland Hospital.

ELDERKIN, M., Nurse, Aux. Hospital, Norfolk.

ELIOT, K., Exeter War Hospital.

ELLAND, M., 5th Northern Gen. Hospital, Leicester.

ELLICE, M., S. Nurse, Aux. Hospital, Warwick.

ELLIOTT, C., Nurse, 1st Eastern Gen. Hospital, Cambridge.

ELLIS, E., Sister, Endsleigh Palace Hospital, N.W.

ELLIS, MRS. P., Nurse, Amb. Col. London District.

ELLISON, M., Ward Sister, Mill Road, Liverpool.

ELLISON, M., N. Mem., Filey Aux. Hospital, Yorks.

ELMS, J., Matron, Sussex Eye Hospital, Brighton.

ELPHICK, M., Sister, Lewisham Mil. Hospital, S.E.

ELTRINGHAM, MRS., Mt., 7th Northd. Aux. Hospital, Whitley Bay.

ELWES, MRS. M., Aux. Hospital, Wimborne.

EMBY, N., Sister, St. George's, Harrogate.

EMERY, V., N. Mem;, R. Vic. Hospital, Netley.

EMMOTT, MRS. D., Comdt., Woodfield Aux. Hospital, Lancs.

ENRIGHT, E., Sister, 3rd London Gen. Hospital, Wandsworth.

ENSOR, F., Sister, Mil. Hospital, Cannock Chase.

EPPS, E., Supt., Rauceby Aux. Hospital, Grantham.

ETHERIDGE, N., Nurse, Bleakdown Hospital, Surrey.

EVANS, E., Matron, Welsh Hospital, Netley.

EVANS, E., S. Nurse, Sec. 2, Reading War Hospital.

EVANS, G., Sister, Aux. Hospital, Hull.

EVANS, M., Nurse, Aux. Hospital, Nr .Warrington.

EVESON, MRS. W., Nurse Aux. Hospital, Bourneville, Worcs.

EVERITT, I., R. Victoria Hospital, Netley.

EWENS, I., Nurse, Red Cross Hospital, Richmond.

EXHAM, A., Mil. Hospital, Catterick.
EYTON, MRS. F., Qrmr., Aux. Hospital, Ruthin, Flints.

FAIRBAIRN, W., Sister, Amcn. Hospital for English Soldiers, N.
FAIRWEATHER, D., Aux. Hospital, Southampton.
FANSHAWE, MRS. C., N. Mem., Craghead Aux. Hos., Bournemouth.
FARDELL, A., 1st Western Gen. Hospital, Liverpool.
FARQUHAR, G., Sister, St. Bartholomew's, Rochester.
FEARN, F., S. Nurse, 2nd Western Gen. Hospital, Manchester.
FEATHERSTONE, MRS. M., Qrmr., Aux. Hospital, Middlesex.
FEILDING, THE LADY C., Nurse, Warwick.
FERGUSON, MRS. C., Comdt., Aux. Hospital, Tunbridge Wells.
FIDDIAN, H., Mil. Mas. Cps., London Com. Depot.
FIELD, F., Sister, Princess Chris. Mil. Hos., Englefield Green.
FIELDEN, M., Sister, Endsleigh Place Hospital, N.W.
FIELDER, K., Mil. Mas. Cps., 2nd Southern Gen. Hospital, Bristol.
FIELDHOUSE, N., Nurse, Aux. Hospital, Warwick.
FIELDING, MRS. M., Member Aux. Hospital, Gloucester.
FINCH, M., Sidcup Aux. Hospital, Kent.
FINDLAY, A., Mil. Mas. Cps., 4th London Gen. Hospital, Chelsea.
FIRTH, MRS. C., Matron, Mil. Hos., West Didsbury, Manchester.
FIRTH, L., Nurse, Hazlewood Aux. Hos., I. of W.
FISCHER, H., Supt., Chard Aux. Hospital, Somerset.
FISHER, MRS. J., Comdt., Aux. Hospital, Breckenham.
FISHWICK, A., Sister, 3rd London Gen. Hospital, Wandsworth.
FITZGIBBON, G., Mem. Aux. Hospital, Roehampton.
FITZMAURICE, E., Mil. Mas. Cps. Com. Depot, Alnwick.

FITZNER, P., Sister, Myrtle Aux. Hospital, Liverpool.
FLEMING, K., Nurse, 27, Grosvenor Square, W.
FLETCHER, E., A. Nurse, Cliff Mil. Hospital, Felixstowe.
FLETCHER, K., Night Supt., No. 111 Sec. Grouped Hos., Exeter.
FLETCHER, S., Sister, Cumberland Inf. Carlisle.
FLIXON, J., Prob., 2nd Birmingham War Hospital, Northfield.
FLOOD, M., Matron, Charlton Cottage Hospital.
FLYNN, M., Matron, Cen. Mil. Hospital, Belfast.
FOREMAN, M., Sister, Princess Christian Hospital, Norwood, S.E.
FORREST, S., Nurse, Sec. 2, Reading War Hospital.
FORSTER, D., Sister, Northd. War Hospital, Gosforth.
FORSTER, D., Prob., War Hospital, Bradford.
FORSTER, MRS. N., Matron, St. Andrew's Sec., Penrith Aux. Hos.
FOSBERY, H., Prob., Tooting Military Hospital.
FOSTER, A., Cmdt., Beaulieu Aux. Hospital, Harrogate, Yorks.
FOSTER, E., E. Leeds War Hospital.
FOWLER, E., Nurse, Toxteth Park Aux. Hospital, Liverpool.
FOWLER, L., 4th London Gen. Hospital, Chelsea.
FOWLER, M., Nurse, Yeovil Aux. Hospital, Somerset.
FOWLIE, R., Mil. Mas. Cps., New End Sec. Mil. Hos., Hampstead.
FOX, M., Nurse, Aux. Hospital, Whalley Range.
FRASER, M., A. Nurse, Stanley Hospital, Liverpool.
FRECKNALL, M., Sister, Tooting Military Hospital, S.W.
FREEMAN, L., Coleshill Aux. Hospital, Warwick.
FREEMAN, W., Nurse, No. 1 Reading War Hospital.
FRENCH, Hon. Miss E., Military Mas. Cps.
FRIEND, K., Comdt., The Castle Aux. Hospital, Ryde.

w

FROST, J., N. Mem., Aux. Hos., Cromer, Norfolk.
FROST, M., Mil. Mas. Cps., Lancs.
FUDGER, M., Nurse, Ascot Aux. Hospital, Berks.
FULBROOK-LEGGATT, V., Nurse, Aux. Hospital, Reading.
FULLER, F., A. Nurse, Aux. Hospital, Oswestry, Salop.
FULLER, V., Exeter War Hospital.
FULLERTON, J., S. Nurse, Catterick Mil. Hospital.
FURLONG, E., 1st Western Gen. Hospital, Liverpool.

GADD, MRS. H., Comdt., Aux. Hos., Gravesend.
GAINS, H., Nurse, 1st Western Gen. Hospital, Liverpool.
GALE, M., Staff Nurse, Aux. Hospital, Middlesex.
GALL, E., Sister, 1st Southern Gen. Hospital, Worcs.
GALLAGHER, E., S. Nurse, 2nd Birmingham War Hospital, Northfield.
GALLAWAY, C., Nurse, R. Free Hospital, W.C.
GALLIE, H., 1st Western Gen. Hospital, Liverpool.
GALLOWAY, J., Comdt., No. 16 Aux. Hospital, Northumberland.
GAPE, MRS. K., Nurse, Aux. Hospital, St. Albans, Herts.
GARNET, L., Matron, Borough Isol. Hospital, Weymouth.
GARNETT, MRS. E., Nurse, Aux. Hospital, Clitheroe, Lancs.
GARNETT, M., Mil. Mas. Cps., London Com. Depot.
GARROD, J., Qrmr., Aux. Hos., Suffolk.
GARTIN, MRS. E., N. Mem., Aux. Hospital, Thorpe, Norfolk.
GARTSIDE, R., Sister, War Hospital, Keighley.
GASKELL, MRS. M., Nurse, Woolton Aux. Hospital, Lancs.
GASKIN, E., Matron, Aux. Hospital, Coventry.
GATES, M., Sister, Q. Alexandra's Hospital, Highgate.

GATES, M., Sister, Aux. " A " Cottage Hospital, Oswestry.
GAUL, U., Aux. Hospital, Town Close Lodge, Norwich.
GAY, F., S. Nurse, 4th London Gen. Hospital, Chelsea.
GAYTHEN, L., Sister, Aux. Hospital, Cheshire.
GEE, A., Mil. Mas. Cps., Eastern Com. Depot.
GEE, B., Asst. Nurse, Bermondsey Mil. Hospital, London.
GELL, C., Nurse, Aux. Hospital, Warwick.
GEM, G., 4th Northern Gen. Hospital, Lincoln.
GEORGE, A., Nurse, 1st London Gen. Hospital, Chelsea.
GEORGE, F., Trd. Nurse, 9, Cedars Road, Clapham Common.
GEORGE, MRS. J., 18th Durham Aux. Hospital, Hebhurn-on-Tyne.
GERMANY, E., Sister, Springfield War Hos., Upper Tooting, S.W.
GERRARD, J., Mc.C. Sister, St. Mary's Con. Aux. Hospital, York.
GERSTLEY, MRS. A., Comdt., Aux. Hospital for Officers, S.W.
GIBB, A., Nurse, Aux. Hospital, Timberley, Cheshire.
GIBBS, A., Nurse, Johnson Aux. Hospital, Lincoln.
GIBBS, MRS., Qrmr., 25th Durham Aux. Hospital, Ashburne.
GIBERT, E., Sister, 1st London Gen. Hospital, Chelsea.
GIBSON, MRS. J., Comdt., Con. Home, Westmorland.
GIBSON, MRS. L., Comdt., Seely Aux. Hospital, Newport.
GILL, E., Matron, Ear and Throat Hospital, Shrewsbury.
GILLIAT, M., N. Mem., Aux. Hospital, Norwich.
GILLOTT, M., Sister, Mil. Hospital, Sutton Veny, Wilts.
GILMOUR, I., Bermondsey Military Hospital, London.
GIMSON, M., Comdt., Witham Aux. Hospital, Essex.
GLADSTONE, MRS. M., Comdt., Barton Court Aux. Hos., Berks.
GLADWIN, J., A. Nurse, Mil. Hos., Catterick Camp, Yorks.

GLASS, G., Sister, Aux. Mil. Hospital, Liverpool.

GLOSSOP, E., N. Mem., Hill House Hospital, Guildford.

GLOSSOP, G., Nurse, Bricket House Aux. Hospital, Herts.

GLOVER, N., S. Nurse, 1st Southern Gen. Hospital, Birmingham.

GLOYER, MRS. B., Amb. Sister, Amb. Col. London District.

GODOLPHIN-OSBORNE, LADY, M., Nurse, 5, Nottingham Place, W.

GODSON, F., Nurse, Cheadle House Aux. Hospital, Cheshire.

GOLD, J., Nurse, Smithson War Hospital, Scotland.

GONIG, M., N. Mem., Littlehampton Aux. Hospital, Sussex.

GOOCH, LADY M., Comdt., Hylands Aux. Mil. Hospital, Chelmsford.

GOODALL, A., Comdt., 4, Lyndhurst Gardens, Hampstead.

GOODALL, A., Comdt., Aux. Hos., Lyndhurst Gdns., Hampstead.

GOODBODY, A., A.P. Mil. Mas. Cps., Aldershot.

GOODMAN, H., Nurse, Binefield, Oxted.

GOODWIN, F., S. Nurse, Huddersfield War Hospital.

GORDON, G., Mil. Mas. Cps., Irish Com. Dpt., Tipperary.

GORDON, L., Sister, Met. Hospital, London, N.E.

GORDON-BOYD, S. Nurse, No. 1, N.Z. Gen. Hos., Brockenhurst.

GORING, P., N. Mem., R. Vic. Hospital, Netley.

GOSCHEN, .M, The Mickie Aux. Hospital, London.

GOSDEN, M., Sister, Normanhurst Aux. Hospital, Sussex.

GOSDEN, M., Nurse, Malvern Aux. Hospital, Worcs.

GOSS, MRS. E., Supt., Palace Aux. Hospital, Gloucester.

GOSS, V., Nurse, The Priory Aux. Hospital, Cheltenham.

GOTCH, V., Aux. Hospital, Chigwell, Essex.

GOULD, M., N. Prob., Mil. Hospital, London, W.C.

GOULDBURNE, E., Sister, Mil. Hospital, Ripon.

GOWAN, G., Matron, Calne Aux. Hospital, Wilts.

GRAHAM, H., Nurse, No. 1, Reading War Hospital.

GRAHAM, K., Nurse, Aux. Hospital, Lady's Close, Watford.

GRANAGE, MRS., N. Mem., 4th Nth'd. Aux. Hos., Corbridge-on-Tyne.

GRANT, MRS. A., S. Nurse, 17, Durham Aux. Hospital, Durham.

GRAVES, L., 2nd Western Gen. Hospital, Manchester.

GREATHED, MRS. J., Qrmr.. Aux. Hospital, Waltham Abbey, Essex.

GREEN, A., Sister, Aux. Hospital, Frodsham, Cheshire.

GREEN, M., Prob., Bethnal Green Aux. Hospital.

GREEN, MRS. P., N. Mem., Aux. Hospital, Norfolk.

GREEN, W., Nurse, Wardown Aux. Hospital, Bedford.

GREENWOOD, E., Prob., Queen Mary's Mil. Hospital, Whalley.

GREGORY, M., Mem., Filsham Aux. Hospital, Sussex.

GREGORY, M., Nurse, Polefield Aux., Hospital, Prestwich.

GREGORY, R., Matron, Mil. Sec., Hampstead Gen. Hospital, N.

GREEN, B., S.-in-Charge, Badminton Aux. Hospital, Glos.

GREEN, MRS. M., Comdt., Aux. Hospital, Luton.

GREENLESS, M., African Hospital, Richmond Park, Surrey.

GREENWOOD, E., Nurse, Aux. Hospital, Cheadle.

GREY, LADY C., Qrmr., Aux. Hospital, Stourbridge.

GREY, H., Nurse, Aux. Hospital, Cheshire.

GREY, M., A.P., Mil. Mas. Cps., Com. Dpt., Heaton Park.

GRIFFITHS, H., Matron, Polefield Hospital, Prestwich.

GRIFFITHS, M., S. Nurse, 2nd Western Gen. Hospital, Manchester.

GRIMSHAW, MRS., Norton-sub-Hamden Aux. Hospital, Somerset.

GROOM, E., Sister, Lewisham Mil. Hospital, S.E.

GROUNDS, N., Matron, St. John Hospital, Cheltenham.

GURNEY, C., Qrmr.. Aux. Hospital, Norwich.
GURNEY, MRS. E., Comdt., Biggleswade Aux. Hospital, Beds.
GUTHRIE-SMITH, MRS. O., A.P. Mil. Mas. Cps., Lond. Com. Dpt.
GWILLIM, M., Marlborough Aux. Hospital, Wilts.

HABLUTZEL, R., Sister, Wharncliffe War Hospital.
HACKFORTH, B., S. Nurse, Aux. Hospital, Warwick.
HACON, H., S.-in-Charge, Aux. Hospital, Cranleigh.
HADDON, M., Sister, 1st Southern Gen. Hospital, Birmingham.
HADDON, L., Nurse, Aux. Hospital, Cheshire.
HAGGAR, L., Nurse, Aux. Hospital, Ipswich, Suffolk.
HAGUE, M., Mil. Mas. Cps., Woolwich.
HAIG, I., Kinmel Park Mil. Hospital, Rhyl.
HAILE, E., S. Nurse, Bethnal Green Mil. Hospital, E.
HAILSTONE, Z., Sister, 3rd Southern Gen. Hospital, Oxford.
HALAHAN, D., Mil. Mas. Cps., The Curragh.
HALES, M., N. Mem., Aux. Hospital, Letheringsett, Norfolk.
HALKITT, M., Matron, Aux. Hospital, Stafford.
HALL, A., Sister, Aux. Hospital, Stafford.
HALL, A., Sister, Charing Cross Hospital, London.
HALL, E., Sister, 1st Southern Gen. Hospital, Birmingham.
HALL, F., Trd. Nurse, Aux. Hospital, Birmingham.
HALL, G., 4th London Gen. Hospital, Chelsea.
HALL, K., Nurse, Naunton Aux. Hospital, Cheltenham.
HALL, M., 3rd London Gen. Hospital, Wandsworth.
HALL-HOUGHTON, A., A. Nurse, 2nd Southern Gen. Hos., Bristol.
HALL-WALKER, MRS. S., Comdt., Sussex Lodge, London, N.W.

HALLIWELL, MRS. J., Qrmr., Aux. Hospital, Gloucester.

HALMSHAW, M., Mil. Mas. Cps., Huddersfield War Hospital.

HAM, B., Nurse, Eye and Ear Infirmary, Liverpool.

HAMILTON, HON. MISS C., Dublin Castle Aux. Hospital, Dublin.

HAMILTON, D., Nurse, U.V.F. Hospital, Belfast.

HAMILTON, DUCHESS OF M., Comdt., Aux. Hospital, Suffolk.

HAMILTON-HOSKINS, L., Nurse, Rose Hill Aux. Hospital, Herts.

HAMILTON-RUSSELL, THE HON. MRS. O., No. 7, Aux. Hos., Durham.

HAMMOND, N., Graylingwell Mil. Hospital.

HAMPSON, D., Sister, N. Staffordshire Infirmary.

HANAN, S. Nurse, No. 2, N.Z., Gen. Hospital, Walton-on-Thames.

HANCOCK, MRS. A., S. Nurse, VI. Dur. Aux. Hospital, Durham.

HARDIMAN, MRS. E., Chippenham, Aux. Hospital, Wilts.

HARDING, MRS. E., Supt., Aux. Hospital, Willesden, London.

HARDY, A., Comdt., Convent Hospital, Sussex.

HARDY, E., Nurse, Gt. Northern Gen. Hospital, London, N.

HARFORD, MRS. R., Matron, Holt Aux. Hospital, Liverpool.

HARGREAVE, E., Prob. Mil. Hos., Mont Dore, Bournemouth.

HARGREAVES, MRS. E., N. Mem., Aux. Hospital, Sherborne.

HARGREAVES, G., Sister, War Hospital, Duston.

HARKER, MRS. M., Comdt., Aux. Hospital, Norwich.

HAROLD, G., Netley Aux. Hospital, Hants.

HAROLD, W., Sister, 3rd Western Gen. Hos., Newport Section.

HARPER, M., Nurse, Henham Hall, Wangford, Suffolk.

HARRIES, K., 1st London Gen. Hospital, Chelsea.

HARRIES, S., Nurse, Mil. Hospital, Pembroke Dock.

HARRIS, E., Nurse, Aux. Hospital, Cooden, Sussex.

HARRIS, E., Nurse, Upperton Aux. Hospital, Sussex.
HARRIS, E., Comdt., Aux. Hospital, Co. Dublin.
HARRIS, E., Sister, No. 1, N.Z., Gen. Hospital, Brockenhurst.
HARROP, F., Sister, Aux. Hospital, Aberford.
HARROWELL, L., A.P. Mil. Mas. Cps., Yorks.
HART, C., Sister, Chester R. Infirmary, Chester.
HART, MRS. S., Actg. Sister, No. IV. Sec. Grouped Hos., Exeter.
HARTLAND, D., Sister, Mil. Hospital, Ripon.
HARTLEY, K., A.P. Mil. Mas. Cps., 2nd Westn. Gen. Hos., Manchester.
HARVEY, C., 4th Southern Gen. Hospital, Plymouth.
HASLIP, V., Nurse, Red Cross Hospital, Middlesex.
HASLIP, V., Nurse, Hanworth Park Aux. Hospital, Middlesex.
HASTINGS, H., Sister, 4th Sec. Gen. Hospital, Glasgow.
HATCH, M., Nurse, Aux. Hospital, Southport.
HATCLIFFE, N., Aux. Hospital, Lincoln.
HATTERSLEY-SMITH, R., Aux. Hospital, Cheltenham.
HATTON, K., Sister, Aux. Hospital, Weir, Surrey.
HATTON, MRS. L., S.-in-Charge, Aux. Hospital, Rugeley.
HAWKINS, M., 2nd London Gen. Hospital, Chelsea.
HAY, E., Sister, Red Cross Hospital, Torquay.
HAY, M., Sister, 3rd Aust. Aux. Hospital.
HAY, M., Graylingwell Military Hospital.
HAYBITTEL, MRS. M., N. Mem., Cornelia Hospital, Poole.
HAYDEN, M., S.-in-Charge, Aux. Hospital, Bishop's Stortford.
HAYES, M., Matron, Aux. Hospital, Beachrock, Co. Dublin.
HEAL, M., Sister, Springfield War Hospital, Upper Tooting, S.W.
HEALEY, E., S.-in-Charge, Thame Aux. Hospital, Oxon.

HEATHER, L., Sister, R. National Orthopædic Hospital, W.

HEATLEY, E., Nurse, St. John's Aux. Hospital, Shrewsbury.

HEATON, H., 2nd Southern Gen. Hospital, Bristol.

HEBERT, H., Aux. Hospital, E. Dereham, Norfolk.

HEBER-PERCY. MRS. G., Comdt., Aux. Hospital, Hodnet.

HEIGHT, M., S.-in-Charge, Aux. Hospital, Malpas.

HELLENS, N., Mil. Hospital, Lewisham, S.E.

HELSHAM-JONES, A., Nurse, Aux. Hospital, Newbury.

HEMMING, M., Nurse, Aux. Hos., Shrewsbury, Salop.

HENDERSON, A., Lady Supt., Aux. Hospital, Leicester.

HENDERSON, E., Ngt. Supt., Keighley War Hospital, Yorks.

HENDERSON, B., S. Nurse, Yorkhill War Hospital, Lanark.

HENDERSON, M., Comdt., 3rd Aux. Hospital, Hexham, Northumbld.

HENDERSON, M., Mil. Mas. Cps., Com. Dpt., Ireland.

HENDRY, MRS. D., Prob., Attd. Mil. Hos., Fovant, Wilts.

HENRICI, M., Matron, Southport Cottage Hospital.

HENRY, R., W. Sister, Alder Hey Hospital, Liverpool.

HEPBURN, MRS. E., 1st Northn. Gen. Hos., Newcastle-on-Tyne.

HERBERT, A., No. 1 N.Z., Gen. Hospital, Brockenhurst.

HERBERT, M., Comdt., Fairlawn Aux. Hospital, London, S.E.

HERDMAN, O., Sister, Hampstead Lane, London, N.

HERRING, MRS. M., Comdt., 40, Weymouth Street, London, W.

HERRON, MRS. E., Actg. Sister, Hampstead Mil. Hospital.

HEWITT, MRS. E., N. Evington War Hospital, Leicester.

HEWLETT, M., Qrmr., Aux. Hospital, Norfolk.

HEYDE, MRS. E., Supt., Balgowan Aux. Hospital, Kent.

HEYGATE, K., N. Mem., Aux. Hospital, Norfolk.

HEYWOOD-LONSDALE, HON. MRS. M., Comdt., Aux. Hospital, Salop.
HEYWORTH, T., Comdt., Aux. Hospital, Essex.
HICKLEY, A., Sister, 3rd Northern Gen. Hospital, Sheffield.
HICKS, L., Sister, Aux. Hospital, Birmingham.
HIGGIN-BOTHAM, B., 2nd Western Gen. Hospital, Manchester.
HIGGINS, G., Nurse, Aux. Hospital, Much Hadham, Herts.
HILDEBRAND, G., N. Mem., Aux. Hospital, Dorchester.
HILEY, MRS. M., Comdt., Aux. Hospital, Lincoln.
HILL, A., S. Nurse, Mil. Hospital, W. Didsbury, Manchester.
HILL, A., Matron, Keighley War Hospital, Yorks.
HILL, M., N. Mem., Middlesex War Hospital, St. Albans.
HILL, M., Nurse and Actg. Qrmr., Aux. Hospital, Oxon.
HILL, N., N. Mem., Foye House Aux. Hospital, Bristol.
HILL-JOSEPH, MRS. G., Nurse, Aux. Hospital, Sussex.
HIMSCOOTE, MRS. M., Sister, Bermondsey Mil. Hospital, S.E.
HINGESTON-RANDULPH. G., E. Com. Dpt., Shoreham-by-Sea.
HINTON, MRS. K., Chippenham Aux. Hospital, Wilts.
HIRD, M., 1st London Gen. Hospital, Warwick.
HIRON, MRS. J., N. Mem., Aux. Hospital, Leamington, Warwick.
HIRST, MRS. E., Supt., Aux. Hospital, Worcs.
HIRST, L., Sister, Coventry Hospital, Coventry.
HITCHCOCK, E., 3rd Southern Gen. Hospital, Oxford.
HOADLEY, J., Matron, King George V. Hospital, Dublin.
HOAR, E., Nurse, Mil. Hospital, Ripon.
HOARE, M., Comdt., Hampstead Lane, N.
HOCKADAY, E., Lydney Aux. Hospital, Glos.
HOCKEY, M., Qrmr., Aux. Hospital, Gt. Yarmouth, Norfolk.

HODGES, MRS. L., Nurse, Percy House Aux. Hospital, Middlesex.
HODGES, M., Supt., Yeovil Aux. Hospital, Somerset.
HODGSON, A., S. Nurse, Aux. Hospital, Warwick.
HODGSON, E., A. Mem., Aux. Hospital, Birmingham.
HODSON, M., Woolton Aux. Hospital, Lancs.
HODSON, S., Prob., Mil. Hospital, Grimsby.
HOGARTH, A., N. Sister, No. 2 Can. Gen. Hospital, France.
HOGG, J., Sister-in-Charge, Aux. Hospital, Worcs.
HOGG, MRS. M., Qrmr., Aux. Hospital, Essex.
HOGGETT, N., Sister, Durham Aux. Hospital, Durham.
HOLBECHE, K., Malvern Aux. Hospital, Worcs.
HOLCOMBE, C., S. Nurse, 1st Western Gen. Hos., Liverpool.
HOLDSWORTH, E., N. Evington War Hospital, Leicester.
HOLE, D., N. Mem., Aux. Hos., Crewkerne, Somerset.
HOLLAND, M., S. Nurse, Didsbury Aux. Hospital, Lancs.
HOLLAND, M., A. Commdt. Naunton Aux. Hospital, Cheltenham.
HOLLEY, MRS. E., Aux. Hospital, Norfolk.
HOLLISTER, A., Nurse, Aux. Hospital, Droitwich, Worcs.
HOLLOWAY, M., Comdt., Aux. Hospital, Norfolk.
HOLLY, E., Sister, Prince of Wales's Hospital, Staines.
HOLMES, C., Prob. 2nd Birmingham War Hospital, Northfield.
HOLMES, MRS. E., Aux. Hospital, Norfolk.
HOLMES, H., Nurse, Aux. Hospital, Worcs.
HOLMES, G., Sister, 106, Jamaica Road, Bermondsey.
HOLT, M., Prob., Bethnal Green Mil. Hospital, E.
HOME, I., Qrmr., 13, Gros. Crescent Aux. Hospital, S.W.
HOOPER, A., Matron, No. V. Sec. Grouped Hospital, Exeter.

HOPKINS, F., Sister, 9, Grosvenor Gardens, S.W.

HOPPERTON, J., 3rd London Gen. Hospital, Wandsworth.

HOPTON, D., N. Mem., Aux. Hospital, Southampton.

HOPWOOD, E., Trd. Sister, 19th North'd. Aux. Hospital.

HORNE, F., Nurse, 5, Nottingham Place, W.

HORNER, MRS. A., Qrmr., Aux. Hos., Theydon Bois, Epping.

HOSKING, A., Prob., 2nd Birmingham War Hospital, Northfield.

HOW, F., Nurse, Aux. Hospital, Worcs.

HOWARD, E., N. Mem., Aux. Hospital, Norwich.

HOWARD, E., Nght. Supt., Nurse, Union Infirmary, Hartlepool.

HOWARD, MRS. K., Aux. Hospital, Timperley, Cheshire.

HOWARD, L., A. Qrmr., Stildon House Aux. Hospital, Sussex.

HOWARD, M., Matron, Crawley Cottage Hospital, Sussex.

HOWARD, M., Asst. S. Nurse, Norfolk War Hospital, Norwich.

HOWARD-SMITH, MRS. G., Comdt., Highbury Aux. Hos., Birmingham.

HOWARTH, M., Sister, The Welsh Met. War Hospital, Cardiff.

HOWE, R., Dresser, Southwood Aux. Hospital, Eltham.

HOWITT, H., Nurse, Aux. Hospital, Northumberland.

HOYLE, A., Sister, Fulham Mil. Hospital, W.

HUDDLESTONE, B., Sister, 3rd Western Gen. Hospital, Cardiff.

HUDSON, A., S. Nurse, Huddersfield War Hospital.

HUDSON, E., No. 6 Aux. Hospital, Northumberland.

HUDSPETH, MRS. J., S. Nurse, Aux. Hospital, Wallfields, Herts.

HUGH-JONES, P., Qrmr., Aux. Hospital, Denbighshire.

HUGH SMITH, K., Sec. Leader, St. J. A. B., Aux. Hos., Birmingham.

HUGHES, A., Actg. Sister, R. Southern Hos., Liverpool.

HUGHES, H., S. Nurse, Hahnemann Hospital, Liverpool.

HUGHES, M., N. Mem., Aux. Hospital, Anglesey.

HUGHES, M., Qrmr., Aux. Hospital, Ystrad, Denbigh.

HUGHES, M., S. Nurse, 5th Southern Gen. Hos., Portsmouth.

HUGHES, M., Matron, Froome Bank Aux. Hospital.

HUGHES, Sister, 3rd Southern Gen. Hospital, Oxford.

HUGHES-ONSLOW, D., Qrmr. and Nurse, Aux. Hospital, Yorks.

HULBERT, C., Sister, King George Hospital, S.E.

HULBERT, K., Nurse, Aux. Hospital, Salisbury.

HUMPHRIES, F., Mil. Hospital, Musters Road, Notts.

HUNT, A., Sister, Mile End Mil. Hospital, E.

HUNT, A., Comdt., Aux. Hospital, Baschurch, Salop.

HUNTER, D., Nurse, 10, Carlton House Terrace, W.

HURESTON, L., Sister, 184, Queen's Gate, W.

HUTCHISON, V., 4th Northern Gen. Hospital, Lincoln.

HUTCHISON, H., N. Mem., St. J.A.B., Aux. Hos., Newcastle-on-Tyne

HUTCHISON, N. B., Sister, Mil. Hospital, Weymouth.

HYNDMAN, D., Nurse, Aux. Hospital, Battle.

INGOLDBY, MRS. M., Comdt., Aux. Hospital, Louth, Lincoln.

INGRAM, B., Nurse, Aux. Hospital, Worcs.

INGRAM, R., Supt., Aux. Hospital, Ampton Hall, Suffolk.

INMAN, G., Sister, Huddersfield War Hospital.

INSTON, B., Sister, Aux. Hospital, Stafford.

ISAAC, A., N. Sister, St. John Hospital, Cheltenham, Glos.

ISAACS, A., Aux. Hospital, Brondesbury, London.

ISAACS, M., Comdt., 184, Queen's Gate, London.

IVES, R., Matron, Infec. Dis. Hospital, Dover.

IVESON, I., Qrmr., 3rd Aux. Hospital, Hexham, Northumberland.

JACK, I., N. Sister, Univ. War Hospital.

JACKLIN, D., Aux. Hospital, Herts.

JACKSON, A. de B., Matron, Aux. Hospital, Herefordshire.

JACKSON, D., Evington Ex. Hospital, Leicester.

JACKSON, D., Sister, Tranmere Hospital, Birkenhead.

JACKSON, D., N. Evington War Hospital, Leicester.

JACKSON, K., Supt., Aux. Hospital, Cheltenham.

JACKSON, I., Nurse, Aux. Hospital, Bexhill-on-Sea.

JACKSON, L., Sister, Welsh Met. War Hospital, Cardiff.

JACKSON, M., N. Mem., Aux. Hospital, Birkenhead.

JACOB, MRS. E., Qrmr., Hungerford Aux. Hospital, Berks.

JACQUES, E., St. James Aux. Hospital, Herts.

JAMES, A., Qrmr., Stroud Aux. Hospital, Glos.

JAMES, C., Nurse, Ashcombe House, Weston-super-Mare.

JAMES, H., Nurse, Founders Col. Aux. Hospital, Ackworth, Yorks.

JAMES, M., Sister, No. 14, Aux. Hospital, Montgomery.

JAMESON, MRS. A., Nurse, Aux. Hospital, Beds.

JAMESON, MRS. L., Comdt., The Convent, Rye.

JAMESON, MRS. M., Nurse, Ascot Aux. Hospital, Berks.

JAMIESON, L., Prob. No. 2 N.Z., Gen. Hospital, Walton-on-Thames.

JASPER, E., Matron, Aux. A. Cottage Hospital, Oswestry.

JEFFREYS, K., Sister, The Welsh Met. War Hospital, Cardiff.

JEMMITT-BROWNE, G., N. Mem. Aux. Hospital, Warwick.

JENKINS, B., Nurse, Struan Aux. Hospital, Reading.

JENKINS, I., Prob., Attd. Mil. Hospital, Fovant.

JENNINGS, MRS. I., Comdt., Aux. Hospital, Northampton.

JERMY, R., Asst. S. Nurse, Norfolk War Hospital, Norwich.

Johns, A., A. Qrmr., Hornsea Aux. Hospital, Yorks.

Johnson, D., A.P. Mil. Mas. Cps., Com. Dpt., Heaton Park.

Johnson, G., R. Naval Hospital, Hull.

Johnson, G., Trd., Nurse, Town Hall Aux. Hospital, Essex.

Johnson, I., Nurse, Mil. Hospital, Surrey.

Johnson, M., King George Mil. Hospital, London.

Johnson, W., Spec. Prob., War Hospital, Lanark.

Johnston, J., Sister, Graylingwell Mil. Hospital.

Johnston, M., Sur. Sister, Aux. Hos., Gt. Langhall, Cheshire.

Johnston, Mrs. R., Sister, Aux. Mil. Hospital, Liverpool.

Johnstone, Hon. Mrs. R., S. Nurse, War Hospital, London, W.

Jollands, Mrs. B., S. Nurse, Aux. Hospital, Wallfields, Herts.

Jones, C., Nurse, 45, Devonshire St., W.

Jones, D., Sister, 1st Southern Gen. Hospital, Birmingham.

Jones, E., Night. Sister, Welsh Met. Hospital, Cardiff.

Jones, E., 3rd Western Gen. Hospital, Cardiff.

Jones, E., Matron, Aux. Hospital, Oxford.

Jones, H., S. Nurse, 3rd Western Gen. Hospital, Cardiff.

Jones, Mrs. E., Lady Supt., Aux. Hospital, Staffs.

Jones, E., Matron, Wingfield Aux .Hospital, Oxford.

Jones, H., 1st Eastern Gen. Hospital, Cambridge.

Jones, M., Sister, Bethnal Green Mil. Hospital, E.

Jones, M., Cannock Chase Mil. Hospital, Staffs.

Jones, R., 2nd London Gen. Hospital, Chelsea.

Jones, R., Matron, The Guest Hospital, Dudley.

Joyce, E., Nurse, St. Anne's Aux. Hospital, Caversham.

Joyce, L., Prob., 1st Southern Gen. Hospital, Birmingham.

JOYCE, M., Prob., 1st Southern Gen. Hospital, Birmingham.
JULIAN, A., Mil. Mas. Cps., Mil. Orthopædic Hospital, London.
JULL, MRS. E., N. Evington War Hospital, Leicester.
JUPP, MRS. D., Nurse, Syon Red Cross Hospital, Brentford.

KATTERICK, A., Nurse, Aux. Hospital, Lancs.
KEARNEY, M., Sister, St. Andrew's Hospital, Dollishill.
KEORY, M., Red Cross Hospital, Torquay.
KEATES, C., Nurse, Hampstead Lane, N.W.
KEATS, A., N. Mem., Colliton Aux. Hospital, Dorchester.
KEELING, MRS. F., Nurse, Aux. Hospital, Norfolk.
KEENE, B., Comdt., Aux. Hospital, Denbighshire.
KELLS, M., Sister, R. Vic. Hospital, Belfast.
KEMBLE, MRS. A., Qrmr., Aux. Hos., East Lodge, Crawley Down.
KEMBLE, K., Qrmr., Struan Aux. Hospital, Reading.
KEMPE, R., Graylingwell Mil. Hospital.
KENDALL, A., Supt., Abbey Mnr., Aux. Hospital, Worcs.
KENDALL, E., Nurse, Aux. Hospital, Rainhill, Nr. Liverpool.
KENDALL, L., Exeter Grouped Hospital.
KENNEDY, A., 1st London Gen. Hospital, Chelsea.
KENNEDY, K., Nurse, U.V.F., Hospital, Belfast.
KENT, M., Mil. Mas. Cps., Com. Dpt., Alnwick.
KENYON-SLANEY, S., Nurse, Aux. Hospital, Shifnal, Salop.
KERMAN, E., S. Nurse, Cen. Mil. Hospital, Fort Pitt.
KERSHAW, M., S. Nurse, Mil. Hospital, Pembroke Dock.
KETTLE, L., Aux. Hospital, Winchmore Hill, Middlesex.
KING, B., Sister, East Sussex Aux. Hospital, Hastings.

KING, E., Mil. Mas. Cps., Southern Com. Dpt., Ireland.
KING, G., Nurse, Ampthill Aux. Hospital, Beds.
KING, MRS. K., N. Sister, Ear Hospital, Folkestone.
KINGHAM, N., Nurse, Aux. Hospital, Lady's Close, Watford.
KINGSBURY, MRS. M., Sister, Mil. Hospital, Grantham.
KING-SMITH, M., Nurse, Aux. Hospital, Watford, Herts.
KINMOND, N., 2nd Western Gen. Hospital, Manchester.
KINNEAR, F., S. Nurse, Queen Mary's Mil. Hospital, Whalley.
KINROSS, G., Sister, Mil. Hospital, Cannock Chase, Staffs.
KIRK, M., Matron, Woodclyffe Aux. Hospital, Wargrave, Berks.
KIRKLAND, J., Prob., Hursley Park Mil. Hospital, Winchester.
KITCHENER, M., Nurse, Lady Ridley's Hospital, London.
KITSON, MRS. E., N. Sister, St. John's Hospital, Cheltenham.
KNAPTON, E., Matron, School House, Lewes.
KNIGHT, A., Aux. Hospital, Coombe Lodge, Colchester.
KNIGHT, M., Aux. Hospital, West Dene, St. Leonards-on-Sea.
KRABBE, H., N. Mem., Northlands Aux. Hospital, Emsworth.

LABBETT, E., N. Mem., No. 1, Grouped Hospital, Exeter.
LACE, T., Qrmr., Chelsea Aux. Hospital, London, S.W.
LAING, MRS. C., Matron, Ardwick Div. Aux. Hospital, Manchester.
LAMBE, G., S.-in-Charge, Aux. Hospital, Corbridge-on-Tyne.
LAMBERT, L., Nurse, 17th Aux. Hospital, Whittingham.
LAMBERT, M., Sister, Cornelia Hospital, Poole.
LAMBTON-GIBSON, E., Sister, Aux. Hospital, Suffolk.
LAMOTTE, D., Seeley Aux. Hospital, Newport, I. of W.
LANCASTER, B., Sister, New End Sect., Hampstead.

LANCHESTER, C., Nurse, Aux. Hospital, Cooden, Sussex.

LANE, E., 2nd Western Gen. Hospital, Manchester.

LANG, D., Nurse, Red Cross Hospital, Richmond.

LANGDON, NURSE, Aux. Hospital, Nr. Liverpool, Lancs.

LANGFORD, M., S. Nurse, Didsbury Aux. Hospital, Didsbury.

LANGLEY, C., Nurse, 1st Eastern Gen. Hospital, Cambridge.

LANGLEY, MRS. E., Nurse, Cornelia Hospital, Poole.

LANGMAN, THE HON. MRS. E., Aux. Hospital, Wincanton.

LARDELLI, F., Nurse, Sec. 3, Reading War Hospital.

LARGE, E., Nurse, Marsden Green Aux. Hospital, Warwick.

LARKWORTHY, F., Nurse, Gt. Northern Gen. Hospital, London, N.

LASCELLES, M., Nurse, Aux. Hospital, Forest Row, Sussex.

LASLETT, G., Sister Supt., Aux. Hospital, Essex.

LAUGHTON, Hampstead Lane, N.

LAWLEY, HON. I., Nurse, 5, Nottingham Place, W.

LAURENCE, MRS. C., Matron and Qrmr., Aux. Hospital, Norfolk.

LAWRENCE, G., Sister, War Hospital, Upper Tooting, S.W.

LAWSON, C., Matron, Aux. Hospital, Reading.

LAWSON, J., Nurse, R. Victoria Hospital, Folkestone.

LAWTON, D., Qrmr., Aux. Hospital, Sussex.

LAWTON, Sister, Mil. Hospital, Endell Street, W.C.

LAY, L., Qrmr., Kempston Aux. Hospital, Sussex.

LAYCOCK, M., Staff Nurse, 3rd Western Gen. Hos., Newport.

LAYLAND BARRATT, D., Nurse, Aux. Hospital, Norfolk.

LAYTON, H., S. Nurse, Alexandra Hospital, Cosham.

LAYTON, M., Mil. Mas. Cps., 3rd London Gen. Hos., Wandsworth.

LEA, B., Comdt., Aux. Hospital, Hereford.

LEAH, MRS. G., S.-in-Charge, Stoke Newington Hospital, London.
LEATHAM, M., Stapleton Park Aux. Hospital, Yorks.
LEATHER, MRS. E., Comdt., Aux. Hospital, Hereford.
LEE, D., Cook, Aux. Hospital, Pontefract, Yorks.
LEE, I., S. Nurse, Union Infirmary, Hartlepool.
LEE, M., Comdt., Aux. Hospital, Clapham-Common.
LEECH, E., Prob., 2nd Birmingham War Hospital, Northfield.
LEEDER, C., Nurse, Broadwater Aux. Hospital, Ipswich.
LEEKE, U., A. Comdt., Aux. Hospital, Leamington.
LEGGE, L., Sister, Endsleigh Palace Hospital, N.W.
LEIGH-PEMBERTON, E., Nurse, 5th Southern Gen. Hos., Portsmouth.
LEIGHTON, Qrmr., Aux. Hospital, Cheltenham.
LEITCH, M., Mil. Mas. Cps., Croydon War Hospital.
LEITH-MURRAY, MRS. D., Qrmr., Aux. Hospital, Holyhead.
LEMAY, MRS. E., Nurse, Aux. Hospital, Norwood, S.E.
LENNAN, A., Mil. Hospital, The Curragh, Dublin.
LE MESSURIER, S. Nurse, 1st Aust. Aux. Hospital.
LENG, M., Sen. Nurse, Union Infirmary, Hartlepool.
LENNOX, E., Matron, Waveney Hospital, Ireland.
LEON, M., N. Mem., Red Cross Hospital, Torquay.
LESLIE, L., Qrmr., Aux. Hospital, Lindfield, Sussex.
LETT, E., Sister, Mile Road, Liverpool.
LENCHARS, J., Nurse, 6, Grosvenor Place, W.
LEVEY, MRS. C., A. Qrmr., Summerlee Aux. Hospital, Middlesex.
LEVITT, M., N. Sister, St. John's Hospital, Lewisham, S.E.
LEWIN, MRS. L., Comdt., St. Mary's Aux. Hospital, Bromley.
LEWIS, MRS. F., Aux. Hospital, Llandovery.

LEWIS, MRS. M., Nurse, Aux. Hospital, Hereford.

LEWIS, M., Kinmel Park Mil. Hospital, Rhyl.

LEWIS, M., Nurse, Ley Aux. Hospital, Cheshire.

LINCHAM, MRS. F., Matron, St. John's Aux. Hos., Nr. Chester.

LINDSAY, F., N. Mem., 5th Northern Gen. Hospital, Leicester.

LINDSAY, J., Sister, Cornelia Hospital, Poole.

LINTOLL, W., S.-in-Charge, Aux. Hospital, Roehampton.

LINTON, L., Prob., Mil. Hospital, Mont Dore, Bournemouth.

LINTON, L., Mil. Mas. Cps., R. Vic. Hospital, Netley.

LISTER, N., N. Mem., Aux. Hospital, Rutland.

LITTLE, F., Nurse, Lutterworth, Warwick.

LITTLEWOODS, A., Sec. Lead., Clayton Aux. Hospital, Wakefield.

LIVESEY, Sister, No. 1 N.Z., Gen. Hospital, Brockenhurst.

LLOYD, G., Univ. War Hospital, Southampton.

LLOYD, K., Matron, 1st Southern Gen. Hospital, Birmingham.

LLOYD, S., Nurse, 3rd London Gen. Hospital, Wandsworth.

LLORD PARRY, B., Qrmr., Aux. Hospital, Mold, Flints.

LOAKES, MRS. G., Sister, Aux. Hospital, Cawston, Norfolk.

LOCKE-KING, MRS. E., Brooklands Aux. Hospital, Weybridge.

LODGE, M., Nurse, Aux. Hospital, Woodhall Spa.

LONG, A., Matron, Aux. Hospital, Cliff House, Norfolk.

LONG, K., Aux. Hospital, Wincanton, Somerset.

LONGSON, M., Mil. Mas. Cps., 5th Northern Gen. Hos., Leicester.

LOONEY, E., A. Matron, Borough Hospital, Birkenhead.

LORICK, M., Nurse, Ware Aux. Hospital, Herts.

LOUSADA, F., Nurse, 3rd Durham Aux. Hospital, Sunderland.

LOVETT, I., Matron, Mil. Hospital, Park Hill Cmp., Oswestry.

LOW, E., Nurse, Hungerford Aux. Hospital, Berks.

LOWRY, C., Nurse, 1st Western Gen. Hospital, Liverpool.

LOWSON, E., S. Nurse, 3rd Sco. Gen. Hospital, Glasgow.

LOXSTON, E., S.-in-Charge, Aux. Hospital, Mayfield, Sussex.

LOYNES, H., Nurse, Aux. Hospital, Norwich.

LUMLEY, MRS. E., Matron, Aux. Hospital, Talbot's Inch, Kilkenny.

LYE, A., Supt., Birch Hill Hospital, Rochdale.

LYNDON, J., Nurse, Mil. Hospital, Lincoln.

LYNN, D., Mil. Hospital, Lewisham.

LYON, A., Nurse, Hornsea Aux. Hospital, Yorks.

LYON, L., Asst. S. Nurse, Norfolk War Hospital, Norwich.

LYON, MRS. M., Qrmr., Aux. Hospital, Wimborne.

LYTHGOE, MRS. L., Supt., Aux. Hospital, Crewe, Cheshire.

MACALISTER, C., Matron, Can. Officers Hospital, Broadstairs.

MACALISTER, M., MacD. Qrmr., Aux. Hospital, Cambridge.

McALLISTER, W., N. Mem., Aux. Hos., Ingham Old Hall, Norwich.

MACBETH, C., Nurse, R. Vic. Hospital, Folkestone.

McCALL, MRS. D., Nurse, Aux. Hospital, Sussex.

MacCALL, J., S. Nurse, 2nd Western Gen. Hos., Manchester.

McCARTHY, H., A. Matron, Waterloo and District Hospital, Lancs.

McCAUSLAND, B., Nurse, 16, Bruton Street, W.

MacCAUSLAND, D., 4th Southern Gen. Hospital, Plymouth.

McCLEARY, A., Nurse, Aux. Hospital, Cheadle.

McCOSH, J., 2nd Southern Gen. Hospital, Bristol.

McCREERY, MRS. E., Qrmr., Greenhill Aux. Hospital, Sherborne.

MacDERMOTT, A., S.-in-Charge, Aux. Hospital, Brondesbury.

MACDONALD, A., N. Sister, No. 9, Can. Stat. Hospital, Bramshott·
McDONALD, O., Prob., Mil. Hospital, Yorks.
McDONALD, F., S. Nurse, Mil. Hos., Kinmel Park, Denbighshire.
MacDONALD, M., S.-in-Charge, Aux. Hos., Potter's Bar, Herts.
MACDONALD, M., House Sister, Welsh Met. War Hos., Nr. Cardiff.
MACDONALD, M., Matron, Con. Hospital, Cross-in-Hand, Sussex.
MacDONELL, H., Sister, Met. Hospital, Kingsland Road, N.E.
McELLEN, A., Nght. Supt., Aux. Hospital, Nr. Wigan.
McEWEN, MRS. I., Sis. Aux. Hos., Atd. 1st Sthn. Gen. Hos., Brmgm.
McFARLANE, A., Matron, Kidderminster Infirmary.
McFADDEN, K., 1st Western Gen. Hospital, Liverpool.
McGAW, J., S. Nurse, R. Free Hospital, W.C.
McGAW, M., Nurse, Mil. Hospital, Surrey.
McGOVERN, A., Nurse, Hartlepools Hospital.
McGOVERN, Sco. Gen. Hospital, Glasgow.
McHARDY, A., N. Mem., Aux. Hospital, Petersfield, Hants.
McHUGH, N., Sister, 48, Bryanston Square, W.
MacINTOSH, Mil. Hospital, Lewisham, S.E.
McINTYRE, M., S. Nurse, 4th Sco. Gen. Hospital, Glasgow.
McINTYRE, R., East Leeds War Hospital.
MacISAAC, Matron, No. 9 Can. Stat. Hospital, Bramshott.
McKEE, N. Sister, Westcliffe Can. Hospital, Folkestone.
MACKERDY, M., Spec. Prob., Gen. Mil. Hospital, Colchester.
MacKENZIE, B., Sister, Infirmary and District, Bolton.
MACKENZIE, C., N. Sister, No. 9 Can. Stat. Hospital, Bramshott.
MACKENZIE, E., Qrmr., New Court Aux. Hospital, Cheltenham.
MacKENZIE, J., Sister, Mile End, Mil. Hospital, E.

MACKERN, G., Nurse, De Walden Court Aux. Hospital, Eastbourne.
MACKINNON, L., Matron, 184, Queen's Gate, S.W.
McKINSTRY, L., Qrmr., Beach Aux. Hospital, Holyhead.
McLACHIE, MRS. M., Prob., Pollock's Hospital, London, W.
McLAREN, E., Sister, Crumpsall Infirmary, Manchester.
MacLEAN, MRS. L., N. Mem., War Hospital, Napsbury, St. Albans.
MACLEAR, E., Hdqrs., Mil. Mas. Cps.
MacLEOD, J., Sister, 1st Southern Gen. Hos., Birmingham.
McLUCKIE, A., 3rd Sco. Gen. Hospital, Glasgow.
McMILLAN, M., Sister, 4th Sco. Gen. Hospital, Glasgow.
MacNAB, A., Prob., King George Hospital, S.E.
McNAB, A., Actg. Matron, Cober Hill Hospital, Yorks.
MACNAMARA, MRS. H., Qrmr., Aux. Hospital, Southampton.
McNAUGHT, MRS. S., Comdt. and Matron, Aux. Hos., Bootle, Lancs.
McNAUGHTON, G., Nurse, Princess Christian's Hos., London.
McNELLY, M., W. Sister, Aux. Hospital, Nr. Wigan.
McPHERSON, L., Sister, The Coulter Hospital, London, W.
MacPHERSON, L., S. Nurse, Stoke-on-Trent War Hospital, Staffs.
MacRAE, C., Sister, Woodside Cen. Hospital, Lanark.
MacRAE, M., Matron, Heatherdene, Harrogate.
McSWEENEY, S., Sister, New End Sec., Hampstead.
McVICKER, J., Prob., 1st Birmingham War Hospital, Worcs.
MABERLEY, M., Lancs. Aux. Hospital, Worsley.
MADDEN, A., Hd. Sister, Eccleston Hospital, London, S.W.
MADDISON, P., 1st Eastern Gen. Hospital, Cambridge.
MADDISON GREEN, MRS. C., Nurse, Aux. Hospital, Herts.
MAGGS, MRS. F., Nurse, Goring Aux. Hospital, Oxon.

MAGNESS, R., N. Sister, I.O.D.E. Hospital.

MAGNOR, MRS. F., Comdt., Hylands Aux. Hospital, Writtle.

MAHON, MRS. L., Comdt., V.A.D. Hospital, Norwich.

MAJOR, A., S.-in-Charge, Aux. Hospital, Belfast.

MANCHESTER, N. Sister, King's Can. Con. Hos., Bushey Park.

MANN, G., Sister, London Hospital.

MANN, K., Sister, U.V.F. Hospital, Belfast.

MANN, W., A. Nurse, 2nd Northern Gen. Hospital, Leeds.

MANN, MRS. M., Sister, Welsh Met. War Hospital, Cardiff.

MANNERS, LADY D., Rutland Hospital.

MANNING, E., Prob., 1st Birmingham War Hospital, Worcs.

MANSFIELD, H., Mil. Prob., Univ. War Hospital, Southampton.

MARGERISON, E., 1st Southern Gen. Hospital, Birmingham.

MARGERISON, E., Prob. 1st Southern Gen. Hospital, Birmingham.

MARKHAM, MRS. E., Qrmr., Aux. Hospital, Woodford Green, Essex.

MAROTT, D., 1st Southern Gen. Hospital, Birmingham.

MARRIAGE, H., Aux. Hospital, Ongar, Essex.

MARX, G., 2nd Western Gen. Hospital, Manchester.

MARSDEN, E., S. Nurse, R. Vic. Hospital, Netley.

MARSDEN, MRS. E., Matron, Aux. Hospital, Brondesbury.

MARSDEN, MRS. J., Sec. Ldr., Aux. Hospital, Lancs.

MARSDEN, MRS. I., A. Qrmr., Red Cross Hospital, Torquay.

MARSDEN, W., Comdt., Aux. Hospital, Dorchester.

MARSH, MRS. A., Rochester Priv. Hospital.

MARSHALL, MRS. A., Aux. Hospital, Lincoln.

MARSHALL, MRS. A., No. 2 Birmingham War Hospital, Northfield.

MARSHALL, B., Aux. Hospital, Lincoln.

MARSHALL, E., Sister, S. Matron, St. John Hospital, Southport.
MARSHALL, H., Qrmr., Aux. Hospital, Waltham Abbey, Essex.
MARSHALL, MRS. J., Sister, Sco. Nat. Red Cross Hospital, Bella.
MARSLAND, H., Sister, 4th Southern Gen. Hospital, Plymouth.
MARSTON, D., Comdt., Aux. Hospital, Ludlow, Salop.
MARSTON, M., Sister, London Hospital.
MARTIN, E., 1st Officer, Aux. Hospital, Dublin.
MARTINDALE, MRS. E., Comdt., Aux. Hospital, Westmoreland.
MARY, H., Mil. Orthopædic Hospital, London.
MASON, MRS. E., Actg. Matron, Naval Aux. Hospital, Cornwall.
MASON, M., Spec. War Prob., Mil. Hospital, Chatham.
MATANLE, MRS. F., Qrmr., Aux. Hospital, Yorks.
MATHER, H., 1st Southern Gen. Hospital, Birmingham.
MATHER, M., S. Nurse, Stanley Hospital, Lanarkshire.
MATHEWS, C., S.-in-Charge, No. 5 Aust. Aux. Hospital, Welwyn.
MATTINGLY, D., Trowbridge Aux. Hospital, Wilts.
MAUDE, E., Matron, Underwarth Aux. Hospital, I. of W.
MAUDSLEY, M., Sister, Salford Union Hospital, Manchester.
MAUDSLEY, M., 2nd Grade Mil. Con. Hospital, Eastern Com.
MAUGHAN, S., Mil. Hospital, Tidworth.
MAUNDERS, C., East Leeds War Hospital.
MAWBY, L., Comdt., Aux. Hospital, Northampton.
MAWDSLEY, J., W. Sister, Alder Hey Hospital, Liverpool.
MAWSON, MRS. A., Sister, War Hospital, Upper Tooting, S.W.
MAXWELL, MRS. N., S. Nurse, Aux. Hospital, London.
MAY, MRS. K., Comdt., Aux. Hospital, Hampstead Heath.
MAYALL, S., Mil. Hospital, Winchester.

z

MAYNARD, O., S.-in-Charge, Roehampton Aux. Hospital.

MAYO, K., Nurse, Cornelia Hospital, Poole.

MAYORS, A., S.-in-Charge, Ld. Dunleath's Hospital, Ballywater.

MAYS, C., S. Nurse, Cornelia Aux. Hospital, Poole.

MEADE, S., War Hospital, Bath.

MEADOWS, E., Matron, Wolverhampton.

MEESON, E., Nurse, Gen. and Aux. Hospital, Chelmsford.

MEGSON, I., Nurse, E. Lancs. Aux. Hospital, Worsley.

MELLERSH, C., Nurse, 11, Palace Green, W.

MELLOR, A., S. Nurse, Didsbury Aux. Hos., Didsbury, Lancs.

MELVILLE, E., N. Mem., War Hospital, Lanark.

MELVIN, P., A. Nurse, War Prob., North'd. War Hospital, Gosforth.

MENDELSSOHN, M,. N.Z., Con. Hos., Hornchurch.

MENZIES, N., Theatre Nurse, Aux. Hospital, Southall, Middlesex.

METTERR, M., Nurse Aux. Hospital, Herts.

MERRET, M., Croydon War Hospital.

MERRITT, E., Prob., Tarporley, Cheshire.

MESS, M., Dundee War Hospital.

MIDDLETON, M., Prob. Nurse, Wharncliffe War Hos., Sheffield.

MILDRED, E., Matron, St. John Hospital, Southport.

MILLAR, D., Comdt., Aux. Hospital, Co. Dublin.

MILLER, C., Sister, Clock House, Chelsea.

MILLER, E., S.-in-Charge, Aux. Hospital, Lindfield.

MILLER, G., Sister, Aux. Hospital, Essex.

MILLER, H., Actg. Sister, No. 4 Sect., Grouped Hos., Exeter.

MILLER-HALLETT, W., N. Mem., R. Vic. Hospital, Netley.

MILLS, M., Sister, 1st Southern Gen. Hospital, Birmingham.

MILWARD, N., Prob., 1st Southern Gen. Hospital, Birmingham.

MOAKSON, C., Staff, Southern Gen. Hospital, Oxford.

MOGGIE, M., S. Nurse, 10, Palace Green, W.

MOIR, J., Sister, Adelaide Hospital, Dublin.

MONCK, L., Comdt., Heatherside Aux. Hospital, Wellington Col.

MONCK-MASON, E., Prob. Nurse, Mil. Hospital, Winchester.

MONCKTON, L., No. 2 N.Z. Gen. Hospital, Walton-on-Thames.

MONTAGUE, A., Sister, R. Vic. Hos., Belfast.

MONTFORD, C., Qrmr., No. 14 Aux. Hospital, Montgomery.

MONTFORD, E., Matron & Comdt., Aux. Hospital, Montgomery.

MOON, E., S. Nurse, Norfolk War Hospital, Thorpe.

MOORE, E., Sister, R. Salop Infirmary, Shrewsbury.

MOORE, C., N. Mem., Aux. Hospital, Rutland.

MOORE, G., Sister, Cameron Hos., W. Hartlepool.

MOORE, M., 1st Sco. Gen. Hospital, Old Mill.

MOORE, N., Aux. Hospital, Bray, Co. Wicklow.

MOORE, W., St. Nicholas, Harrogate.

MOORES, N., Sister, Stepping Hill Hospital, Stockport.

MOORHOUSE, E., Brookfield House Aux. Hospital, Cheshire.

MORFEY, D., Spev. Prob., R. Herbert Hospital, Woolwich.

MORGAN, G., Nurse, Aux. Hospital, Hendon, Middlesex.

MORGAN, G., 3rd Western Gen. Hospital, Cardiff.

MORGAN, N., Sister, The Infirmary, Rochdale.

MORLEY, J., A. Nurse, War Prob., North'd. War Hos., Gosforth.

MORLEY, MRS. O., Actg. Nurse, Tooting Mil. Hospital, S.W.

MORRISON, S., Nurse, Aux. Hospital, 17, Breeze Hill, Lancs.

MORSHEAD, B., Exeter War Hospital.

MORTIMER, MRS. R., Qrmr., Exeter Grouped Hospital.

MORTON, MRS. F., Actg. Matron, Mil. Hospital, Scarborough.

MORTON, J., Mil. Hospital, Endell Street.

MORTON, S., 3rd Sco. Gen. Hospital, Glasgow.

MOSTYN, LADY M., Comdt., Aux. Hospital, Holywell.

MOULD, MRS. E., Comdt., Aux. Hospital, Colwyn Bay.

MOUNT, E., Qrmr., Edmonton Aux. Hospital, Middlesex.

MOUNTFIELD, M., N. Mem., Aux. Hospital, Norwich.

MOWBRAY, C., N. Sister, C.A.M.C.I.O.D.E. Hospital.

MOYLE, E., 1st Southern Gen. Hospital, Stourbridge Sec.

MULLALLY, A., A. Matron, Aux. Hospital, Bray, Co. Wicklow.

MULLALLY, M., S. Nurse, King George V. Hospital, Dublin.

MUNRO, M., Matron, Aux. Hospital, Swanley.

MUNRO, M., Prob., Nurse, Gen. Military Hospital, Edmonton.

MURDOCH, MRS. A., Aux. Hos., under 2nd Eastn. Gen. Hos. Brighton.

MURGATROYD, B., Qrmr., Aux. Hos., Colwyn Bay, N. Wales.

MURRAY, A., Sister, Mil. Hospital, Mont Dore, Bournemouth.

MURRAY, E., Sister, Aux. Hospital, Willesden, London.

MURRAY, I., Nurse, Aux. Hospital, Balcombe, Sussex.

MURRAY, M., Sister, Aux. Hospital, Timperley, Cheshire.

MURRAY-BROWNE, O., 1st Western Gen. Hospital, Liverpool.

MUSGROVE, E., Sister, No. 2 Sect.. Grouped Hospital, Exeter.

MUSSETT, E., Matron, Miller Gen. Hospital, Greenwich.

MUSSON, E., Princ. Matron, 1st Southern Gen. Hos., Birmingham.

MUSTARD, R., Sister, 4th Sco. Gen. Hospital, Glasgow.

NAPIER-MILES, MRS. S., Comdt., Aux. Hospital, Gloucester.

NASH, F., N. Mem., War Hospital, Guildford.

NASH, H., N. Mem., Aux. Hospital, Weymouth.

NASH, M., Marlborough Aux. Hospital, Wilts.

NEALE, MRS. C., Qrmr., Aux. Hospital, Hewell, Worcs.

NEALE, M., Aux. Hospital, Hastings, Sussex.

NEAME, M., Nurse, Aux. Hospital, Hampstead.

NEAVE, S., A. Staff Nurse, War Hospital, Norwich.

NEILAN, MRS. S., 22nd Durham Aux. Hospital, New Seaham.

NELSON, M., Mile End Mil. Hospital.

NESBITT, Matron, Shorncliffe Mil. Hospital.

NEW, M., Theatre Nurse, Aux. Hospital, Worcs.

NEWBURY, E., Aux. Hospital, Battle, Sussex.

NEWITT, I., Nurse, Aux. Hospital, Northampton.

NEWLANDS, I., Theatre Sister, 5, Nottingham Place, W.

NEWMAN, E., Southwood Aux. Hospital, Eltham.

NEWPORT, E., 2nd Western Gen. Hospital, Manchester.

NEWSON, A., N. Mem., Aux. Hos., Calton Hall, Norwich.

NEWTON, G., Bethnal Green Mil. Hospital.

NICCOLL-SEARANCKE, C., Mil. Com. Hospital, Blackpool.

NICHOLLS, E., Prob., No. 2 N.Z. Gen. Hospital, Walton-on-Thames.

NICHOLLS, R., Sister, 8, Lennox Gardens, S.W.

NICHOLLS, MRS. M., Office of Co. Director, Dorset.

NICHOLS, MRS. M., Supt., Aux. Hospital, Banff.

NICHOLSON, E., Mil. Mas. Cos., Mil. Hospital, Dover.

NICHOLSON, H., Nurse, Tooting Mil. Aux. Hospital, S.W.

NICHOLSON, J., S. Nurse, Cen. Mil. Hospital, Belfast.

NICOL, A., N. Mem., Yorkhill War Hospital, Lanarkshire.

NICOL, G., Sister, Cumberland Infirmary, Carlisle.
NIGGERMAN, H., St. J. A. A. 1st Western Gen. Hospital, Liverpool.
NIGHTINGALE, F., Nurse, Hornbrook Aux. Hospital, Chislehurst.
NIGHTINGALE, R., Nurse, Timberhurst Aux. Hospital, Bury.
NIVEN, A., W. Sister, Mill Road, Liverpool.
NIXON, A., S. Nurse, Northumberland War Hos., Gosforth.
NIXON, A., Nurse, Hartlepool Hospital.
NOBLE, M., Sister, No. 1 Sect. Grouped Hospital, Exeter.
NOLAN, L., Nurse, 5th Southern Gen. Hospital, Portsmouth.
NORBURY, M., N. Mem., 2nd Western Gen. Hospital, Manchester.
NORMAN, A., 1st Eastern Gen. Hospital, Cambridge.
NORTH, MRS. E., Prob. Aux. Hospital, Wrexham.
NORTHCOTE, S. Nurse, 1st Aust. Aux. Hospital.
NORTON, A., Croydon War Hospital.
NORTON, E., Kitebrook Aux. Hospital, Glos.
NORTON, MRS. E., Qrmr., Aux. Hos., Crawley Down, Sussex.
NORTON, M., N. Mem., Craghead Aux. Hospital, Bournemouth.
NOWLAND, L., 5th Southern Gen. Hospital, Gosport.
NUGENT, E., Comdt., Aux. Hospital, Norfolk.
NUSSEY, H., Comdt., Aux. Hospital, Harrogate.

O'BRIEN, M., S.-in-Charge, Aux. Hospital, Hampstead.
O'CONNOR, MRS. A., Sister, No. 4, London Gen. Hospital, Chelsea.
OGDEN, M., Sister, Salford Union Hospital, Worcs.
OGILVY-DALGLEISH, M., Nurse, Aux. Hospital, Wokingham, Berks.
O'HARA, E., Sister, Mil. Hos., Mont Dore, Bournemouth.
OLDROYD, M., Huddersfield War Hospital.

OLIVER, E., Nurse, Aux. Hos., under 2nd Eastern Gen. Hos., Brighton
OLIVER, L., No. 6 Aux. Hospital, Northumberland.
OMEROD, J., A. Comdt., Aux. Hospital, Cheltenham.
OPENSHAW, MRS. F., Comdt., Aux. Hospital, Herne Bay.
O'REILLY, H., Linden Con. Aux. Hospital, Co. Dublin.
O'REILLY, M., S.-in-Charge, Aux. Hospital, Herts.
O'REILLY, T., Sister, Edmonton Mil. Hospital, London.
ORMEROD, A., Supt., Aux. Hospital, Rochdale.
OSBORNE, A., S. Nurse, 1st Southern Gen. Hospital, Birmingham.
OSWALD, S. Nurse, Cirencester Aux. Hospital, Glos.
OSWALD, E., Mil. Con. Hospital, Epsom.
OWEN, R., S. Nurse, N. Staff Infirmary.
OWENS, A., A. Matron, Billinge Aux. Hospital, Nr. Wigan.

PAGAN, G., R. Vic. Hospital, Edinburgh.
PAGE, A., Sister, " Binefield " Oxted.
PAGE, J., Nurse, 5th Southern Gen. Hospital, Portsmouth.
PAGE, MRS. M., Qrmr., Aux. Hos., Chorlton-cum-Hardy, Lancs.
PAINE, D., Mil. Orthopædic Hospital, London.
PALAOLOGUS, MRS. N., A. Qrmr., Aux. Hospital, Norwich.
PALEY, H., Heatherdene, Harrogate.
PALIN, D., Sister, Aux. Hos., Gloucester.
PALMER, J., S/Nurse, 5th Southn. Gen. Hos., Portsmouth.
PALMER, MRS. M., Comdt., 1st Durham Aux. Hos., Gateshead.
PALMER, N., Sister, War Hos., Shrewsbury.
PAMPHLETT, M., A/Qrmr., Aux. Hos., Crewkerne.
PARK, S., Sister, 4th Scottish Gen. Hos., Glasgow.

PARKER, K., Ch./Sister, Aux. Hos., Nr. Malton, Yorks.
PARKER, Mrs. M., 2nd Westn. Gen. Hos., Manchester.
PARKES, Mrs. A., Qrmr., Aux. Hospital, Bourneville, Worcester.
PARKES, E., Sister-in-Charge, Aux. Hospital, Worcester.
PARMETER, Mrs. E., Asst. Comdt. and Qrmr., 18th North'd Aux. Hos.
PARR, Mrs. G., Nurse, Roland Gdns. Hospital, London.
PARRY, M., 1st Westn. Gen. Hospital, Liverpool.
PARRY, W., Sister, Aux. Hospital, Clopton, Warwick.
PARSON, A., Royal Vict. Hospital, Netley.
PARSONS, S., Nurse, Aux. Hospital, Willesden.
PARTRIDGE, D., Nurse, Aux. Hospital, Burnham-on-Crouch.
PARTRIDGE, M., Aux. Hospital, Prince Edward Home, Norfolk.
PATEHALL, Mrs. C., Comdt., Higham Ferrers, Northants.
PATER, W., Nurse, 3rd Durham Aux. Hospital, Sunderland.
PATON-SMITH, H., Nurse, No. 1 Reading War Hospital.
PAUL, R., Matron, Wellington Infrmy. Aux. Hospital.
PAULL, K., Nurse, Aux. Hospital, St. Mary's Road, London.
PAULSEN, J., S/Nurse, Yorkhill War Hospital, Lanarkshire.
PAYNE, G., Mtrn., Mil. Hospital, Pembroke Dock.
PAYNE WILLIAMS, Mrs. J., Comdt., Aux. Hospital, Bedfordshire.
PEACEY, E., Nurse, Urnston Aux. Hospital, Eastbourne.
PEARSON, E., Sister, War Hospital, Berrington.
PEARSON, E., Nurse, Mil. Hospital, Hampstead Heath, N.W.
PEDLEY, Mrs. M., Nurse, Eccleston Hospital, S.W.
PEEL, A., Matron, Girstley Hall Aux. Hospital, London.
PEERS, F., S/Nurse, Royal Free Hospital, London.
PEMBROKE, N., Nurse, Clock House, Chelsea.

PENROSE, E., A.P. Mil. Mas. Cps., Irish Com. Dpt., Tipperary.

PEPPER, M., Matron, Aux. Hospital, Burford, Oxon.

PERCIVAL, Mrs. K., Comdt., Aux. Hospital, Towcester.

PERCY, Lady V., Matron, Aux. Hospital, Northumberland.

PERCY, The Lady, Matron, Mil. Hos., Alnwick, Northumberland.

PERKINS, H., Nurse, Wells Aux. Hospital, Somerset.

PERKINS, Mrs. M., S/Nurse, Aux. Hospital, Southall, Middlesex.

PERRY, A., Nurse, Cameron, Hospital, West Hartlepool.

PERRY, G., A.P. Mil. Mas. Cps., War Hospital, Bristol.

PERRY, Mrs. V., Aux. Hospital, Northwood, Middlesex.

PESCOD, F., Graylingwell, Mil. Hospital, Chichester.

PETER, E., A.P. Mil. Mas. Cps., 3rd Southn. Gen. Hospital, Oxford.

PETER, M., Sister, 18, Cadogan Gardens, S.W.

PETIT, L., A.P. Mil. Mas. Cps., Mil. Con. Hospital, Epsom.

PETRE, The Hon. B., Amb. Sister, Amb. Col., London District.

PETTER, Mrs. E., Comdt., 6th Durham Aux. Hospital, Darlington.

PHELP, J., Nurse, Aux. Hospital, Loughton, Essex.

PHELPS, G., Sister, 1st Southern Gen. Hospital, Birmingham.

PHIBBS, S., A.P. Mil. Mas. Cps., Richmond Hill Hospital.

PHILBRICK, M., Struan Aux. Hospital, Reading.

PHILLIMORE, M., Qrmr., Aux. Hospital, Stonehouse, Gloucester.

PHILLIP, F., Soldiers' Aux. Hospital, Royston, Herts.

PHILLIPS, E., Asst.-Qrmr., Soldiers' Aux. Hospital, Royston.

PHILLIPS, P., Sister, Officers' Hospital, London.

PHILPPOT, D., Nurse, Empire Hospital, Vincent Square, London.

PICKFORD, Mrs. J., S/Nurse, 5th Dur. Aux. Hospital, Darlington.

PICTOR, D., Corsham Aux. Hospital, Wilts.

AA

PIDGEON, M., Nursing Mem., Aux. Hospital, Cheshire.
PIERSON WEBBEL, Mrs. M., Qrmr., Aux. Hospital, Kingston.
PIKE, Mrs. F., Matron, Cork Steamship Hospital, Cork.
PILKINGTON, Mrs. M., Supt., Aux. Hospital, Hayes End, Middlesex.
PIM, Mrs. V., Commandant, Grantham Aux. Hospital, Lincoln.
PIPER, H., Matron, R. Hospital, W.
PIRIE, H., Sister, Empire Hospital, S.W.
PIRRIE, E., Sister, 48, Bryanstone Square, W.
PITMAN, Mrs. M., Qrmr., Red Cross Hospital, Torquay.
PITTAWAY, M., S/Nurse, King George Hospital, S.E.
PITT-TAYLOR, N., Nurse, " Moray Lodge " Hospital, W.
PITTS, D., Nurse, Aux. Hospital, Northampton.
PITTS, E., Nurse, Gen. and Aux. Hospital, Chelmsford.
PIXTON, Mrs. E., A.P. Mil. Mas. Cps., Comd. Dpt., Heaton Park.
PLANTE, E., Nurse, Aux. Hospital, Hove, Sussex.
PLUNKET, E., Sister, Lady Evelyn Mason's Hospital, W.
POINTER, L., Amb. Sister, Amb. Col., London District.
POLLARD, M., Nurse, Aux. Hospital, Willesden.
POLLOCK, A., Nurse, U.V.F. Hospital, Belfast.
POLLOCK, C., A.P. Mil. Mas. Cps., Dublin.
POOLE BERRY, W., Nurse, Aux. Hospital, Grantham, Lincoln.
PORRETT, M., Nurse, 20th Dur. Aux. Hospital, Sunderland.
PORTER, D., Seeley Aux. Hospital, Newport, I. of W.
PORTER, G., Nurse, Aux. Hospital, Northiam, Sussex.
PORTER, Mrs. E., Nurse, Aux. Hospital, Gravesend, Kent.
POTTER, V., S/Nurse, Aux. Hospital, Sussex.
POTTINGER, D., 184, Queen's Gate, S.W.

POULTON, Mrs. S., Qrmr., Aux. Hospital, Reading.
POVALL, A., Sister, Crumpsall Infm., Manchester.
POWELL, M., Nursg. Mem., Aux. Hospital, Wrexham, N. Wales.
POWELL-REES, Mrs. C., Comdt., Aux. Hospital, Abergavenny.
POWER, D., Nurse, Aux. Hospital, Ottershaw, Surrey.
POWER, L., Matron, St. J.A.A., Park House Hospital, Newbury.
POWER, Mrs. L., Comdt., St. J.A.B., Park House Hospital, Newbury.
PRAGNELL, A., Sister, War Hospital, Duston.
PRATT, M., Mil. Hospital, Clipstone Camp, Notts.
PRENDERGAST, M., Comdt., Red Cross Hospital, Richmond.
PRESSLY-SMITH, V., Mil. Hospital, Clipstone Camp, Notts.
PRETTY, E., Home Sister, Queen Mary's Hospital, Whalley.
PRICE, A., Mil. Hospital, Cork.
PRICE, E., N/Mem., Middlesex War Hospital, St. Albans.
PRIDDY, D., A/Nurse, Aux. Hospital, Gloucester.
PRIEST, B., 2nd London Gen. Hospital, Chelsea.
PRITCHARD, M., 1st Westn. Gen. Hospital, Liverpool.
PROCTOR, Mrs. H., Comdt., Aux. Hospital, Merioneth.
PROCTOR, M., Sister, Univsty. Aux. Hospital, Dublin.
PROUDFOOT, J., Nurse, War Hospital, Lanark.
PROUDMAN, A., Sister, Stepping Hill Hospital, Stockport.
PROWTING, A., Sister, Aux. Hospital, Altrincham, Cheshire.
PRYSE-RICE, C., S/Nurse, Aux. Hospital, Carmarthen.
PUGH, Mrs. E., Sister, Woolton, Aux. Hospital, Lancs.
PULLIN, Mrs. E., Aux. Hospital, Ardleigh, Essex.
PUMPHREY, L., Matron, The Queen's Civil Hospital, Birmingham.
PUNCHARD, M., S/Nurse, 2nd Westn. Gen. Hospital, Manchester.

PURCHAS, A., Matron, No. 4 Sec. Exeter Grouped Hospital.
PURVES, M., A.P. Mil. Mas. Cps., Norfolk War Hospital, Norwich.
PYKE-NOTT, Mrs. D., Comdt., Aux. Hospital, Evesham, Gloucester

QUEST, G., Nurse, Aux. Hospital, Westcliffe-on-Sea, Essex.

RABAGLIATI, C., Sister, Aux. Hospital, Ilkley, Yorks.
RADCLIFFE, G., N/Sister, Mil. Hospital, Orpington.
RAE, E., 3rd Westn. Gen. Hospital, Cardiff.
RAE, M., Sister, Hartlepools Hospital.
RAINE, E., Nurse, 3rd Durham Aux. Hospital, Sunderland.
RAMSBOTTOM, E., Sister, 1st Southn. Gen. Hospital, Birmingham.
RAMSELL, H., Sister, War Hospital, Duston.
RANDALL, M., Nurse, 3rd South. Gen Hospital, Oxford.
RANKEN, E., A.P. Mil. Mas. Cps., Mil. Hospital, Edinburgh.
RANS, Mrs. S., Comdt., Aux. Hospital, Ardleigh, Essex.
RANSOM, H., Qrmr., Aux. Hospital, Ipswich, Suffolk.
RATCLIFF, M., Aux. Hospital, Coventry, Warwick.
RATSEY, M., Northwood House Aux. Hospital, Cowes, I. of W.
RAVEN, Mrs. A., Nurse, Aux. Hospital, Forest Hill, S.E.
RAWLINSON, M., Sec. Leader, Aux. Hospital, Lancs.
RAY, M., Nurse, Aux. Hospital, Margate.
RAY, N., Nurse, U.V.F. Hospital, Belfast.
RAYMOND, M., Spec. Prob. Royal Herbert Hospital, Woolwich.
RAYNER, M., Sister, Aux. Hospital, Suffolk.
READ, A., Sister, Mil. Hospital, W.C.
READ, A., 11th Durham Aux. Hospital, Sunderland.

READER, H., 2nd Westn. Gen. Hospital, Manchester.

REAH, Mrs. R., Comdt., 10th North'd Aux. Hospital, Pendower.

REAKES, I., Sister, Maida Vale, London.

REDFERN, Mrs. C., Sister-in-Charge, Aux. Hospital, Stafford.

REDFERN, C., Sister, Aux. Hospital, Mold, Flintshire.

REDMOND, E., N/Sister, Mil. Hospital, Orpington.

REED, Mrs. J., N/Mem., 4th North'd Aux. Hos., Corbridge-on-Tyne.

REES, F., 2nd Westn. Gen. Hospital, Manchester.

REES, M., 1st Southern Gen. Hospital, Birmingham.

REEVE, R., Matron, Conv. Hospital, Knaphill, Bisley.

REEVE, N., 3rd Northn. Gen. Hospital, Sheffield.

REEVES, Mrs. H., Nurse, Aux. Hospital, Henley, Oxon.

REID, A., Nurse, Llandaff House.

REID, C., Aux. Hospital, Co. Dublin.

REID, M., Asst. Qrmr., Aux. Hospital, Rainhill, Lancs.

REID, T., Sect. Ldr., Aux. Hospital, Rainhill, Lancs.

REILLY, S., Comdt., Aux. Hospital, Essex.

RENAUT, E., Matron, Northern Hospital, Liverpool.

RENDALL, A., S/Nurse, Royal Vic. Hospital, Netley.

RENWICK, E., 1st Western Gen. Hospital, Liverpool.

RHIND, Krs. G., Queen Vic. Hospital, Bristol.

RHODES, Mrs. C., Comdt., Aux. Hospital, Wargrave.

RHODES, K., Mil. Mas. Cps., London Com. Dpt.

RICARDO, V., Nurse, Christchurch Aux. Hospital, Hants.

RICE, B., Sister, War Hospital, Keighley.

RICHARDS, C., Red Cross Hospital, Torquay.

RICHARDS, E., A.P. Mil. Mas. Cps., Southn. Comd. Dpt., Birmingham

RICHARDS, M., Qrmr., Aux. Hospital, Carmarthen.
RICHARDSON, E., 1st Southn. Gen. Hospital, Birmingham.
RICHARDSON, Mrs, J., Comdt., Dollis Hill House, N.W.
RICHARDSON, L., Mil. Hospital, Dublin.
RICHLEY, L., Aux. Hospital, Shotley Bridge, Durham.
RIDEAL, H., N/Mem., Aux. Hospital, Glossop.
RIDING, G., Night Sister, Mill Road, Liverpool.
RIDSDALE, E., N/Mem., Aux. Hospital, Anglesey.
RIGBY, Mrs. A., Comdt., Aux. Hospital, Denbigh.
RIGGS, H., Qrmr., Prince of Wales's Hospital, Staines.
RING, Mrs. K., N/Sister, Ear Hospital, Folkestone.
ROBB, Mrs. C., Qrmr., Aux. Hospital, Brecondale, Norwich.
ROBERTS, C., Nurse, 1st Western Gen. Hospital, Liverpool.
ROBERTS, E., Sister, Aux. Hospital, Cromer.
ROBERTS, L., A.P. Mil. Mas. Cps., Comd. Dpt., Ripon.
ROBERTSON, C,. Sister, Aux. Hospital, Preston, Lancs.
ROBERTSON, Mrs. E., Qrmr., Aux. Hospital, Nr. Warrington.
ROBERTSON, E., S/Nurse, 3rd Scottish Gen. Hospital, Glasgow.
ROBERTSON, M., Sister, 2nd Westn. Gen. Hospital, Manchester.
ROBEY, D., 3rd London Gen. Hospital, Wandsworth.
ROBINSON, C., Amb. Sister, Amb. Col., London District.
ROBINSON, D., Mil. Hospital, Denbighshire.
ROBINSON, E., Wharncliffe War Hospital, Sheffield.
ROBINSON, L., Sister, 17th Aux. Hospital, Northumberland.
ROBINSON, M., 2nd Westn. Gen. Hospital, Manchester.
ROBINSON, M., Mil. Hospital, Tidworth.
ROBINSON, M., Sister, Tranmere Hospital, Birkenhead.

ROBINSON, Mrs. W., Monkstown Red Cross Hospital, Co. Dublin.
ROBSON, A., 4th Southern Gen. Hospital, Plymouth.
ROBSON, I., Sister, Mil. Hospital, Grimsby.
ROBSON, R., Comdt., 5th Durham Aux, Hospital, Durham.
RODGERS, E., Nurse, U.V.F., Hospital, Gilford.
RODWAY, E., Sister, Longfield Aux. Hospital, Warwick.
ROGERS, Mrs. J., N/Mem. Aux. Hospital, Doncaster.
ROGERSON, F., Sister, Southport Infirmary.
ROME, M., Nurse, Goring Aux. Hospital, Oxon.
ROPER, Mrs. E., Asst. Qrmr., Aux. Hospital, Loughton.
ROSE, E., Prob., S/Nurse, War Hospital, Yorks.
ROSS, A., Prob. Nurse, Edmonton Mil. Hospital, London.
ROTTEN, Mrs. M., Comdt., Aux. Hospital, Salop.
ROTHERA, A., A.P. Mil. Mas. Cps., 2nd Eastn. Gen. Hos., Brighton.
ROTHWELL, J., Matron, The Infirmary, Rochdale.
ROWE, H., Sister, Branksome Gate, Bournemouth.
ROWELL, M., No. 5 Aux. Hospital, Tynemouth.
ROWLAND-HALL, Mrs. A., 1st London Gen. Hospital, Chelsea.
ROWLANDSON, E., East Leeds War Hospital.
ROWLEY, A., Lady, Vice-Pres., Aux. Hospital, Guildford.
ROYCE, E., 3rd Southern Gen. Hospital, Oxford.
RUDD, E., Sistsr, Aux. Hospital, Norwich.
RUDGE, B., Qrmr., Aux. Hospital, Evesham, Worcs.
RUSSELL, A., Prob. Nurse, Gen. Mil. Hospital, Edmonton.
RUSSELL, A., Comdt., Aux. Hospital, Reading.
RUSSELL, R., R.R.C. Matron, Can. Red Cross Hospital, Taplow.
RUSSELL, M., N/Mem., Red Cross Hospital, Torquay.

Rust, M., Sister, 9, Cedars Road, Clapham Common.
Rutherford, E., N/Mem., Aux. Hospital, Essex.
Rutherford, E., Sister, Aux. Hos., Myrtle St., Liverpool.
Rutherford, M., Mil. Hospital, Tidworth.
Ryde, A., Sister, Royal Nat. Orthpd. Hospital.
Rygate, Mrs. M., Qrmr., Aux. Hospital, Norfolk.
Ryland, M., 1st Southern Gen. Hospital, Birmingham.

Saffrey, G., Sister, Brondesbury Park Hospital, London.
Saint George, E., 1st Western Gen. Hospital, Liverpool.
Saint Johnston, Mrs. M., Qrmr., Aux. Hospital, Gloucester.
Sale, G., Aux. Hospital, Warwick.
Salmon, D., Nurse, 1st Western Gen. Hospital, Liverpool.
Salmond, E., Sister-in-Charge, Aux. Hospital, Thame, Oxon.
Salmond, M., Asst. Nurse, Mil. Hospital, Dovercourt.
Salter, F., Sister, 4th Southern Gen. Hospital, Plymouth.
Sambridge, M., N/Mem., Aux. Hospital, Harborne, Birmingham.
Samuel, A., N/Mem., Aux. Hospital, Wrexham, N. Wales.
Samuel, Lady F., Private Hospital, Kent.
Sandbrooke, M., Sister, 3rd Western Gen. Hospital, Cardiff.
Sandell, A., Supt., Aux. Hospital, Bromley, Kent.
Sanders, E., Sister, Mil. Hospital, Sutton Veney, Wilts.
Sanders, N., Sister, Salford Union Hospital, Manchester.
Sanderson, S., Nurse, Merryflats War Hospital.
Sapwell, D., N/Mem., Aux. Hospital, Norfolk.
Sara, M., Beechwood Aux. Hospital, Hereford.
Sargant, Lady A., St. Anselm's, Walmer.

SARGENT, A., Aux. Hospital, Rugby.

SARGENT, L., Prob., War Hospital, Bradford.

SAVAGE, D., Nurse, Aux. Hospital, Harrow.

SAVILE, Mrs. A. A., Nurse, Aux. Hospital, Cheltenham.

SAYER, M., Nurse, Woolton Aux, Hospital, Lancs.

SCARBOROUGH, S., Sister, The Infirmary, Rochdale.

SCARLETT, K., Nurse, Aux. Hospital, Barton Court, Berks.

SCHIFF, M., 184, Queen's Gate, London.

SCHOALES, L., Matron, Aux. Hospital, Co. Dublin.

SCHOFIELD, S., A.P. Mil. Mas. Cps., Stoke-on-Trent.

SCHOLES, E., Matron, Aux. Hospital, Bolton.

SCHLICH, E., Nurse, Univ. Aux. Hospital, Oxford.

SCONCE, K., Head Sister, 11, Palace Green, W.

SCOTT, E., N/Mem., Aux. Hospital, Guildford.

SCOTT, G., 3rd Western Gen. Hospital, Cardiff.

SCOTT, H., Sister, Gen. Hospital, Tunbridge Wells.

SCOTT, M., Sister, 11, Palace Green, W.

SCOTT, M., Sister, Royal Infirmary, Manchester.

SCOTT, M., N/Mem., Aux. Hospital, Guildford.

SCOTT, N., Qrmr., Aux. Hospital, Burnham-on-Sea.

SCOTT-GATTY, M., 5th London Gen. Hospital, Chelsea.

SCREECH, B., Sister, The Welsh Met. Hospital, Cardiff.

SEAMAN, D., Sister, Hartlepools Hospital.

SEATON, D., Nurse, 3rd Lond. Gen. Hospital, Wandsworth.

SEDDON, J., Sister, 1st Southern Gen. Hospital, Birmingham.

SEDGWICK, M., Asst. Comdt. and Nurse, Aux. Hospital, Grantham.

SEELEY, Mrs. V., Comdt., Aux. Hospital, Gloucester.

AB

SELFE, O., Nurse, Aux. Hospital, Hampstead.
SELLS, C., Nurse, Aux. Hospital, Hayling Island, Hants.
SENIOR, H., Aux. Hospital, Wincanton.
SEWELL, Mrs. E., Nurse, Aux. Hospital, Carlisle.
SEWELL, E., Nurse, Mayfair, W.
SHALDERS, M., Sister, Aux. Hospital, Cheltenham.
SHARPE NATORS, E., 2nd Northn. Gen. Hospital, Leeds.
SHARPLES, M., Bethnal Green Mil. Hospital.
SHAW, A., Asst. Nurse, Mil. Hospital, Fargo.
SHAW, Mrs. B., Comdt., Aux. Hospital, Flixton, Lancs.
SHAW-BOND, Mrs. N., Sister-in-Charge, 7, Mandeville Place, W.
SHEBBEARE, C., Kingston Barracks.
SHELCOTT, M., Sen. Prob., Royal Nat. Orthopædic Hospital.
SHELFORD, W., Aux. Hospital, Gt. Chesterfield.
SHELTON, M., Sister, 3rd Westn, Gen. Hospital, S.W.1.
SHEPPARD, O., Mil. Hospital, S.W.1.
SHEPHERD, D., Nurse, 1st Eastn. Gen. Hospital, Cambridge.
SHEPHERD, Mrs. E., Nurse, Aux. Hospital, Steventon, Berks.
SHEPHERD, S., 1st Westn. Gen. Hospital, Liverpool.
SHERINGHAM, M., N/Mem., Aux. Hospital, Norfolk.
SHERWOOD, G., Nurse, Rothesay Hospital, Hants.
SHIELD, Mrs. M., Matron, 20th Durham Aux. Hospital, Sunderland.
SHIELDS, Mrs. E., Theatre Sister, Mile-end Mil. Hospital.
SHINN, E., S/Nurse, 3rd Westn. Gen. Hospital, Newport Sec.
SHIRLEY, Mrs. E., Matron, 4, Lyndhurst Gardens, Hampstead.
SHIRT, M., Sister, Crumpsall Infirmary, Manchester.
SHOOLBRED, Mrs. N., Comdt., Aux. Hospital, Halstead, Essex.

SHORROCK, S., Prob., 2nd Birmingham War Hospital, Northfield.

SHORT, E., Sister, No. 1, Station Grouped Hospitals, Exeter.

SHREEVE, M., Sister, Norfolk War Hospital, Norwich.

SHROSBREE, J., 1st Southern Gen. Hospital, Birmingham.

SIMMONS, A., Nurse, Mil. Hospital, Hampstead Heath.

SIMMONS, Mrs. M., Nurse, Mil. Hospital, Sutton Veney.

SIMPSON, E,. A.P. Mil. Mas. Cps., Stob Hill, Glasgow.

SIMS, J., Sister, Oakenshaw, Surbiton.

SINCLAIR, M., A.P. Mil. Mas. Cps., Prescot.

SINGER, Mrs. A., Lady Supt., Aux. Hospital, Steventon, Berks.

SINTON, J., Sister, 53, Cadogan Square, London.

SKIPWORTH, Mrs. S., Comdt., Aux. Hospital, Doncaster.

SKINNER, E., Matron, 9, Grosvenor Gardens, S.W.

SKINNER, N., Nurse, Hoole Bank Aux. Hospital, Chester.

SKIPWITH, F., Qrmr., Aux. Hospital, Doncaster.

SLADE, E., 4th Southern Gen. Hospital, Gosport.

SLANEY, N., Staffordshire Infirmary.

SMART, M., Nurse, Latchmere, Ham Common.

SMEETON, E., Sister, 2nd Northern Gen. Hospital, Leeds.

SMITH, A., Sister, Aux. Hospital, Saffron Walden, Essex.

SMITH, A., 3rd Southern Gen. Hospital, Oxford.

SMITH, B., Nurse, Fishmongers' Hall Hospital, E.C.

SMITH, C., Sister, London Hospital, Whitechapel.

SMITH, E., Sister, 4th Southern Gen. Hospital, Plymouth.

SMITH, Mrs. E., Supt., Aux. Hospital, Radcliffe, Lancs.

SMITH, E., 2nd London Gen. Hospital, Chelsea.

SMITH, E., A.P. Mil. Mas. Cps., Derby.

SMITH, E., Nurse, Aux. Hospital, Linton.

SMITH, F., Matron, Aux. Hospital, Chelmsford.

SMITH. F., Comdt., Aux. Hospital, Lincoln.

SMITH CRAN, G., Aux. Hospital, Stratford-on-Avon.

SMITH, H., Nurse, Aux. Hospital, Oxon.

SMITH. H., Nurse, Aux. Hospital, Westcliffe-on-Sea.

SMITH, M., Sister, Aux. Hospital, Sale, Cheshire.

SMITH, M., Matron, The Lady Forester Hospital, Salop.

SMITH, M., Matron, Aux. Hospital, Leek, Staffs.

SMITH, Acting Matron, Mil. Hospital, Orpington.

SMITH, M., A.P. Mil. Mas. Cps., Mil. Hospital, Canterbury.

SMITH, N., Qrmr., Aux. Hospital, Doncaster.

SMITH, N., S/Nurse, 1st Southern Gen. Hospital, Birmingham.

SMYTHE, I., Sister, Stoke-on-Trent War Hospital.

SMYTHE, A., N/Mem., Aux. Hospital, Hitchin, Herts.

SNEYD-KYNERSLEY, R., N/Mem., Aux. Hospital, Dorset.

SNOW, D,. S/Nurse, Mil, Hos., Fort Pitt, Chatham.

SNOW, J., S/Nurse, 1st Southern Gen. Hospital, Birmingham.

SOKELL, G., Nurse, Aux. Hospital, Leeds.

SOMERVELL, J. J., Bethnal Green Mil. Hospital.

SOMERVILLE, Hon. M., Theatre Nurse, Aux. Hospital, Battle.

SOMMERS, Mrs. R., Comdt., Aux. Hospital, Birmingham.

SORBY, G., Wharncliffe War Hospital, Sheffield.

SOUTHCOTT, C., Qrmr., Aux. Hospital, Woodford Green.

SOWERBY, L., N/Mem., Aux. Hospital, Hitchin.

SOWERBY, V., N/Mem., Aux. Hospital, Hitchin.

SPALDING, A., Nurse, 1st Borough Aux. Hospital, Cambridge.

SPARKES, E., N/Mem., Aux. Hospital, Sussex.

SPARROW, E., N/Mem., Aux. Hospital, Leamington Spa.

SPEIGHT, E., Matron, Aux. Hospital, Hampton.

SPEIR, J., Nurse, 20th Durham Aux. Hospital, Sunderland.

SPENCER, E., Spec. Prob., Mil. Hospital, S.W.

SPENCER, G., Matron, 5, Nottingham Place, W.

SPENDER, Mrs. M., Comdt., Tankerton Hospital, Whitstable.

SPILLANCE, M., A.P. Mil. Mas. Cps., Ireland.

SPRECKLEY, Mrs. J., Qrmr., Aux. Hospital, Worcs.

SPRINGMAN, Mrs. V,. Comdt. and Matron, Aux. Hospital, Ruthin.

SQUAIR, Mrs. E., 13th Durham Aux. Hospital, Seaham Harbour.

SQUIRE, E., 2nd London Gen. Hospital, Chelsea.

SQUANCE, E., Nurse, 3rd Durham Aux. Hospital, Sunderland.

STACEY, B., Holborn Mil. Hospital.

STACEY, Mrs. E., Comdt., Aux. Hospital, Monmouth.

STAGG,, M., N/Mem., Aux. Hospital, Norfolk.

STAINTHORPE, I., Mil. Hospital, Bagthorpe, Notts.

STAIRMOND, R., Ward Sister, Milll Road, Liverpool.

STANFORD, K., Nurse, Aux. Hospital, Reading.

STANIER, C., Sister, Mile End Mil. Hospital, E.

STANNARD, Mrs. F., Comdt., Willesden Lane.

STAPLEY, E., Sister, 5, Grosvenor Square.

STEEL, A., Prob., Aux. Hospital, Weir, Surrey.

STEEL, Mrs. D., Qrmr., Aux. Hospital, Norwich.

STEELE, Mrs. L., Comdt., 338, King Street, Hammersmith.

STEELE, M., Matron, Hereford Gen. Hospital.

STEERS, M., Matron, Hereford Gen. Hospital.

Stein, E., Qrmr., Aux. Hospital, Shipston-on-Stour.
Stell, C., Prob., War Hospital, Keighley.
Stephen, M., Nurse, 5, Nottingham Place, W.
Stephens, C., Nurse, Stroud Aux. Hospital, Glos.
Stephens, J., 17, Durham Aux. Hospital, Durham.
Stephenson, A., 1st Northern Gen. Hospital, Newcastle-on-Tyne.
Stevens, Mrs. E.. Comdt., Aux. Hospital, Beds.
Stenens, I., Comdt., Aux. Hospital, Newport.
Stevens, Q., Nurse, Aux. Hospital, Sevenoaks.
Stevenson, K., S/Nurse, Mil. Hospital, Prees Heath Camp.
Stevenson, M., Sister, 4th Southern Gen. Hospital, Plymouth.
Steward, E., Nurse, Aux. Hospital, Gloucester.
Stewart, A., Asst. Qrmr., Aux. Hospital, Herts.
Stewart, C., S/Nurse, Caterham Mil. Hospital.
Stewart, E., Theatre Sister, Mill Road, Liverpool.
Stewart, Mrs. E., No. 1, N.Z. Gen. Hospital, Brockenhurst.
Stewart, K., Qrmr., Fairfield Aux. Hospital, Eastbourne.
Stewart, M., Qrmr., Red Cross Hospital, Brentford.
Stileman, A., Acting Sister, St. George's Hill Hospital.
Stileman, A., Sister, Aux. Hospital, Surrey.
Stinton, E., Sister, Stepping Hill Hospital, Nr. Stockport.
Stirrat, J., Nurse, Woodside Gen. Hospital, Lanark.
Stobart, D., Qrmr., 17th Durham Aux. Hospital, Durham.
Stobart, J., 17th Durham Aux. Hospital, Durham.
Stockdale, A., 1st Western Gen. Hospital, Liverpool.
Stockwood, W., Asst. Matron, Wardell Hospital, Brockley Hill.
Stol, A., Sister, Aux. Hospital, Saffron Walden.

STONEMAN, F., Nurse, Mil. Hospital, Sutton Veney, Wilts.
STOPFORD, Lady E., Aux. Hospital, Dublin.
STOREY, E., S/Nurse, Mil. Hospital, Maghull, Liverpool.
STORR, E., Sister, Tooting Mil. Hospital, S.W.
STORRAR, M., 4th Northern Gen. Hospital, Lincoln.
STORRAR, M., 4th Northern Gen. Hospital, Lincoln.
STORRY, M., Huddersfield, War Hospital.
STOTHARD, H., Sister, Fulham Mil. Hospital, W.
STOTE, Mrs. D., Nurse, Aux. Hospital, Lancs.
STOTT, G., Comdt., Aux. Hospital, Flixton, Lancs.
STOTT, M., Sister, Birch Hill Hospital, Nr. Rochdale.
STOW-GRAHAM, Mrs. E., Matron, Westminster Hospital, London.
STRACHAN, C., Mil. Hospital, Hampstead.
STRACHEY, Mrs, A., Vice-President, Aux. Hospital, Guildford.
STRADBROKE, H., Countess of, Matron, Henham Hospital, Suffolk.
STREATFIELD, M., Comdt., 24, Park Street, W.
STREET, M., Surg. Sister, Grata Quies Aux. Mil. Hos., Bournemouth.
STRETCH, L., Lady Supt., 17, Park Lane, W.
STRICKLAND, L., Mem., 23rd Durham Aux. Hospital, Durham.
STRIKE, M., Sister, Mil. Hospital, Grantham.
STUART, L., Sister, Mil. Sec. Hampstead Gen. Hospital.
STUBBS, M., Sister, Red Cross Hospital, Torquay.
STYLES, E., Sister, Aux. Hospital, Birmingham.
STYLES, M., Prob., 1st Southern Gen. Hospital, Birmingham.
SUFFIELD, W., 25th Durham Aux. Hospital, Sunderland.
SUFFOLK and BERKSHIRE, E., Countess of, Comdt., Aux. Hos., Wilts.
SULMAN, M., Nurse, Aux. Hospital, Sussex.

SUMMER, Mrs. D., Aux. Hospital, Gloucester.

SUMNER, A., Sister, Mil. Hospital, S.E.

SUMPTER, F., A.P. Mil. Mas. Cps., Eastern Command.

SUTCLIFFE, E., N/Mem., Aux. Hospital, Glossop.

SUTHERLAND, M., Nurse, Mil. Hospital, Sutton Veney

SUTTON, G., Nurse, Aux. Hospital, Warwick.

SUTTON, Mrs. W., N/Mem., Aux. Hospital, Middlesex.

SWALLOW, Mrs. C., Comdt., Durham Aux. Hospital, New Seaham.

SWAN, D., No. 5, Aux. Hospital, Tynemouth.

SWANWICK, H., S/Nurse, Aux. Hospital, Glos.

SWIFT, J., Royal Vict. Hospital, Netley.

SWINERTON, K., S/Nurse, 5th Southern Gen. Hospital, Portsmouth.

SWINTON, E., Sister, War Hospital, Bath.

SWIRE, Mrs. I., Nurse, Aux. Hospital, Shrewsbury.

SYRES, F., Sister, Grove End Road, N.W.

SYKES, Mrs. L., Comdt., Aux. Hospital, Denbighshire.

SYKES, M., N/Mem., Aux. Hospital, Manor Hill, Cheshire.

TAAFFE, M., Sister, Royal Infirmary, Liverpool.

TABERSHAM, G., Sister, Mile End Hill Hospital, E.

TABUTEAN, L., Sister, Mercers Hospital, Dublin.

TAITE, S., Sister, War Hospital, Bath.

TALBOT, K., S/Nurse, Aux. Hospital, Warwick.

TALBOT, Mrs. K., Comdt., Aux. Hospital, Durham.

TANNAHILL, E., King George V.'s Hospital, Dublin.

TANNER, M., Sister-in-Charge, Aux. Hospital, Norwich.

TANSLEY, M., Prob., 1st Southern Gen. Hospital, Birmingham.

TAPLEY, M., S/Nurse, Aux. Mil. Hospital, Liverpool.

TAPLEY, M.. Comdt., Aux. Hospital, Cornwall.

TARRATT, Mrs. A., S/Nurse, 6th Durham Aux. Hospital, Darlington.

TAYLOR, A., 1st Eastern Gen. Hospital, Cambridge.

TAYLOR, Mrs. C., Aux. Hospital, Henley.

TAYLOR, Mrs. B., Sister, 10, Carlton House Terrace, W.

TAYLOR, B., A.P. Mil. Mas. Cps., Cardiff.

TAYLOR, E., S/Nurse, St. Mary's Hospital.

TAYLOR, H., Qrmr., Aux. Hospital, Bridlington.

TAYLOR, Mrs. H., A.P. Mil. Mas. Cps., Manchester.

TAYLOR, Mrs, M., Nurse, Aux. Hospital, Sussex.

TAYLOR, Mrs. N., Sec. Leader, Aux. Hospital, Birmingham.

TEASDALE, F., Prob., Mil. Hospital, Whalley, Lancs.

TEASDALE, M., N/Mem., 1st Durham Aux. Hospital, Gateshead.

TEASK, J., Prob., 1st Southern Gen. Hospital, Birmingham.

TEDD, Mrs. B., Sister, Aux. Hospital, Cheshire.

TESSIER, Mrs. M., Comdt., Red Cross Hospital, Middlesex.

TESSIER, Mrs. M., Comdt., Aux. Hospital, Feltham.

THAIN, Mrs. M., N/Mem., 5th Northern Gen. Hospital, Leicester.

THEOBALDS, Mrs. E., Nurse, Aux. Hospital, Wargrave.

THOMAS, A., S/Nurse, Bootle Borough, Hospital Liverpool.

THOMAS, Mrs. A., Sister, Aux. Hospital, Birmingham.

THOMAS. D., Nurse, Aux. Hospital, Newark.

THOMAS, Mrs. E., Aux. Hospital, Gloucester.

THOMAS, Mrs. K., Sister-in-Charge, Te Hire Hospital, Warwick.

THOMAS, L., Sister, King Edward VII. Hospital, S.W.

THOMAS, M., Matron, 1st Southern Gen. Hospital, Birmingham.

AC

THOMAS, T., Qrmr., Aux. Hospital, Anglesey.

THOMAS-RIDLEY, Mrs. S., Comdt., Aux. Hospital, Oswestry.

THOMPSON, A., Sister, North'd War Hospital, Gosforth.

THOMPSON, A., Nurse, Aux. Hospital, Herts.

THOMPSON, E., N/Sister, St. John's Hospital, Lewisham.

THOMPSON, Mrs. E., Asst. Qrmr., Aux. Hospital, Worcs.

THOMPSON, H., 2nd Eastern Gen, Hospital, Brighton.

THOMPSON, I., Sister, Empire Hospital, S.W.

THOMPSON, J., No. 2 N.Z. Gen. Hospital, Walton-on-Thames.

THOMPSON, Mrs, J., Sister, Aux. Hospital, Durham.

THOMPSON, Mrs. M., Comdt., Red Cross Hospital, Bedford.

THOMPSON, Mrs. M., N/Mem., Aux. Hospital, Rutland.

THOMPSON, M., N/Sister, The Welsh Hospital, Netley.

THOMPSON, Mrs, M., Comdt., Aux. Hospital, Durham.

THOMPSON, S., Sister, Central Hospital, Lanark.

THOMSON, Mrs. M., Comdt., Aux. Hospital, Bedford.

THOMSON, N., Nurse, Aux. Hospital, Myrtle Street, Liverpool.

THORNE, E;., Aux. Hospital, Sutton Veney.

THORNTON, A., Netley Aux. Hospital.

THORNTON, C., Nurse, Sister, Herts.

THORP, M., N/Mem., 5th Northern Gen. Hospital, Leicester.

TICEHURST, Mrs. I., Supt., Aux. Hospital, Hitchin.

TIDDERMAN, A., N/Mem., Aux. Hospital, Herts.

TIDSWELL, M., Comdt., Aux. Hospital, Northumberland.

TILLINGS, A., S/Nurse, Aux. Hospital, Bury St. Edmunds.

TODD, D., N/Mem., Aux. Hospital, Norwich.

TODHUNTER, H., Sister-in-Charge, Aux. Hospital, Upton.

TOLHURST, Mrs. M., Sister, Royal Naval Hospital, Yorks.
TOMLINSON, M., Sister, Mil. Hospital, Ripon.
TOMMY, G., Sister, 1st Southern Gen. Hospital, Birmingham.
TONEY, M., Acting Sister, Mil. Hospital, Yorks.
TOWNSEND, Mrs. A., Qrmr., Aux. Hospital, Lincoln.
TRACEY, E., A.P. Mil. Mas. Cps., Tipperary.
TRACY, K., Qrmr., Aux. Hospital, Suffolk.
TRAVERS, M., Sister, Mil. Orthopædic Hospital, London.
TRENERY, M., S/Nurse. King George Hospital, S.E.
TREVOR, The Lady R., Comdt., Aux. Hospital, Denbighshire.
TRIBE, Mrs. C., Nurse, The Coulter Hospital, W.
TROOD, M., N/Mem., Aux. Hospital, Cornwall.
TUBBS, Mrs. L., Comdt., Aux. Hospital, Newbury.
TUCKER, A., Sister, Aux. Hospital, Stratford-on-Avon.
TULLOCH, B., Sister, King Edward VII.'s Hospital, S.W.
TULLY, H., Sister, Mil. Orthopædic Hospital, London.
TUNSTALL, E., Nurse, Mil. Hospital, Warrington.
TURLEY, Med. Sister, Grata Quies Aux. Hospital, Bournemouth.
TURNER, A., Sister, Mil. Hosptal, Denbighshire.
TURNER, A., Nurse, 1st London Gen. Hospital, Chelsea.
TURNER, F., A.P. Mil. Mas. Cps., Chelsea.
TURNER, W., Asst. Qrmr., Aux. Hospital, Norfolk.
TURNER, P., Nurse, Suffolk Aux. Hospital.
TURTON, W., A.P. Mil. Mas. Cps., Hampstead.
TUTE, E., Sister, 3rd Western Gen. Hospital, Cardiff.
TUTTY, F., 1st Western Gen. Hospital, Liverpool.
TYE, M., Sister, War Hospital, Duston.

TYNDALL, M., 1st Southern Gen. Hospital, Birmingham.
TYRIE, M., S/Nurse, Central Mil. Hospital, Chatham.

UNDERWOOD, E., Sister, Aux. Hospital, Wimborne.
UNDERWOOD, F., Sister, Mil. Hospital, S.E.
URQUHART, Matron, No. 8 Can. Stat. Hospital, Hastings.
USHER, C., Sister, 5th Southern Gen, Hospital, Portsmouth.
USLORNE, Mrs. M., Nurse, Aux. Hospital, Harlow.

VALLINGS, V., Aux. Hospital, St. Leonards-on-Sea.
VAN BERGEN, Mrs. E., Comdt., Aux. Hospital, Shrewsbury.
VAN DER HYDE, M., Nurse, St. George's Hill Hospital, Surrey.
VASSER-SMITH, B., Nurse, Aux. Hospital, Cheltenham.
VAUGHAN, E., Aux. Hospital, Essex.
VAUGHAN, M., N/Mem., 2nd Western Gen. Hospital, Manchester.
VAUX, Mrs. M., Comdt., Aux. Hospital, Sunderland.
VAVASOUR, M., Comdt., Aux. Hospital, Southampton.
VEITCH, A., S/Nurse, Aux. Hospital, Liverpool.
VENNING, Mrs. M., Joint Comdt., 44, Eaton Place, S.W.
VERNEY, the Hon. M., Qrmr., Aux. Hospital, Warwick.
VICTOR, M., Matron, Aux. Hospital, Sussex.
VIGIS, E., Sister, War Hospital, Bath.

WAGER, E., Sister, 3rd Western Gen. Hospital, Cardiff.
WAITE, Mrs. E., 1st Southern Gen. Hospital, Birmingham.
WALDEGRAVE, Mrs. A., Qrmr., Aux. Hospital, Dorset.
WALDRON, M., S/Nurse, E. Leeds War Hospital, Worcs.

WALFORD, G., Matron, Wimbledon Hospital.

WALKER, B., Matron, Mil. Hospital, Salop.

WALKER, E., 2nd Western Gen. Hospital, Streatham.

WALKER, E., Nurse, 1st Borough Aux. Hospital, Cambridge.

WALKER, M., Sister, Cornelia Hospital, Poole.

WALKER, M., Harrogate.

WALKER, M., Aux. Hospital, Lincoln.

WALKER, M., S/Nurse, Alexandra Hospital, Cosham.

WALLACE, F., Nurse, Aux. Hospital, Burnham-on-Crouch.

WALLACE, I., Member, Aux. Hospital, Battle.

WALLACE, M., Nurse, War Hospital, Glasgow.

WALLIS, C., Exeter Grouped Hospital.

WALLIS, G., Sister, Lewisham Mil. Hospital.

WALPOLE, K., Comdt., Ottershaw Mil. Hospital.

WALSH, G., Qrmr., No. 2 Sec. Grouped Hospitals, Exeter.

WALSH, V., N/Mem., 2nd Western Ben. Hospital, Manchester.

WALSHE, E., S/Nurse, 1st Southern Gen. Hospital, Birmingham.

WALTER-SMITH, R., Spec. Prob. Gen. Mil. Hospital, Colchester.

WALTERS, Mrs. E., Weir Aux. Hospital, Balham.

WALTERS, H., Matron, Southport Infirmary.

WALTHAM, A., Nurse, Aux. Hospital, Reading.

WARD, Mrs. A., Prob. Nurse, Mil. Hospital, Sheffield.

WARD, A., Sister, Birch Hill Hospital, Nr. Rochdale.

WARD, A., Aux. Hospital, Cheshire.

WARD, Mrs. C., Comdt., Aux. Hospital, Nr. Macclesfield.

WARD, M., 3rd Southern Gen. Hospital, Oxford.

WARDE-ALDAM, Mrs. J., Comdt., Aux. Hospital, Doncaster.

WARDEN, K., Nurse, Aux. Hospital, Stratford-on-Avon.

WARREN, H., Sister, Aux. Hospital, Cheshire.

WARRINGTON, E., Prob., Stamford Street, S.E.

WATERMAN, A., S/Nurse, Alexandra Hospital, Cosham.

WATKINS, E., Nurse, London Bridge, E.C.

WATSON, A., Qrmr., Aux. Hospital, Newport.

WATSON, I., Nurse, Aux. Hospital, Freshwater, I. of W.

WATSON, J., Prob., Queen Mary's Mil. Hospital, Cromarty.

WATT, A., 1st Western Gen. Hospital, Liverpool.

WATT, J., Sister, Mas. Cps., 5th Southern Gen. Hospital, Portsmouth

WATTS, R., Qrmr., Aux. Hospital, Weymouth.

WAUGH, E., Qrmr., Aux. Hospital, Haywards Heath.

WAVELL, L., N/Mem., Aux. Hospital, Sturminster Newton.

WAYMAN, Mrs. A., Qrmr., Aux. Hospital, Norfolk.

WEBB, J., Trained Nurse, Aux. Hospital, Surrey.

WEBB, K., S/Nurse, 3rd Western Gen. Hospital, Cardiff.

WEBB, R., Nurse, Aux. Hospital, Worcs.

WEBBER, I., Sister, No. 1 Sec. Grouped Hospitals, Exeter.

WEBSTER, S., Nurse, Aux. Hospital, Bournville.

WELCHMAN, E., Prob., Mil. Hospital, Oswestry.

WELDRON, F., Nurse, Aux. Hospital, Berks.

WELLER, G., A.P. Mil. Mas. Cps., Mil. Gen. Hospital.

WELLINGHAM, Mrs. M., Qrmr., Aux. Hospital, Norfolk.

WELLS, E., Nurse, Aux. Hospital, Nr. Chelmsford.

WELLS, Mrs. M., N/Mem., Aux. Hospital, Portsmouth.

WELLS, R., Sister, Aux. Hospital, Birmingham.

WELLSTED, A., Sister, 5th Southern Gen. Hospital, Portsmouth.

WELSH, M., No. 3 N.Z. Gen. Hospital, Codford.

WELTON, Mrs. B., Aux. Hospital, Coventry.

WENSLEY, A., Prob., King George's Hospital, S.E.

WERNER, J., Nurse, Aux. Hospial, Harrow.

WEST, Mrs, C., Nurse, Aux. Hospital, Herts.

WEST, E., Prob., Mil. Hospital, Bournemouth.

WEST, M., Qrmr., Cluny Aux. Hospital, Swanage.

WESTERN, Mrs. A., Comdt., Aux. Hospital, Woking.

WESTON, A., N/Mem., Aux. Hospital, Norwich.

WEYMAN, E., Aux. Hospital, Newcastle-on-Tyne.

WHARTON, Mrs. D., Qrmr., Te Hire Aux. Hospital, Rugby.

WHARTON, M., N/Mem., Aux. Hospital, Norwich.

WHEATCROFT, F., Asst. Comdt., Aux. Hospital, Eastbourne.

WHEELER, H., Nurse, Myrtle Aux. Hospital, Liverpool.

WHITAKER, Mrs. E., Matron, 13, Grosvenor Crescent, S.W.

WHITE, E., Sister, Aux. Hospital, Weston-super-Mare.

WHITE, Matron, 3rd Southern Ben. Hospital, Oxford.

WHITE, J., Sister, Swedish War Hospital, W.

WHITEHEAD, M., Comdt., Aux. Hospital, Escrick.

WHITEHORN, M., Qrmr., and Nurse Aux. Hospital, Oxon.

WHITELEY, Mrs. A., Nursing Sister, No. 10, Stat. Hos., Eastbourne.

WHITFIELD, Mrs. A., Sister, Aux. Hospital, Woodford Green.

WHITFIELD, Mrs. E., Comdt., Aux. Hospital, Birmingham.

WHITTAM, J., Sister, 4th Southern Gen. Hospital, Plymouth.

WHITTING, M., Sister-in-Charge, Aux. Hospital, Dorchester.

WHITTLE, V., Nurse, Aux. Hospital, Latchford.

WHITWAN, R., Huddersfield War Hospital.

WICKES, Mrs. F., N/Mem., Aux. Hospital, Northwood.

WICKSTED, J., Mil. Orthopædic Hospital, London.

WIDDOWS, A., Acting Sister, Mil. Hospital, Yorks.

WILKES, D., Prob., 1st Southern Gen. Hospital, Birmingham.

WILKINSON, Aux. Hospital, Runcorn, Cheshire.

WILKINSON, E., Sister, Aux. Hospital, Leeds.

WILKINSON, Mrs. E., Comdt., Aux. Hospital, Kemsing.

WILKINSON, M., S/Nurse, Norfolk War Hospital.

WILLDER, N., S/Nurse, 2nd Brmghm. War Hospital, Northfield.

WILLIAMS, A., Sster, Belmont Road, Liverpool.

WILLIAMS, B., Sister, 3rd Western Gen. Hospital, Cardiff.

WILLIAMS, E., Sister, Gen. Hospital, Tunbridge Wells.

WILLIAMS, E., Sister, 1st Southern Gen. Hospital, Birmingham.

WILLIAMS, E., S/Nurse, 3rd Western Gen. Hospital, Cardiff.

WILLIAMS, G., Nurse, Univ. Aux. Hospital, Oxford.

WILLIAMS, L., Prob., Nurse Welsh Met. Hospital, Cardiff.

WILLIAMS, L., Sister, 1st Southern Gen. Hospital, Birmingham.

WILLIEMS, M., Ngt. Sister, Royal Infirmary, Liverpool.

WILLIAMS, M., Sen. Nurse, Percy House Aux. Hospital, Isleworth.

WILLIAMS, Mrs. M., Asst. Comdt., Aux. Hospital, Eastbourne.

WILILAMS, M., Sister-in-Charge, Aux. Hospital, Steventon.

WILLIAMS, S., Sister, 1st Southern Gen. Hospital, Stourbridge.

WILLIAMSON, J., S/Nurse, 3rd Western Gen. Hospital, Cardiff.

WILLIAMSON, S., North'd War Hospital, Gosforth.

WILLMOT, G., Nurse, Aux. Hospital, Warwick.

WILLOUGHBY, F., Cheveley Park Aux, Hospital, Cambridge.

WILSON, Mrs. R., Comdt., Aux. Hospital, Grantham, Lincoln.

WILSON, A., Nurse, Aux. Hospital, Wilts.

WILSON, A., Nurse, Aux. Hospital, Bury St. Edmonds.

WILSON, B., Nurse, Aux. Hospital, Cheshire.

WILSON, Mrs. B., N/Sister, No. 10, Can. Stat. Hospital, Eastbourne.

WILSON, D., Spec. Mil. Prob., 2nd Northern Gen. Hospital, Leeds.

WILSON, F., Sister, 1st Southern Gen. Hospital, Birmingham.

WILSON, J., Sister, 6, Grosvenor Place, S.W.

WILSON, Lady L., Comdt., Aux. Hospital, Eastbourne.

WILSON, Mrs. L., N/Mem., Aux. Hospital, East Dereham.

WILSON, M., 1st Western Gen. Hospital, Liverpool.

WILSON, N., Sister, Warneford Hospital, Leamington.

WILSON-FITZGERALD, O., 5th London Gen. Hospital, Wilts.

WINDEBANK, Mrs. A., Nurse, Aux. Hospital, Herefordshire.

WINDEMER, M., Matron, Freemasons' War Hospital.

WINKWORTH, L., Nurse, 5th Southern Gen. Hospital, Portsmouth.

WINTER DRYLAND, Mrs. D., Supt., Aux. Hospital, Kingston.

WINTLE, F., Sister, Aux. Hospital, Cheltenham.

WINTOUR, M., Nurse, Aux. Hospital, Bradford.

WISE, L., Heatherdene, Harrogate.

WISEMAN, C., 2nd Southern Gen. Hospital, Bristol.

WITKINSHAW, M., Nurse, Aux. Hospital, Ryde, I. of W.

WOLTERS, K., 4th London Gen. Hospital, Chelsea.

WOOD, A., 4th Southern Gen. Hospital, Plymouth.

WOOD, A., Sister, 3rd Western Gen. Hospital, Cardiff.

WOOD, M., Nurse, Aux. Hospital, Worcs.

WOOD, M., S/Nurse, Mil. Hospital, Bournemouth.

WOOD, R., S/Nurse, 1st Southern Gen. Hospital, Birmingham.

AD

WOODFIN, M., Sister, Aux. Hospital, Moor Park, Preston.
WOODHAMS, L., N/Mem., Aux. Hospital, Sussex.
WOOD-HILL, Mrs. A., Comdt., Hospital, Beccles, Suffolk.
WOODHOUSE, Mrs. D., Sister, Bermondsey Mil. Hospital, S.E.
WOODINGS, M., Matron, Hale End Aux. Hospital, Essex.
WOODROW, M., Matron, Mil. Hospital, Surrey.
WOODWARD, E., S/Nurse, Sect. 5 Reading War Hospital.
WOODWARD, I., Qrmr., St. John Hospital, Cheltenham.
WOOLCOTT, K., Nurse, Aux. Hospital, Somerset.
WOOLDRIDGE, J., Comdt., Aux. Hospital, Berks.
WREN, Mrs. E., Comdt., Aux. Hospital, Colchester.
WRIGHT, C., Mil. Hospital, Prees Heath Camp.
WRIGHT, E., S/Nurse, 1st London Gen. Hospital, Chelsea.
WRIGHT, F., N/Mem., Aux. Hospital, Burton-on-Trent.
WRIGHT, K., Sister, Met. Hospital, N.E.
WRIGHT, M., Nurse, Aux. Hospital, Liverpool.
WRIGHT, S/Nurse, No. 3, N.Z. Gen. Hospital, Codford.
WRIGLEY, Mrs. L., Aux. Hospital, Bollington, Cheshire.
WURTZBURG, M., Qrmr., Aux. Hospital, Hampstead.
WYNNE, C., S/Nurse, Aux. Hospital, Woolton.
WYNNE, F., 1st Western Gen. Hospital, Liverpool.
WYTOCK, R., S/Nurse, 2nd Western Gen. Hospital, Manchester.

YATES, E., Matron, Aux. Hospital, London.
YATES, J., Prob., 1st Western Gen. Hospital, Birmingham.
YATES, R., 1st Western Gen. Hospital, Liverpool.
YEATMAN, F., Nurse, 3rd Northern Gen. Hospital, Sheffield.

YEOMAN, D., N/Mem., Aux. Hospital, Dorset.
YORKE, Mrs. B., Qrmr., Aux. Hospital, Norton.
YORKE, Hon. Mrs., The Coulter Hospital, W.
YOUNG, C., A.P. Mil. Mas. Cps., Eastern Command.
YOUNG, F., Sister, No. 2 N.Z. Gen. Hospital, Walton-on-Thames.
YOUNG, E., Sister, 3rd Northern Gen. Hospital, Sheffield.
YOUNG, Mrs. E., Sister-in-Charge, Aux. Hospital, Cheshire.
YOUNG, Mrs. M., Qrmr., Aux. Hospital, Wargrave.
YOUNGHUSBAND, H., Qrmr., Aux. Hospital, Braintree.
YOUNGMAN, S., S/Nurse, 2nd London Gen. Hospital, Chelsea.

ZEHETMAYR, L., Nurse, Percy House Aux. Hospital, Middlesex.

Lightning Source UK Ltd.
Milton Keynes UK
UKOW06f0202151114

241610UK00013B/209/P

9 781847 346797